Student Study Guide

to accompany

Creswell's

Educational Research

Planning, Conducting, and Evaluating
Quantitative and Qualitative Research

Third Edition

Prepared by

Vicki L. Plano Clark
University of Nebraska–Lincoln

PEARSON

Merrill
Prentice Hall

Upper Saddle River, New Jersey
Columbus, Ohio

Vice President and Executive Publisher: Jeffery W. Johnston
Publisher: Kevin M. Davis
Development Editors: Autumn Benson, Christina Robb
Editorial Assistant: Sarah N. Kenoyer
Production Editor: Mary Harlan
Design Coordinator: Diane C. Lorenzo
Cover Design: Ali Mohrman
Cover Image: SuperStock
Production Manager: Laura Messerly
Director of Marketing: David Gesell
Marketing Manager: Autumn Purdy
Marketing Coordinator: Brian Mounts

This book was printed and bound by Bind-Rite Graphics. The cover was printed by Phoenix Color Corp.

Pearson Education Ltd.
Pearson Education Singapore Pte. Ltd.
Pearson Education Canada, Ltd.
Pearson Education–Japan

Pearson Education Australia Pty. Limited
Pearson Education North Asia Ltd.
Pearson Educación de Mexico, S.A. de C.V.
Pearson Education Malaysia Pte. Ltd.

10 9 8 7 6 5 4 3 2 1
ISBN-13: 978-0-13-159296-4
ISBN-10:   0-13-159296-3

This work is dedicated to my parents

Jack C. and Ellen L. Plano

who taught me that happiness is writing a book.

Hints for Using This Student Study Guide

This Study Guide has been designed to help you, the student, to learn the important concepts and topics relevant to educational research that are introduced in the textbook: *Educational Research: Planning, Conducting, and Evaluating Quantitative and Qualitative Research* (3rd edition) by John W. Creswell.

As with any new subject, in order for you to learn the concepts, you must work with them and practice applying them. This Study Guide has been designed to assist you in identifying the important concepts of each chapter, applying the ideas in practice activities, and testing your understanding of the concepts. In addition, the Study Guide includes six complete educational research studies, which augment the chapters and form the basis of many of the practice activities for the different chapters. Here is a brief description of the four sections that you will find in the Study Guide chapters as well as a few hints of how to put this guide to best use.

Student Study Guide Chapter Content

Each chapter in the Study Guide has four main sections.

1. Chapter Learning Objectives

Each chapter begins by stating the chapter learning objectives identified in the textbook. You are encouraged to read these learning objectives before and after you read each chapter. Use them to help you see the overall structure of the chapter and to identify the big ideas of each chapter.

2. Practice in Understanding Key Concepts

This section provides three different kinds of activities that require you to practice using the key concepts of the chapter. (1) You will record definitions for the important terms and concepts identified in the chapter. Put these definitions in your own words to make them more meaningful to you. (2) You will apply these terms and concepts to actual research situations as a "consumer of research." Many of these activities will ask you to read the provided sample research studies and interpret and evaluate how the concepts have been applied within these examples. (3) You will consider these terms and concepts in the context of a new research scenario that you design as a "producer of research." Be creative and select topics that are of interest to you. This will make studying more interesting and will make you more critical of your own understanding as you practice using the ideas.

Each chapter includes at least one *Activity Hint!* to help you master the new material. These hints point you to key sections in the textbook that will assist you in completing the activities. As you work, keep in mind that most activities in this section do not have clear right and wrong answers. Look for *Activity Feedback!* notes to receive feedback on select activities in Parts I and II. In addition, discuss your answers and ideas with other students when possible. You will never learn more than when you are explaining your thoughts to someone else.

3. Practice Test Items

Each chapter contains ten questions for you to check your understanding of the major terms and concepts. See if you can answer these questions based on your own understanding and the notes that you have made.

4. Practice Test Items – Answer Key

The chapters end by providing the solutions to the practice test items. Each solution also contains a suggested section in the textbook to review for the concept behind the question. As you check your understanding with the answer key, you should not only see if you marked the "right" answer, but also ask yourself under what conditions the other answers would have been best.

Other Key Features of the Student Study Guide

The Study Guide includes sample studies and reviews of the research designs in addition to the 18 content chapters.

Sample Studies

Six complete educational research studies are provided in this Study Guide. These articles represent a range of educational topics (music education, children with Asperger Syndrome, eating disorders, preservice teaching, study abroad programs, and leadership), participant types, and approaches to research. They are presented exactly as they appeared when published in their respective journals so you can practice reading "real" research studies. They also serve as the basis for activities where you will apply the important concepts as a consumer of research.

Reviews of the Research Designs

In Part III on Research Designs, the Study Guide includes brief reviews for the Quantitative, Qualitative, and Combined research designs. These reviews ask you to summarize what you have learned across multiple chapters and give you an opportunity to compare and contrast the difference designs.

New Features in the Third Edition

You will find several new features included in this third edition.

- Six complete published educational research studies are embedded throughout the Study Guide. These articles serve as examples of published research and form the basis of many of the chapter's application activities.

- Each chapter now includes advice to assist students working on their own to better master the content and check their understanding. These features can be identified under the headings of *Activity Hints!* and *Activity Feedback!* These features point the reader to sections of the textbooks that are relevant for understanding a given topic and provide solutions to certain activities so students can check their work.

- Three reviews of the research designs have been included to help students compare and contrast the major types of research designs discussed in the textbook.

Acknowledgments

I am indebted to many who have assisted with the completion and revisions of the Study Guide. Of course, the Study Guide would not exist without the writings of John W. Creswell, but I also thank him for his insights on teaching research methods and his careful eye when reviewing this material. I am also grateful to my colleagues in the Office of Qualitative and Mixed Methods Research at the University of Nebraska-Lincoln, who have shared their feedback, suggestions, and edits. These individuals include Ronald Shope, Amanda Garrett, and Denise Green. Finally, I express my sincerest thanks for the assistance and guidance I have received from the personnel at Pearson Education. I thank my editor, Kevin Davis, and my development editors, Autumn Benson and Christina Robb, for their enthusiasm and continued support for this project.

Contents

Chapter 1

The Process of Conducting Research

Learning Objectives

After completing your study of Chapter 1, you should be able to:

1. Define educational research.

2. Identify three reasons for the importance of research.

3. Name the six steps typically undertaken by researchers in the process of research.

4. Identify important ethical issues in conducting research.

5. Reflect on the skills you bring to the research process.

Practice in Understanding Key Concepts

Important Terms and Concepts

The following items represent important concepts relating to the process of conducting research. Using your own words, record definitions for the items in the space provided.

Research: _____

_____

_____

_____

Adding to knowledge: _____

_____

_____

_____

Chapter 1

Process of research: _____

_____

_____

_____

Identifying a research problem: _____

_____

_____

Reviewing the literature: _____

_____

_____

Purpose for research: _____

_____

_____

Collecting data: _____

_____

_____

Analyzing and interpreting the data: _____

_____

_____

Reporting research: _____

_____

_____

Evaluating research: _____

_____

_____

Ethical issues: _____

_____

_____

_____

Applying the Concepts as a Consumer of Research

Carefully consider your definitions and descriptions of the key concepts for this chapter as you complete the following application activities.

Read the following abstract provided for the research study "*The State of Music in the Elementary School: The Principal's Perspective*" and answer the three questions that follow.

Abstract #1

This study is an examination of school principals' perceptions of the elementary school music curriculum. A survey, mailed to 350 elementary school principals (61% response rate), was designed to answer the following questions: What are principals' perceptions of music learning outcomes and broad educational goals that result from school music instruction at their respective schools? How do they believe these should exist in ideal conditions? Is there a difference between principals' ratings for current and ideal conditions? To what degree do certain variables affect the music program? Results revealed that principals were generally satisfied with their music programs' ability to meet music education standards and broad educational goals. However, significant differences between the current and ideal conditions imply that they believe improvement is possible. Principals reported that the No Child Left Behind Act, budgets, standardized tests, and scheduling had the most negative effects on their music programs. (Abril & Gault, 2006, p. 6)

1. Explain in what ways this study appears to meet the definition of research. _____

_____

_____

_____

_____

_____

2. How might this study be viewed as important or valuable? _____

_____

_____

_____

_____

3. What ethical practices might the researchers have observed when researching this topic? _____

_____

_____

_____

_____

Chapter 1

Read the following abstract provided for the research study "*Adolescents with Asperger Syndrome and Perceptions of Friendship*" and answer the three questions that follow.

Abstract #2

This qualitative study investigated the perceptions of friendship faced by teenagers diagnosed with Asperger syndrome. This research aimed to provide teachers with an insight into the social world of Asperger syndrome from a student perspective. A multiple-case study approach was used to collect data from 5 secondary school students in Australia. Data were collected through the use of semistructured interviews. An inductive approach to data analysis resulted in a number of broad themes in the data: (a) understanding of concepts or language regarding friendships, (b) description of what is a friend, (c) description of what is not a friend, (d) description of an acquaintance, and (e) using masquerading to cope with social deficits. The insights provided by the participants in this study are valuable for teachers, parents, and anyone else involved in inclusive education. (Carrington, Templeton, & Papinczak, 2003, p. 211)

4. Explain in what ways this study appears to meet the definition of research. _____

_____

_____

_____

_____

_____

5. How might this study be viewed as important or valuable? _____

_____

_____

_____

_____

6. What ethical practices might the researchers have observed when researching this topic? _____

_____

_____

_____

_____

_____

Activity Feedback!

- ▪ Note how the authors indicate their use of a research process by stating or implying a question, reporting the collection of data to answer the question, and discussing results to the question based on the data.
- ▪ Review Chapter 1 sections "*What Is Research?*", "*Why Is Research Important?*", and "*What Ethical Practices Should You Observe?*" in the textbook for additional information.

Now apply the research process to two actual studies. Read carefully the two articles at the end of this chapter (Study Guide [SG] pages 11–25 and 26–33). They are:

> **Sample Study #1:** Abril, C. R., & Gault, B. M. (2006). The state of music in the elementary school: The principal's perspective. *Journal of Research in Music Education, 54*(1), 6–20.

> **Sample Study #2:** Carrington, S., Templeton, E., & Papinczak, T. (2003). Adolescents with Asperger syndrome and perceptions of friendship. *Focus on Autism and Other Developmental Disabilities, 18*(4), 211–218.

As you read these articles, make annotated notes in the left-side margins indicating where each of the six steps of the research process covered in this chapter is addressed within the studies.

Activity Hint!

- See Chapter 1 sections "***Applying the Research Process to Actual Studies***" and "***Useful Information for Consumers of Research***" for advice on using the sections of an article to help locate the steps of the research process.

7. List the major section headings of the article (e.g., "Introduction," "Method," "Results," or "Discussion") where you found each of the steps discussed:

Sample Study #1 (Abril & Gault, 2006):

Identifying a research problem: _____

Reviewing the literature: _____

Specifying a purpose for research: _____

Collecting data: _____

Analyzing and interpreting the data: _____

Reporting and evaluating research: _____

Sample Study #2 (Carrington et al., 2003):

Identifying a research problem: _____

Reviewing the literature: _____

Specifying a purpose for research: _____

Collecting data: _____

Analyzing and interpreting the data: _____

Reporting and evaluating research: _____

Chapter 1

Applying the Concepts as a Producer of Research

You will now practice applying the important concepts of this chapter to a new research problem relevant to you.

8. What is an example of a topic or question that you would like to study? _____

_____

_____

_____

_____

9. Why would research on this topic be valuable to educators or other specific audiences? _____

_____

_____

_____

_____

10. What skills do you have that will help with the research process? _____

_____

_____

_____

_____

11. What skills do you need to further develop for conducting research? _____

_____

_____

_____

_____

12. In what ways will you ensure that you observe ethical practices while conducting your study? _____

_____

_____

_____

_____

Practice Test Items

Answer the following items to check your understanding of the important concepts related to the process of research. Once you have answered all of the items, you can check your ideas with the provided solutions.

1. What is research?

   _____

   _____

   _____

   _____

2. Consider the question "What format should be used when writing up research results?" This question would be addressed by which step in the process of research? Circle the letter to the left of the correct response.

   a. Collecting data
   b. Analyzing and interpreting the data
   c. Reporting and evaluating research
   d. Specifying a purpose for research
   e. Identifying a research problem
   f. Reviewing the literature

3. Consider the question "How do researchers convey the need for a study?" This question would be addressed by which step in the process of research? Circle the letter to the left of the correct response.

   a. Collecting data
   b. Analyzing and interpreting the data
   c. Reporting and evaluating research
   d. Specifying a purpose for research
   e. Identifying a research problem
   f. Reviewing the literature

4. Consider the question "How do researchers gather information from participants?" This question would be addressed by which step in the process of research? Circle the letter to the left of the correct response.

   a. Collecting data
   b. Analyzing and interpreting the data
   c. Reporting and evaluating research
   d. Specifying a purpose for research
   e. Identifying a research problem
   f. Reviewing the literature

5. Consider the question "How do researchers decide whether or not a published journal article is relevant to a study?" This question would be addressed by which step in the process of research? Circle the letter to the left of the correct response.

   a. Collecting data
   b. Analyzing and interpreting the data
   c. Reporting and evaluating research
   d. Specifying a purpose for research
   e. Identifying a research problem
   f. Reviewing the literature

6. Consider the question "How do researchers convey the major intent of their study?" This question would be addressed by which step in the process of research? Circle the letter to the left of the correct response.

   a. Collecting data
   b. Analyzing and interpreting the data
   c. Reporting and evaluating research
   d. Specifying a purpose for research
   e. Identifying a research problem
   f. Reviewing the literature

7. Consider the question "How do researchers make sense out of the numerical scores and textual words that they collect?" This question would be addressed by which step in the process of research? Circle the letter to the left of the correct response.

   a. Collecting data
   b. Analyzing and interpreting the data
   c. Reporting and evaluating research
   d. Specifying a purpose for research
   e. Identifying a research problem
   f. Reviewing the literature

8. Suppose you are about to undertake a research study. Put the following steps in order, starting with the first step. Use the letters to the left of the choices to designate each step in the provided blanks.

   a. Collecting data
   b. Analyzing and interpreting the data
   c. Reporting and evaluating research
   d. Specifying a purpose for research
   e. Identifying a research problem
   f. Reviewing the literature

   First step _____ _____ _____ _____ _____ _____ Last step

9. List three types of ethical issues to consider when conducting research.

   a. _____
   b. _____
   c. _____

10. List three reasons why research can be important.

a. _____

b. _____

c. _____

Practice Test Items - Answer Key

1. What is research? A possible answer is:

   Research is a cyclical process of steps used to collect and analyze information in order to increase our understanding of a topic or issue.

   Review section "What Is Research?" in the textbook

2. Consider the question "What format should be used when writing up research results?" This question would be addressed by which step in the process of research?

   c. Reporting and evaluating research

   Review section "Reporting and Evaluating Research" in the textbook

3. Consider the question "How do researchers convey the need for a study?" This question would be addressed by which step in the process of research?

   e. Identifying a research problem

   Review section "Identifying a Research Problem" in the textbook

4. Consider the question "How do researchers gather information from participants?" This question would be addressed by which step in the process of research?

   a. Collecting data

   Review section "Collecting Data" in the textbook

5. Consider the question "How do researchers decide whether or not a published journal article is relevant to a study?" This question would be addressed by which step in the process of research?

   f.   Reviewing the literature

   Review section "Reviewing the Literature" in the textbook

6. Consider the question "How do researchers convey the major intent of their study?" This question would be addressed by which step in the process of research?

   d.   Specifying a purpose of research

   Review section "Specifying a Purpose for Research" in the textbook

7. Consider the question "How do researchers make sense out of the numerical scores and textual words that they collect?" This question would be addressed by which step in the process of research?

   b.   Analyzing and interpreting the data

   Review section "Analyzing and Interpreting the Data" in the textbook

8. Suppose you are about to undertake a research study. Put the following six steps in the order that you would do them, starting with the first step.

   First step: e.   Identifying a research problem
                  f.   Reviewing the literature
                  d.   Specifying a purpose of research
                  a.   Collecting data
                  b.   Analyzing and interpreting the data
   Last step: c.   Reporting and evaluating research

   Review section "What Are the Steps in Conducting Research?" in the textbook

9. List three types of ethical issues to consider when conducting research. Possible answers include:

   a.   Respecting the rights of participants
   b.   Honoring research sites
   c.   Reporting research fully and honestly

   Review section "What Ethical Practices Should You Observe?" in the textbook

10. List three reasons why research can be important. Possible answers include:

   a.   It can add to knowledge about educational issues
   b.   It can lead to improved practice
   c.   It can inform important policy debates

   Review section "Why Is Research Important?" in the textbook

6 JRME (SPRING 2006), VOLUME 54, NUMBER 1, PP. 6–20

This study is an examination of school principals' perceptions of the elementary school music curriculum. A survey, mailed to 350 elementary school principals (61% response rate), was designed to answer the following questions: What are principals' perceptions of music learning outcomes and broad educational goals that result from school music instruction at their respective schools? How do they believe these should exist in ideal conditions? Is there a difference between principals' ratings for current and ideal conditions? To what degree do certain variables affect the music program? Results revealed that principals were generally satisfied with their music programs' ability to meet music education standards and broad educational goals. However, significant differences between the current and ideal conditions imply that they believe improvement is possible. Principals reported that the No Child Left Behind Act, budgets, standardized tests, and scheduling had the most negative effects on their music programs.

Carlos R. Abril, *Northwestern University*
Brent M. Gault, *Indiana University*

The State of Music in the Elementary School: The Principal's Perspective

Throughout history, philosophers, religious leaders, aristocrats, and civic officials have described music education as a necessary component of society (Mark, 2002). Today, principals, school boards, and other community leaders are responsible for making curricular decisions based on a variety of beliefs and rationales. Within a school, the principal often facilitates the implementation of the curriculum and monitors its ability to meet broad educational goals. Teachers often depend on the support of the principal to meet their specific objectives and enhance their programs. This assistance is especially crucial in music education programs, where the building principal can help establish schoolwide support for the music curriculum. Clark (1999) states, "unless the value of music education is recognized within a school, adequate resources, funding, and equipment will not be committed. Principals play a vital role in creating a supportive environ-

Carlos R. Abril is an assistant professor of music education at Northwestern University School of Music, 711 Elgin Road, Evanston, IL 60208; e-mail: c-abril@northwestern.edu. Brent M. Gault is an assistant professor of music education in the Indiana University School of Music, 1201 East Third Street, Bloomington, IN 47405; e-mail: bgault@indiana.edu. Copyright © 2006 by MENC: The National Association for Music Education.

Sample Study #1

**Steps in the
Research Process**

**Quantitative
Characteristics**

JRME 7

ment for music" (p. 43). For elementary music educators to garner
this support from school administrators, it is important to understand administrators' perceptions of the learning outcomes and
broad curricular goals in music education.

Researchers have investigated administrators' perceptions of the
school music curriculum. Punke (1972) compared the views of
school administrators and music teachers in Colorado about the role
of music in the public school curriculum. Respondents completed a
survey, organized into five specific areas: (a) music's role in public
relations, (b) music as a discipline of the mind and body, (c) music
as a social activity, (d) music as an aesthetic art, and (e) music as a
leisure time activity. Results indicated significant differences for
three items: Principals believed that winning athletic teams were
more effective at fostering improved school-community relations
than outstanding musical performing groups; music teachers indicated that music should be taught as an academic subject while
administrators did not; and music teachers suggested that students
were not given enough opportunities to create their own music,
whereas administrators remained uncertain. Music teachers thought
that music had greater potential for building community relations,
fostering creativity, and curricular equality. In a replication of
Punke's study, Liddell (1977) compared the attitudes of school board
presidents, superintendents, principals, and music teachers toward
school music. Mean scores for the music teachers were significantly
higher than all other respondents in all areas except responses related to music's role in public relations. As a result of these findings,
Liddell suggested that music educators consider keeping administrators and school board members informed about the importance of
music in the curriculum.

Payne (1990) asked administrators and music teachers to rank a
series of music education justification statements. Results indicated
that while music teachers and school superintendents rated the
statement related to music education as "aesthetic education" highest, school board presidents and building principals rated the utili-
tarian benefit of developing "self-esteem" highest. Hanley (1987)
also investigated the attitudes of music teachers and administrators,
but included teachers of other subjects as well. Subjects were asked
to perform two Q-sorts in which they ranked a series of statements
corresponding to one of four philosophical approaches to music
education (music for fun, referentialism, formalism, absolute
expressionism). For the first Q-sort, respondents ranked statements
based on what they observed as current practice. For the second,
respondents ranked statements based on what they considered the
ideal situation. Results revealed a difference between actual and
ideal situations, with more respondents labeling the absolute expres-
sionist position ["the essential nature of music is its ability to provide
rich, significant, feelingful experiences without referring to something outside the music" (p. 43)] as the ideal approach for music
education.

8 ABRIL/GAULT

While the researchers in the aforementioned studies sought to investigate administrators' opinions for public school music broadly, investigators in other studies have looked at school administrators' perceptions of specific curricular programs in music. Greenwood (1991) examined the perceptions of secondary school principals about the role of music and school bands in the school curriculum. Principals generally agreed that music programs and bands should be responsible for helping students reach both musical and nonmusical goals. Respondents considered teaching cooperation, encouraging self-discipline, and promoting good public relations as the most important nonmusical goals for a music/band program. Teaching performance skills and musical concepts, providing opportunities for self-expression, and identifying the musically gifted were the highest-rated musical goals. These findings are consistent with Milford's (1995) survey of high school principals in Ohio. Stroud (1980) surveyed principals' attitudes toward elementary general music. Results indicated that over 97% of the principals believed all children should be exposed to music. Respondents also indicated strong agreement with the idea that use of leisure time, development of good citizenship, and integration into other school subjects were important outcomes of an elementary school music program. The aforementioned studies support the idea that while school administrators seem to support music in the schools, their goals and objectives may differ from those of music educators.

Other researchers have looked at the way values manifest themselves in specific aspects of the music curriculum. Rogers (1985) surveyed high school band directors and principals across the United States to determine their attitudes toward marching band contests. Band directors rated the personal benefits for students highest and the musical benefits lowest. In contrast, principals rated improving public relations highest and improving financial support for the band lowest. Principals rated the areas of general education experience, personal benefits to students, motivation and recruitment, and improving public relations significantly higher than did band directors.

Another aspect of the music program in which perceived values about elements of the curriculum can be seen is grading. McCoy (1991) investigated how choral and band directors at high schools in Illinois determined grades for students in their performing organizations, and how these grading systems compared with those proposed by principals. Results indicated that principals considered performance technique to be the most important criterion, while ensemble directors weighted concert attendance most heavily when assigning grades. Overall, directors relied more on nonmusical criteria to determine grades, while principals assigned more weight to musical criteria.

Many of the reviewed studies examined the implementation of curricular values in music education practice in broad terms or focused on the secondary level. These investigations involved examining how administrators apply value for music programs

Sample Study #1

**Steps in the
Research Process**

**Quantitative
Characteristics**

JRME 9

given specific situations. In addition, researchers in previous studies have attempted to capture a "snapshot" of a school administrators' beliefs regarding the place of music in the school curriculum. It is possible that a difference exists between administrators' self-reported value for music education and the implementation of these values given current educational realities. There is a need for research to focus this sort of examination on the elementary general music curriculum.

A recent Gallup poll (2003) indicated that 95% of respondents believed music to be a key component in a child's well-rounded education, and more than three-quarters of those same respondents thought that schools should mandate music education (Gallup, 2003). In a similar vein, in-service elementary educators have been shown to value specialized instruction in music as an important part of the school curriculum (Abril & Gault, 2005). However, an overall increase in music programs has not been noted in current investigations related to this issue. A recent study conducted by the Music for All Foundation (2004) used data from the California Basic Educational Data System to examine and compare the amount of music instruction in California schools over a 5-year period from 1999–2000 through 2003–2004. A comparison of enrollment figures, percentage of student involvement, and total number of music teachers indicated a 50% decline in student involvement in music education courses and a 26.7% decline in the number of music teachers. Based on the interviews of educators and policymakers, researchers speculated that this could be attributed to the current California budget crisis and the implementation of the No Child Left Behind Act.

A survey of 956 elementary and secondary school principals from Illinois, Maryland, New Mexico, and New York indicated that three-quarters of respondents noted an increase in instructional time for reading, writing, and mathematics as a result of the No Child Left Behind Act (Council for Basic Education [CBE], 2004). Twenty-five percent indicated a decline in instructional time for the arts, with 33% anticipating further decreases as a result of the legislation. In Byo's (1999) survey of classroom teachers' and music specialists' perceived ability to implement the National Standards for Music Education, respondents in both groups ranked instructional time, equipment, and materials for music instruction as extremely limited. Byo concluded that "curriculum planners and administrators are strongly encouraged to design curricular models that result in increased instructional contact time for both generalists and music teachers, while increasing the resources available to generalists to implement the standards" (p. 121). An investigation of how principals see legislative, budgetary, and other restraints affecting their ability to implement what they perceive to be the most effective music education curriculum would provide further insight regarding how educational goals are often revised as a result of outside influences.

10 ABRIL/GAULT

The purpose of this study was to investigate principals' perceptions of the elementary general music curriculum. The following questions guided the study: (1) What are elementary school principals' perceptions of music learning outcomes as they are currently being met and as they should be met under ideal conditions? (2) Is there a difference between principals' perceptions of current and ideal conditions? (3) What are elementary school principals' perceptions of broad educational goals as they are currently being met and as they should be met under ideal conditions? (4) Is there a difference between principals' perceptions of current and ideal conditions? and (5) What are principals' perceptions about the degree to which certain variables affect music education in their respective schools?

METHOD

Survey Instrument

A survey was designed to measure respondents' beliefs regarding general music education in the elementary school. The construction of the survey was informed by reviewed research, the National Standards in Music Education, and discussions with local music educators and principals. A draft of the survey was examined by individuals with expertise in either elementary school administration, elementary school music curriculum, arts policy, or research. Comments and suggestions provided were considered in the revision of the survey.

The final version of the survey was divided into four sections. Section 1 was used to collect demographic information about the principal's professional and educational experience, school, and music program. Section 2 consisted of a list of seven music-learning outcomes, modeled after the National Standards in Music Education (e.g., create and compose music, understand music in relation to culture and history). Using a Likert-type scale (strongly agree = 5; strongly disagree = 1), principals indicated the degree to which they believed the music program was able to facilitate students in meeting these learning outcomes. They also indicated the degree to which they believed the music program should meet these outcomes in ideal circumstances. Principals were given the option to check a "Can't Answer" box if they did not have enough background to provide an informed answer. A Cronbach's alpha coefficient was calculated to measure internal consistency of the survey items (α = .86). In the third section, principals responded to a list of 14 broad educational goals that might arise from school music instruction in both current and ideal conditions (i.e., develop creativity, transmit cultural heritage, improve intelligence) (α = .96). In the fourth section, principals determined the degree (strongly positive = 5; strongly negative = 1) to which they believed 10 variables currently affect their music programs (e.g., music teacher, research, parents, standardized tests) (α = .79). The overall alpha coefficient for all three sections of the survey was .94.

Sample Study #1

**Steps in the
Research Process**

**Quantitative
Characteristics**

JRME 11

The final section of the survey consisted of two open-ended items: (a) describe the greatest obstacles hampering your ability to support the music program at your school, and (b) describe anything you think might assist you in alleviating those obstacles. Principals were asked to complete the survey independently and return it anonymously using a self-addressed return envelope enclosed in the mailer.

Sample

A random sample of 350 was drawn from a list of 8,506 active elementary public school principals enrolled as members of the National Association of Elementary School Principals. An initial mailing, a follow-up, and two reminders yielded a 61% response rate. Surveys were returned from principals representing various regions of the United States: Midwest (32%), Northeast (27%), South (26%), and West (15%). These proportions closely reflected the membership of the population from which the sample was drawn. One of the responses was not used because the principal no longer worked at the elementary level. Respondents ($N = 214$) reported the length of their service as elementary school administrators to be as follows: under 1 to under 5 years (28.5%),[1] 5 to under 10 years (30.8%), and 10 or more years (40.7%). Most principals worked in suburban (40.7%) and rural (39.3%) locations, with a smaller percentage in urban settings (20%). The majority of schools (92.5%) required music education, a handful offered it as an option, and only one school failed to offer any music instruction. Most schools employed music specialists (94.9%), whereas some used classroom teachers (4.7%). The decision to employ a music specialist rested with the school board and/or superintendent (69.3%), the principal (24.9%), or a combination of both of these (5.4%). Four principals reported that a school committee/council was responsible for deciding whether to hire a music specialist. Contact hours for those that offered music instruction at the primary level (K–2nd grade) were as follows: less than 1/2 hour per week (4.2%), 1/2 hour to under 1 hour per week (54.7%), 1 hour or more (39.3%). Contact hours at the intermediate level (3rd–5th grade) were: under 1/2 hour (6.1%), 1/2 hour to under 1 hour (48.6%), 1 hour or more (44.4%).

RESULTS

Preliminary analysis of survey results by school setting (rural, suburban, urban) revealed similar means and variances among groups. Since populations from which subjects are drawn can be assumed to be equal if there is homogeneity of variance, all subsequent analyses were conducted without stratifying the sample (Keppel, 1991). In the first research question, we sought to determine principals' perceptions of music learning outcomes as they are currently being met and as they should be met in ideal conditions. Table 1 presents descriptive statistics for these results. Responses were generally positive, with

12 ABRIL/GAULT

Table 1

Mean, Standard Deviation, and Rank for Music Learning Outcomes in Current and Ideal Conditions

	Listen	Perform	Relate Culture/ History	Read & Write Music	Relate to Other Subjects	Analyze	Create & Compose
Current							
M	**4.29**	3.82	3.68	3.62	3.54	3.31	**2.87**
SD	(0.66)	(0.98)	(0.93)	(1.01)	(0.94)	(1.02)	(1.14)
Rank	1	2	3	4	5	6	7
Ideal							
M	**4.57**	4.41	4.46	4.20	4.52	4.26	**4.00**
SD	(0.51)	(0.66)	(0.60)	(0.75)	(0.60)	(0.75)	(0.84)
Rank	1	4	3	6	2	5	7

Note. Bold numbers indicate the highest and lowest means for each condition.

all mean scores above the midpoint (2.5). The highest mean (and lowest standard deviation) in regard to current conditions was "listening to music attentively." Principals seemed to be aware that music instruction focused on developing listening skills in students. The lowest mean score (and highest standard deviation) was "creating and composing music." Principals seemed to be less aware that students were composing and creating music in the classroom. Listening and creating were also rated highest and lowest in ideal conditions, respectively. "Performing music" had the second-highest mean for current conditions but was fourth in ideal conditions. While "understanding music in relation to other subjects" had the fifth-highest mean for current conditions, it had the second-highest mean in ideal conditions. Mean scores for each variable were rank-ordered, and a Spearman correlation was calculated to measure the degree of consistency between current and ideal conditions. Results indicated a moderately positive relationship in which increases in current conditions were accompanied by increases in ideal conditions ($r_s = .68$).

With the second research question, we examined the differences between current and ideal conditions for music learning outcomes. The "ideal" mean ratings were consistently higher than the "current" mean ratings for all variables measured. Repeated measures t-tests were used to test for statistical significance. Results indicated that there were significant differences ($p < .01$) between current and ideal states of music education for all variables under investigation. The

17

JRME 13

magnitude of the effect was calculated for each variable using a Cohen d value. The variables that had a large effect size were: "understanding music in relation to other subjects" ($d = 1.10$); "creating and composing music" ($d = 1.04$); "analyzing, evaluating and describing music verbally and in writing" ($d = .97$); and "understanding music in relation to culture and history" ($d = .86$). The following variables had medium effect sizes: "listen to music attentively," "read and write musical notation," and "perform music."

In Question 3, we sought to determine principals' perceptions of broad educational goals as they were currently being met and as they should be met in ideal conditions. Table 2 (on the following page) presents a descriptive summary of these data. Mean scores for every goal were generally positive. The lowest mean score was "fostering critical thinking" in the current music program; the highest were "developing creativity" and "transmitting cultural heritage." The lowest score for the ideal music program was "providing students with a pleasant diversion during the school day"; the highest score was "developing creativity in students." Most of the scores between current and ideal conditions closely paralleled one another except for "transmit cultural heritage" and "teach students to work cooperatively."

As in the previous part of the survey, means were consistently higher for the ideal versus the current conditions. Correlation analysis revealed a strong positive relationship between current and ideal conditions ($r_s = .81$). Repeated measures t-tests yielded significant differences ($p < .01$) between current and ideal conditions on all broad educational goals. However, none of these differences had a high effect size. Those with medium effect sizes were: "foster critical thinking," "facilitate learning in other subjects," and "improve tolerance, understanding, and acceptance of other cultures."

The final section of the survey measured the degree to which 10 variables were perceived to affect the music program. Means and standard deviations for these ratings are shown in Table 3. There were no variables that posed strongly negative effects. Four of them had means that indicated a neutral to negative effect on music education. The percentage of principals who responded with either negative or strongly negative responses was as follows: "budget/finances" (55.2%), "No Child Left Behind Act" (45.1%), "scheduling" (40.1%), and "standardized tests" (34.4%). The factors that were perceived to pose positive or strongly positive effects on the program included: "students" (92%), "parents" (90.1%), and "the music teacher" (87.8%). These results were compared to the open-ended responses that asked principals to describe the greatest obstacles they face in supporting the music program and anything that might assist them in alleviating these obstacles.

One hundred sixty-seven of 214 principals provided responses for the first open-ended question. Several respondents provided multiple answers, resulting in a total of 231 statements. These statements fell into six general categories: (1) financial/budgetary (31.6% of

14 ABRIL/GAULT

Table 2
Mean, Standard Deviation, and Rank for Each Broad Educational Goal in Current and Ideal Circumstances

	Creativity	Transmit Culture	Sensitivity to Arts	Cooper-ative Learning	Lifelong Learning	Self-Esteem	Understand Music in Life	Future Involvement in Arts	Self-Expression	Intelli-gence	Understand Other cultures	Learning in Other Subjects	Diversion	Critical Thinking
Current														
M	4.16	4.16	4.13	4.09	4.08	4.08	4.06	4.04	4.03	3.91	3.91	3.87	3.82	3.73
SD	(.88)	(.80)	(.75)	(.83)	(.84)	(.83)	(.81)	(.80)	(.87)	(.87)	(.81)	(.92)	(1.03)	(1.02)
Rank	1.5	1.5	3	4	5.5	5.5	7	8	9	10.5	10.5	9.5	13	14
Ideal														
M	4.69	4.58	4.63	4.54	4.61	4.54	4.51	4.59	4.59	4.45	4.47	4.51	4.06	4.44
SD	(.58)	(.65)	(.63)	(.66)	(.64)	(.68)	(.69)	(.65)	(.65)	(.80)	(.76)	(.80)	(1.15)	(.80)
Rank	1	5.5	2	7.5	3	7.5	9.5	4	4	12	11	9.5	14	13

Sample Study #1

**Steps in the
Research Process**

**Quantitative
Characteristics**

JRME 15

Table 3
Means and Standard Deviations for the Effect of Each Factor on the Music Program

	No Child Left Behind	Financial/ Budgetary	Standardized Test	Scheduling/ Time	Upper Administration	Research	Classroom Teachers	Students	Parents	Music Teachers
M	**2.54**	**2.67**	**2.74**	**2.87**	3.63	3.70	4.01	4.20	4.21	4.37
SD	(.81)	(1.16)	(.82)	(.98)	(.86)	(.73)	(.73)	(.98)	(.82)	(.86)

Note: Bold numbers indicate factors that were below a mean of three.

16 ABRIL/GAULT

total responses), (2) scheduling/time (22.5% of total responses), (3) staffing (13.4% of total responses), (4) outside pressures (testing, legislation, upper administration, community attitudes) (12.99% of total responses), (5) no obstacles (11.26% of total responses), and (6) facilities/equipment (7.79% of total responses). Many responses that cited pressures outside the school as the greatest obstacle preventing the implementation of an ideal music program cited the No Child Left Behind Act ("We spend more money on unfunded mandates than ever before. Especially NCLB ...") or specific state standards/tests ("The state mandated tests—time is filled with preparation for testing in 4 core areas," and "There's increasing accountability in reading and math"). This is consistent with the findings of section four of the survey in which these two items were rated as having a neutral/negative effect on the music program. Respondents also had many comments related to the other two items rated in the neutral/negative category on the survey: budget/finance-related issues ("Budget crunch is the biggest obstacle facing the arts") and scheduling issues ("Scheduling to ensure all mandated courses are in first"). A few principals addressed staffing problems ("There is a lack of certified teachers in music"). When asked to describe anything or anyone that could assist them in eliminating the obstacles described in the first open-ended response, 102 principals provided 140 statements. Like the statements from the first item, responses providing solutions were organized into six categories: (1) monetary (increased funding, grants, etc) (35.71% of total responses), (2) legislative, testing, mandates, attitudes toward the arts (25% of total responses), (3) teacher-related (15.71% of total responses), (4) scheduling (14.29% of total responses), (5) facilities/equipment (5% of total responses), and (6) no suggestions (3.57% of total responses). As with the first statement, many of the responses addressed the four issues receiving neutral/negative ratings in section four of the survey: (1) No Child Left Behind Act and standardized tests ("Consideration of standards-based teaching as only one means of determining school effectiveness; there need to be multiple avenues of determining efficacy"), (2) budget ("Fund schools equally—our school receives about $1,000 per student less than the state average"), and (3) scheduling ("More time for music class-more than one hour per week").

DISCUSSION

In this study, we investigated school principals' perceptions of learning outcomes arising from elementary general music education. A second purpose was to ask them to rate the degree to which certain variables affected music programs at their schools. Positive ratings for all learning outcomes indicated that principals believe music programs at their schools were meeting various music education standards. These ratings for learning outcomes were even higher when measuring them as they should be met in ideal circumstances, indicating that principals in this investigation placed a high value on these standards.

JRME 17

The fact that "listen to music attentively" had the highest mean rating for both current and ideal conditions indicated a strong value for this learning outcome. Principals may consider listening to be an essential skill in music, as well as in most other curricular subjects. Principals may have also observed these behaviors, which are common in general music classrooms. As such, they may have come to expect listening to be a substantial facet of a music curriculum. There were significant differences between the current and ideal conditions, with four learning outcomes resulting in large effect sizes: "understand music in relation to other subjects," "create and compose music," "analyze, evaluate, and describe music verbally and in writing," and "understand music in relation to history and culture." These variables had the greatest mean differences between what principals believe is happening and what they think should be happening. The difference between current and ideal conditions with regard to the variable "understand music in relation to history and culture" supports previous findings (Stroud, 1980). Principals seem to value the ways music can connect with other subjects, such as writing, history, and multicultural studies. Music teachers might consider these matters to be peripheral to music, so they figure less prominently within their music curriculums. Alternatively, they may be a part of the curriculum that is less obvious and visible to those observing the program from the outside. Music teachers might consider finding more effective ways to share student achievements in these areas in order to provide administrators with an accurate perception of learning arising from music education.

Similar results were uncovered for the broad educational goals. While all mean scores were positive, ideal ratings were consistently higher than current ratings. This seems to indicate that principals consider music education to have greater potential for meeting both musical and nonmusical goals. Under ideal conditions, "developing creativity" was considered to be the most important of broad educational goals, yet "create and compose music" was considered to be the least important music learning outcome. There are several plausible explanations for these seemingly contradictory results. Principals might consider "creating and composing music" to be a narrow view of creativity. They might also consider performing music to be a form of creating. However, "developing creativity," in the broad sense, might seem to have applications in other subjects and contexts. A greater effort on the part of music teachers to demonstrate the link between creating music and the development of general creativity might help raise the value of these activities in the eyes of school administrators.

The significant difference between the current and ideal conditions for all the broad educational goals is consistent with results reported by Hanley (1987). However, none of these differences produced a large effect size. The following variables with medium effect sizes are worth noting: "foster critical thinking," "facilitate learning in other subjects," and "improve tolerance, understanding, and acceptance of

18 ABRIL/GAULT

other cultures." Alternately, principals may consider these goals important enough to warrant continued improvements. The lowest rating provided for the ideal condition was "provide students with a pleasant diversion during the school day." It seems that principals do not object to music being fun, but they do not think it should be a primary goal of a music program. These results are consistent with the views of in-service elementary school teachers (Abril & Gault, 2005).

The final section of the survey revealed that principals were aware that certain factors had a negative effect on the music program: No Child Left Behind Act, budget, standardized tests, and scheduling. A large percentage of principals considered these factors to have a negative impact on their music programs. These findings are consistent with studies conducted by the Music for All Foundation (2004) and the Council for Basic Education (2004). It seems that the pressures imposed by current legislation and state budget problems do have an effect on elementary school music programs. Open-ended responses provided corroborating evidence. A longitudinal study of specific music programs to measure the effect of these variables over a number of years might yield some specific evidence of how music programs are coping in the current educational landscape. In looking at solutions that would lead to greater support of music programs, administrators cited increased funding, possibly through outside sources, and increased awareness of the benefits of arts programs as possible options. Comments such as "a greater awareness of our stakeholders on the benefit of a strong music program" and "education of school board members and parents" indicate that many principals felt the need for more education for parents and upper administration as to the goals of a music program. Principals considered music teachers, parents, and students to have a positive effect on the music program. Arts policymakers should capitalize on these constituents when seeking support for music education. Music teachers can also serve as advocates of music education and their program by providing principals (and other decisionmakers) with evidence of children's learning.

On a positive note, most principals surveyed (92.5%) reported that music education was a required component of the elementary school curriculum. Furthermore, 94.9% claimed to employ a music specialist at their school. This is evidence of support for music education by administrators and policymakers at schools represented in this study. It should be noted that 39% of sampled principals failed to return their surveys. Therefore, caution should be exercised when generalizing beyond the 61% of principals who did return the survey. However, similar results were reported in an earlier study (Stroud, 1980). Many of the principals surveyed claimed to be fully charged (24.9%) or partially charged (5.4%) with the decision to hire a music specialist at their school. Therefore, it behooves the profession to gain a better understanding of administrators' goals for music education. Continued advocacy and research efforts can help build increased support for music education.

Sample Study #1

JRME 19

NOTE

1. Percentages do not always equal 100% due to rounding errors and/or responses that were not applicable.

REFERENCES

Abril, C. R., & Gault, B. (2005). Elementary educators' perceptions of elementary general music instructional goals. *Bulletin of the Council for Research in Music Education, 164,* 61–70.

Byo, S. J. (1999). Classroom teachers' and music specialists' perceived ability to implement the National Standards for Music Education. *Journal of Research in Music Education, 47,* 111–123.

Clark, N. (1999). Let there be music. *Principal, 79* (2), 43–45.

Council for Basic Education. (2004). Academic atrophy: The condition of the liberal arts in America's public schools. Retrieved November 28, 2004, from http://music-for-all.org.

Gallup Organization. (2003). American attitudes toward music. Retrieved November 28, 2004, from http://www.amc-music.org/news/pressreleases/gallup2003.htm.

Greenwood, R. A. (1991). Secondary school administrators' attitudes and perceptions on the role of music and school bands. *Dissertation Abstracts International, 52* (10), 3552.

Hanley, B. A. (1987). Educators' attitudes to philosophies of music education: A Q study. *Dissertation Abstracts International, 48* (01), 73.

Keppel, G. (1991). *Design and analysis* (3rd ed.). Upper Saddle, NJ: Prentice Hall.

Liddell, L. (1977). A comparison of attitudes toward music education among school board presidents, superintendents, principals, and music teachers in Mississippi public schools. *Dissertation Abstracts International, 38* (07), 4009.

Mark, M. L. (2002). Nonmusical outcomes of music education: Historical considerations. In R. Colwell & C. Richardson (Eds.) *The new handbook of research on music teaching and learning* (pp. 1045–1052). New York: Oxford University Press.

McCoy, C. W. (1991). Grading students in performing groups: A comparison of principals' recommendations with directors' practices. *Journal of Research in Music Education, 39,* 181–190.

Milford, G. F. (1995). Attitudes of Ohio high school principals toward band. *Dialogue in Music Education, 19* (2), 60–72.

Music for All Foundation. (2004). The sound of silence—The unprecedented decline of music education in California public schools. Retrieved November 20, 2004, from http://music-for-all.org.

Payne, B. S. (1990). Justifying music in the American public school: A survey of selected Ohio school personnel. *Dissertation Abstracts International, 51* (07), 2194.

Punke, W. J. (1972). A comparison of attitudes between Colorado school administrators and Colorado music teachers concerning music education. *Dissertation Abstracts International, 33* (11), 6391.

20 ABRIL/GAULT

Rogers, G. L. (1985). Attitudes of high school band directors and principals toward marching band. *Journal of Research in Music Education, 33,* 259–266.

Stroud, B. S. (1980). A study of the general classroom music programs in the public elementary schools of the Tidewater region of Virginia. *Dissertation Abstracts International, 41* (11), 4640.

Submitted September 15, 2005; accepted November 30, 2005.

Adolescents with Asperger Syndrome and Perceptions of Friendship

Suzanne Carrington, Elizabeth Templeton, and Tracey Papinczak

This qualitative study investigated the perceptions of friendship faced by teenagers diagnosed with Asperger syndrome. This research aimed to provide teachers with an insight into the social world of Asperger syndrome from a student perspective. A multiple–case study approach was used to collect data from 5 secondary school students in Australia. Data were collected through the use of semistructured interviews. An inductive approach to data analysis resulted in a number of broad themes in the data: (a) understanding of concepts or language regarding friendships, (b) description of what *is* a friend, (c) description of what is *not* a friend, (d) description of an acquaintance, and (e) using masquerading to cope with social deficits. The insights provided by the participants in this study are valuable for teachers, parents, and anyone else involved in inclusive education.

Children who have been diagnosed with Asperger syndrome have difficulties in communicating with their peers and developing appropriate relationships with others at school. In spite of this, their intellectual ability can be within or above the normal range (Barnhill, Hagiwara, Myles, & Simpson, 2000). Researchers have agreed that difficulties communicating and learning unspoken social rules contribute to major challenges for children with Asperger syndrome as they develop (Church, Alisanki, & Amanullah, 2000; Frith, 1991; Koning & Magill-Evans, 2001). More specifically, idiosyncratic social skills present an enormous handicap in school, and continuing difficulties may result in aggressive behavior (Simpson & Myles, 1998) and depression (Barnhill, 2001). This is because these students frequently do not have the skills to engage in age-expected reciprocal social interactions (Simpson & Myles, 1998). Rather, these students could be described as socially awkward or self-centered with a lack of understanding of others. One reason social interactions are problematic for people with Asperger syndrome is that they experience difficulty in interpreting subtle social cues, particularly nonverbal body language (Koning & Magill-Evans, 2001). In addition, an inability to "mind read" means that these students will find it difficult to predict others' behavior, read the intentions of others, understand motives behind behavior, understand emotions, and understand how their behavior affects how others think or feel (Baron-Cohen, 1995; Baron-Cohen & Joliffe, 1997). These social and communication difficulties create additional stress for the developing adolescent at secondary school (Carrington & Graham, 2001).

Secondary students are required to cope with changes in routine and in behavioral expectations, engage in complex social interactions with peers and adults, and meet academic learning demands. In adolescence, when fitting in with peers is vitally important, complex, and stressful, students with Asperger syndrome have an increased need for social support and understanding. During their teens, these students generally become more aware of their differences. Carrington and Graham (1999) described how adolescents with Asperger syndrome have a need to fit in but do not know how to do so.

Little research has been conducted describing the perception of friendship and social experiences of adolescents who have Asperger syndrome, and there has been even less qualitative research incorporating children's own words. Church et al.'s (2000) study described characteristics of Asperger syndrome, including social skills and feelings about friends over time and during specific developmental stages. This article contains specific examples and illustrations provided by a group of students who have Asperger syndrome to support the findings in Church et al.'s article.

FOCUS ON AUTISM AND OTHER DEVELOPMENTAL DISABILITIES
—— VOLUME 18, NUMBER 4, WINTER 2003 ——
PAGES 211–218

FOCUS ON AUTISM AND OTHER DEVELOPMENTAL DISABILITIES

212

With this study, we aimed to advance understanding of the social difficulties that are characteristic of individuals with Asperger syndrome while providing a voice to this group of students. We asked the following research question: What are the perceptions of friendship for a group of secondary school students who have Asperger syndrome? Our professional knowledge of Asperger syndrome and the particular social difficulties experienced by this group of secondary school students can be expanded by listening to and reflecting on the voices of the participants in this study.

Description of the Study

This research emphasizes personal reflections about friendship in order to improve our knowledge of the characteristics of teenagers with Asperger syndrome. Interpretative sociology provides a framework by which the researcher can enter the person's world and meanings to get an inside perspective. Specifically, a multiple–case study approach was employed to collect data from five secondary school students. Semistructured interviews were used to obtain information from the participants. This approach enabled the adolescents to describe their own experiences in an open way. Researchers such as Minkes, Robinson, and Weston (1994) and Morris (1998) have discussed the importance of empowering individuals with disabilities by seeking their views. The goal of this type of research is not to explain but to understand the meanings the adolescents have constructed from their own experiences (McPhail, 1995). Ethical standards for research with children, such as attention to informed consent and ethical interview procedures, were considered in planning this study (Mahon, Glendinning, Clarke, & Craig, 1996).

Method

Setting

The setting for the study was a large secondary school in Australia. The school provides support services to students with different learning needs and employs two special education teachers. Services the special education staff members provide include assisting with timetable organization, coordinating special education programs and curriculum modifications for students, supporting general education classroom teachers, advocating for students' needs, coordinating teacher assistants, and communicating with parents and outside agencies.

Participants

One of the special educators facilitated contact between the researchers and the students who have Asperger syndrome and their parents. Letters of information and consent were sent to eight families. Five students and their families agreed to participate in the study. The students agreed to be interviewed regarding their beliefs about and understandings and experiences of friendships. Pseudonyms have been used to protect the true identity of the participants. Characteristics of the participants in the study are summarized in Table 1. The school has a special education center that employs staff members to support students with learning problems and disabilities.

Data Collection

Semistructured interviews were used to collect data regarding students' understanding of friendships. Specifically, in-depth interviewing was used to gather data in this study (Minichiello, Aroni, Timewell, & Alexander, 1995). In-depth interviewing is described by Minichiello et al. as a conversation with a specific purpose "focusing on the informant's perception of self, life and experience, and expressed in his or her own words" (p. 61).

The interviews followed a semistructured format, were approximately 20 to 40 minutes in duration and were audiotaped for later transcription. The interview questions were developed in consultation with the special needs support teacher from the participating school and two adults with Asperger syndrome from a local Asperger syndrome support network. The final list of questions (see the Appendix) were provided to students the week before their interviews were conducted. The aim of this process was to enable discussion of the issues at home or private perusal of the subject by the interviewees. The researchers were aware that these students had not discussed their views on friendship in this manner before and that they therefore needed time to familiarize themselves with the issues in the interview. The special education teacher facilitated planning of interview times and arranged a private space to conduct the interviews at the secondary school. The first and second authors interviewed students over a period of 3 weeks. The researchers had no direct contact with the parents of the participants in the study.

Data Analysis

This research aims to describe and explain a pattern of relationships, which can only be done with a set of conceptually specified categories (Mishler, 1990). The method of constant comparison advocated in seminal work by Glaser and Strauss (1967) influenced the analysis of the interviews. As phenomena were coded and classified, comparison occurred across the categories and previous research findings (Strauss & Corbin, 1994). In this way, relationships were discovered and conceptualizations were refined through classification and analysis.

Interviews were transcribed and imported into QSR NUD*IST (Nonnumerical, Unstructured Data Indexing, Searching, and Theorizing; Richards & Richards, 1994) for coding. This software package is designed for qualitative analysis of unstructured data and assists with the storage, coding, retrieval and analysis of the text of the interviews. Using a computer-based analysis tool such as NUD*IST allows for a more systematic and complete analysis of interview transcripts than is possible using mechanical means (Le Compte & Preissle, 1993). Interviews were coded using a line of text as the text-coding unit. Text units are the smallest units of text recognized by NUD*IST. Defined by the researchers, text units may be lines, para-

VOLUME 18, NUMBER 4, WINTER 2003

TABLE 1
Characteristics of the Participants in the Study

Characteristic	Participant[a]				
	Alice	John	Larry	Jack	Morris
School grade	8	10	10	11	12
Age at time of study (in yrs)	14	15	15	18	17
Ethnicity	Caucasian	Caucasian	Caucasian	Caucasian	Caucasian
Diagnosis	Asperger syndrome	Asperger syndrome	Asperger syndrome	Asperger syndrome	Asperger syndrome
Additional assessment information[b]	•Special interest in and excels at art/portraiture •Strong spelling and vocabulary •Easily stressed and becomes very anxious in new situations •Perfectionist	•Particular interest in motorbikes •Poor concentration in class, struggles academically as a result •At risk of being lead astray socially in order to be seen as one of the crowd	•Very advanced computer skills •Has inserviced with school staff members in areas of information technology •Perfectionist, becomes highly anxious when he does not achieve what he thinks he should	•Special interest in war history and politics •Difficulty with processing and analyzing problems •Poor social skills, few friends	•Advanced skills in the food and hospitality area •Highly developed computer skills •Difficulties in the area of communication and social skills
Support from special education center	•Visits special education center on an as-needed basis to relieve stress •Receives 10 hours of support from special education staff members in the general education classrooms	•Visits special education center on an as-needed basis to relieve stress •Receives 10 hours of support from special education staff members in the general education classrooms •Receives 4 hours of support in the special education class	•Receives 4 hours of support from special education staff members in the general education classrooms	•Receives 4 hours of support from special education staff members in the general education classrooms	•Receives 4 hours of support for English in the special education class •Receives 3 hours of support from special education staff members in the general education classrooms

[a]All names are pseudonyms. [b]For example, particular strengths, weaknesses, or obsessions.

graphs, or words and are automatically numbered for identification and retrieval. NUD*IST is able to organize an index system that has nodes. These can be organized into hierarchies or trees to represent the organization of concepts into categories. The system allows the researchers to store and explore emerging ideas. Students' understandings of friendship in this study were coded in five broad categories:

1. understanding of concepts or language regarding friendships,
2. description of what is *not* a friend,
3. description of what *is* a friend,
4. description of an acquaintance, and

5. using masquerading to cope with social deficits.

Results

Understanding of Concepts or Language Regarding Friendships

Overall, there was a lack of in-depth discussion from all participants about the issues related to friendship. This meant that the interviewers had to use prompts frequently to solicit students' thoughts about friendship. One participant (Alice), had particular difficulty answering the questions, so the interviewer posed them

as sentences for her to complete, rather than as questions. This was preferable to Alice sitting in silence.

Researcher: So when I'm with my friends, the sort of things that don't work are . . . ?

Alice: Having arguments like talking about, like worrying about something that isn't—that's nothing. Arguments over nothing.

Researcher: So there's not really an issue there, it's an argument over nothing? And when I'm with my friends, some other things that don't work are . . . ?

Alice: (long pause with no answer)

FOCUS ON AUTISM AND OTHER DEVELOPMENTAL DISABILITIES

At other times this difficulty seemed to be due to a student's not understanding the words used in the question. For example, in this part of the interview, John did not know the meaning of the word *acquaintance*:

Researcher: Tell me about what you understand about people who are acquaintances.

John: Acquaintances—do you know what that means?

Participants frequently said things such as "It's really hard to explain" and "stuff like that." This supports Myles and Simpson's (1998) findings that individuals with Asperger syndrome may have difficulties with information presented orally. The following two extracts provide further examples of the difficulty these participants had with understanding the language:

Researcher: And what about those people who are not your friends? What are they like?

Larry: They're . . . well . . . define "not friends."

Researcher: That's what I want you to do for me. Describe what you think "not friends" means.

Researcher: If you could look into the future, what would your friends be like?

Jack: I don't know. They would be nice, friendly and nice.

Researcher: What do you mean by "friendly"?

Jack: I don't know.

Researcher: What things would you like to keep the same with friends?

Jack: All the aspects of friendship.

In general, all five participants struggled to describe their own understandings of friendship. Most interviews lasted less than half an hour and required much prompting and rewording of the questions from the interviewers. The interviewers allowed for extra processing time, as suggested by Myles and Simpson (1998); however, it was clear that the students had much difficulty speaking about these issues.

Description of What Is **Not** a Friend

The students were better able to describe a number of characteristics of peers who would not be friends, for instance, "students who are sent to the office" (Alice); students who are "rude, inconsiderate, and thieves" (John); and "the type you wouldn't talk to, never communicate with" (Jack). When asked what people who are not friends would be doing that would make him not want to be around, Jack replied, "Annoying kind of stuff . . . hang around you for too long." In addition, Jack described the mean and unfriendly behavior of some students who were not his friends. He stated, "They'll put me in a situation—like I say something and then they'll say, 'Ha! Just joking!' "

Larry described people who are not friends as "people I don't know and people I don't like." When asked to elaborate, he said that some students were "sort of stuck up," explaining, "They usually for some reason don't like me straight away, pick on me and stuff. But that hasn't happened for about a year and a half." He also suggested that people who were not friends did not share his interests. Similarly, Morris also described people who are not friends as being "different" and said they "like other things."

When asked questions about what happens with peers to make things not go well (i.e., to make that person not a friend), the students reported some of their own experiences. Alice said that one thing that sometimes goes wrong is that friends "break promises." This reflects her rigidity in thinking, which is a characteristic of Asperger syndrome (Szatmari, 1991). John said that it was hard to explain but that things did not go well if students were annoying and behaving in a "stupid" way: "If they're not being nice to me anymore and they're getting really annoying and stuff like that."

Morris described fights and arguments with peers and said that other students sometimes were violent and got drunk. He stated that he did not feel comfortable around these people and therefore they were not his friends. Morris described some situations at school in which students influence what happens in the peer group.

Interviewer: Are there other things that happen at school that make it difficult for you to get on with other people?

Morris: No. I don't know. I suppose it's the other friends that I hang out with that aren't that popular. . . . They just don't like me hanging out with some of them or stuff like that.

Interviewer: So, what do they say?

Morris: I don't know. Just tell them to leave and that I don't really want them to leave. . . . They just tell them to leave and all that. They're friends and all—I don't know.

Description of What Is a Friend

The students had various descriptions of what friends are, but once again they generally found it hard to explain. Alice revealed her inability to fully comprehend the nature of friendship when she described friends as "the ones that could help you and keep in touch" and said, "You grow up with them." Despite the fact that she sought to discuss skating with some of her peers and expressed an interest in going skating with her friends, she failed to reduce her social isolation: "I don't think I have friends . . . not really." In comparison, John stated that a person's friends should be people he or she respects, and Jack said that friends are people one has known for a long time. Jack also described some characteristics of friendship: "Trusting them, not turning their back on you sort of stuff and not fighting with me and my friends . . . sticking up for each other . . . keeping each other's secrets and promises." He said his friendships go well when he and his friends "do the same things."

Sample Study #2

**Steps in the
Research Process**

**Qualitative
Characteristics**

VOLUME 18, NUMBER 4, WINTER 2003

215

Similar Interests. A number of students described friends who had similar interests. This meant that they could talk about the same things and be comfortable with each other. For example, Larry described a friend as "someone who I usually get along with quite well and who shares similar interests with me, and we generally have fun together." Larry also talked about the importance of interest to a friendship when he said, "They are my friends, their interest, their individuality I suppose, everything is important really." This focus on similar interests was reflected in Jack's understanding of friendship as well: "Friends are all really just good because at a POW [prisoner of war] camp, if they didn't have a mate back then, they wouldn't survive. Excuse me. I have an interest in POW camps and the Japanese. I read a lot of war history books." Morris extended the idea of common interests to include feelings of being comfortable. He believed that friends are people "to have a good time with." When asked why he felt comfortable with these people, Morris stated, "You don't get nervous like they're going to criticize what you're going to say." He also preferred that they share his interests.

Larry also brought up the importance of friends' having not only similar interests but similar personalities: "They're really nice people who have got the same interests as me. . . . They're usually weirdos as my parents call them. Yes, so my friends are a bunch of freaks, as they say, and so am I."

Activities with Friends. When asked what they do with their friends, the students discussed a variety of acitivies, including asking people to a birthday party and joining in with others on weekend activities. Alice had difficulty describing other types of activities she engaged in with her friends, although after quite a lot of prompting from the interviewer, she did mention skating and swimming but then could not discuss when this had last happened. Alice also described working on school projects with friends (although the assumption could be made that if they were working on school

group work, the students may not be considered "friends" by most standards).

John, Larry, and Morris described a number of activities involving friends outside of school. For example, John said, "I'm a rider. I ride trail bikes. And I've got a friend that comes out riding with me. And, yeah, that's what we do 'cause it has a partner. Like a friend that comes out and does stuff with me." John's words indicate that he considers a friend someone to accompany him on his weekend activity, similar to a partner.

Jack seemed to take delight in describing "inappropriate" activities he and a friend took part in.

Jack: We played kick the football. We played other outdoor games as well like T-square, or there's another game like handball. This is what you shouldn't do—kill insects.

Researcher: Did you?

Jack: Yeah. Me and my friends did that, used to do naughty things.

Researcher: So, you were doing things together?

Jack: Yeah, we killed them. One of my friends and I had a magnifying glass and the sun was reflecting from it, pssst! Smoke coming from the ant. Yeah, barbequed ant.

The students' focus of activities on interests reflects the need of some students to engage in a restricted range of activities. Larry described activities that enabled him to continue his intense interest in computers: "We talk about stuff like computers, *Dungeons and Dragons.* We play it at school and after school." Larry also ran *Dungeons and Dragons* meetings at school. Such an intense focus on one activity or interest is one of the defining characteristics of Asperger syndrome (Williams, 1995).

Description of an Acquaintance

We asked the participants to describe their perceptions of the term *acquaintance.* Alice made an attempt to describe

her understanding of this word after quite a lot of thinking: "I don't really know what's different, but I think there may be, like they don't match your personality, like I'm quiet and some of them are loud, like they don't match." Alice thought that differences in personality would affect her friendships with her peers. In contrast, John suggested that an acquaintance would know less about him, and Jack explained that he would not mix with people who are just acquaintances. He said, "You don't speak to them as much as you do with your real friends. You don't catch up as much. . . . The ones you speak to at school are acquaintances—I just say, 'Hi.'" Larry agreed with this when he explained that "they're the people who I just meet with a few times, just people I know basically." Similarly, Morris provided a description of his understanding of the term:

> You sort of know them, you talk to them sometimes, but you don't really do stuff. You just see them at school and that. And you talk to them. Things like if you see them through the day, you'd probably say hello or something, but that's it. You don't do nothing else out of school or anything.

The participants' descriptions of an acquaintance indicate an understanding that can be described in unemotional terms. This is contrasted with the lack of qualitative or emotive language in the participants' descriptions of a friend. It seemed much easier for the participants to describe an acquaintance.

Using Masquerading to Cope with Social Deficits

The last theme that emerged from the study data was how these students cope with their social deficits. One way this occurred is through *masquerading,* a characteristic that was also described in Carrington and Graham's (2001) study. High school students with Asperger syndrome may be aware that they do not fit in and try to mask their deficits. John believed that he had many friends and showed evidence of masquerading in the following quote:

FOCUS ON AUTISM AND OTHER DEVELOPMENTAL DISABILITIES

216

I've got the most friends. I'd say I'm probably the one that has the most friends. I don't think I really need to go up there [special education unit] because I think I'm more or less capable of doing things by myself.

Larry also described the vast number of friends he had at school. He said he could talk to anyone, and when the interviewer made the comment that the interview had not taken long, he replied, "That's because we didn't count how many friends I actually have." When asked how many, he said, "Nine . . . at least fifteen. That's why it's hard to keep contact with them all." This "masquerade" is also demonstrated through the following dialogue with Larry:

Researcher: If you could just have perfect friendships, what would those friendships be like?

Larry: The ones I've got now.

Researcher: Just like now. That's lovely, isn't it?

Larry: And no more . . .

Researcher: And no more. You have enough friends?

Larry: Yes, my phone's already going "ring, ring" and then I pick up, "Hello," and it's like, "Gosh, not you again!" And then, "ring, ring" . . . "ring, ring" . . . Gosh! . . . And my phone bill's already far too high.

Larry's stories about the numbers of friends and his interactions with them is a way of masking his communication and interaction difficulties with his peers. This need for interaction with friends is masked by his fictional account of an extensive list of friends.

Discussion

Social dysfunction is perhaps the single most defining and handicapping feature of Asperger syndrome (Rogers, 2000). Friendships may be desired, but the concept of reciprocity and sharing of inter-

ests and ideas inherent in friendship is not often understood (Filipek et al., 1999). The adolescents' words in this study indicate a lack of insight into what constitutes friendship and a general difficulty in using and understanding the language to describe friendship issues.

Individuals with Asperger syndrome have difficulty grasping the subtleties of how people relate to each other (Myles & Simpson, 1998) and understanding the perceptions of others (Myles & Southwick, 1999). As is highlighted in this study, they do not seem to comprehend the nature and reciprocity of friendship. Despite the fact that the participants named friends and discussed activities with friends, we are speculative about the true nature of these friendships. This point is similar to one made by Church et al. (2000), who revealed that although half of all the middle school–age students with Asperger syndrome in their study identified a best friend, this friend may change from time to time and the relationship could be viewed by others as superficial. For example, in this study, John revealed some problems with friendships, despite his insistence that he had "the most friends." John's apparent lack of insight into his social difficulties is typical of adolescents with Asperger syndrome. A study of social problems and adaptive behavior among children and adolescents with Asperger syndrome indicated that although parents generally revealed significant concerns about their children's behavior and social skills, students did not rate themselves as having significant problems in these areas (Barnhill, Hagiwara, Myles, & Simpson, 2000). These results are consistent with the basic features of Asperger syndrome, including an inability to fully consider the perspectives of others and understand one's own feelings and behaviors (Myles & Simpson, 1998).

Some of the behavioral eccentricities associated with Asperger syndrome were also revealed in the study. The restricted range of interests found in persons with Asperger syndrome can take unusual or eccentric forms (Barnhill, 2001). An obsession with computers is particularly prevalent because socializing can be se-

verely limited (Barnhill, 2001). Three of the five adolescents who participated in the study had "best" friendships that seemed to specifically revolve around computers and computer games such as *Dungeons and Dragons*. Church et al. (2000) also found that best friendships among teenagers with Asperger syndrome tend to revolve around very specific interests such as computers and video games.

Another of the core characteristics of Asperger syndrome, cognitive inflexibility, was made apparent by the comments of Alice, John, and Jack in descriptions of who is and who is not a friend. In fact, Alice refused to befriend students who broke school rules. Individuals with Asperger syndrome cannot appreciate that in certain situations, rules may be bent or broken (Szatmari, 1991). Similar information regarding friendships was obtained in a study of experiences of children with Asperger syndrome (Church et al., 2000) in which it was noted that friendships among adolescents could dissolve if rules were broken.

The increasing levels of stress brought about by the characteristics of Asperger syndrome throughout the years of adolescence have been discussed by several authors. Church et al. (2000) noted in particular the anxiety of struggling with social expectations in the late middle school and high school years, and Gilchrist et al. (2001) hypothesized that this increasing difficulty during adolescence may result from the increasing pressure of social expectations on students at this time of development. This helps explain why adolescents with Asperger syndrome masquerade. It is evident that the high school years can represent a huge challenge for students with Asperger syndrome because they must cope with a larger, more diverse student population in which conformity and social competence are emphasised (Adreon & Stella, 2001), along with more rigorous academic work and more copious homework assignments. Students who lack the skills necessary to cope with these demands may experience significant problems and masquerade to hide inadequacies in skills or understanding.

━━ VOLUME 18, NUMBER 4, WINTER 2003 ━━

Conclusions

We conducted this descriptive study with no intent of generalizing the results to all adolescents who have Asperger syndrome. Nonetheless, the words and perspectives shared by these teenagers indicate perspectives of friendship that others with Asperger syndrome may well share. The study specifically provides examples of understandings and perceptions of what is a friend, what is not a friend, and what is an acquaintance; the language difficulties associated with these issues; and data illustrating the concept of masquerading to fit in with peers.

Professionals need to be particularly aware of the possible difficulties experienced by young people who have Asperger syndrome in understanding the language used in discussions about friendships. Sometimes it is easy to presume a level of understanding of terms and concepts associated with friendships. Furthermore, a professional's concept of friendship and what is important in a friendship may be very different from those of young people who have Asperger syndrome. For example, it is evident from the interviews with these students that issues related to society and school rules are important considerations in who is a friend. Although professionals have the goal of helping young people with Asperger syndrome participate in socially acceptable ways, they also have an obligation to recognize and value different people's perspectives about friendship. There is a need for more qualitative research to develop a better understanding of the perceptions and interactions of children and adults who have Asperger syndrome. This type of research will add to the more clinical studies evident in most journals that focus on Asperger syndrome.

ABOUT THE AUTHORS

Suzanne Carrington, PhD, is a lecturer in inclusive education in the School of Learning and Professional Studies at Queensland University of Technology. She is the Coordinator of postgraduate studies in the areas of learning support, inclusive education, and autistim spectrum disorders. She currently assists the Education Department of Queensland, in Australia, in the area of teacher development for inclusive education. Elizabeth Templeton, PhD, is a lecturer in the School of Learning and Professional Studies at Queensland University of Technology. She is the coordinator of the master's degree in education, behavior management, and lectures in behavior management, autism spectrum disorders, and counseling. Dr. Templeton conducts consultancy and private practice for schools, parents, and children in the areas of behavior management and counseling, with particular interest in emotional release counseling, sand play, and symbol work. Tracey Papinczak, MA, currently works in the area of evidence-based medicine at the University of Queensland's School of Population Health. She has a continuing interest in the health of adolescents and children, including children with Asperger syndrome. Address: Suzanne Carrington, School of Learning and Professional Studies, Queensland University of Technology, Victoria Park Road, Kelvin Grove, Brisbane, Queensland, Australia, 4059; e-mail: suzanne.carrington@qed.qld.gov.au

AUTHORS' NOTE

We would like to acknowledge the valuable contribution from Harold Stone in the development of the interview questions. We would also like to thank the special education teacher and students from the secondary school where the study was completed. This research would not have been completed without their valuable involvement.

REFERENCES

Adreon, D., & Stella, J. (2001). Transition to middle and high school: Increasing the success of students with Asperger syndrome. *Intervention in School and Clinic, 36,* 266–271.

Barnhill, G. (2001). What is Asperger syndrome? *Intervention in School and Clinic, 36,* 258–266.

Barnhill, G., Hagiwara, T., Myles, B. S., & Simpson, R. L. (2000). Asperger syndrome: A study of the cognitive profiles of 37 children and adolescents. *Focus on Autism and Other Developmental Disabilities, 15,* 146–153.

Baron-Cohen, S. (1995). *Mindblindness: An essay on autism and theory of mind.* Cambridge, MA: MIT Press.

Baron-Cohen, S., & Joliffe, T. (1997). Another advanced test of theory of mind: Evidence from very high functioning adults with autism or Asperger syndrome. *Journal of Child Psychology and Psychiatry, 38,* 813–822.

Carrington, S., & Graham, L. (1999). Asperger's syndrome: Learning characteristics and teaching strategies. *Special Education Perspectives, 8*(2), 15–23.

Carrington, S., & Graham, L. (2001). Perceptions of school by two teenage boys with Asperger syndrome and their mothers: A qualitative study. *Autism, 5,* 37–48.

Church, C., Alisanski, S., & Amanullah, S. (2000). The social, behavioral, and academic experiences of children with Asperger syndrome. *Focus on Autism and Other Developmental Disabilities, 15,* 12–20.

Filipek, P. A., Accardo, P. J., Baranek, G. T., Cook, E. H., Dawson, G., Gordon, B., et al. (1999). The screening and diagnosis of autistic spectrum disorders. *Journal of Autism and Developmental Disorders, 29,* 439–484.

Frith, U. (1991). Asperger and his syndrome. In U. Frith (Ed.), *Autism and Asperger syndrome* (pp. 1–36).Cambridge, UK: Cambridge University Press.

Gilchrist, A., Green, J., Cox, A., Burton, D., Rutter, M., & Le Couteur, A. (2001). Development and current functioning in adolescents with Asperger's syndrome: A comparative study. *Journal of Child Psychology and Psychiatry, 42,* 227–240.

Glaser, B., & Strauss, A. (1967). *The discovery of grounded theory: Strategies for qualitative research.* New York: Aldine.

Koning, C., & Magill-Evans, J. (2001). Social and language skills in adolescent boys with Asperger syndrome. *Autism, 5,* 23–36.

Le Compte, M. D., & Preissle, J. (1993). *Ethnography and qualitative design in educational research* (2nd ed.). San Diego, CA: Academic Press.

McPhail, J. C. (1995). Phenomenology as philosophy and method. *Remedial and Special Education, 16,* 159–167.

Mahon, A., Glendinning, C., Clarke, K., & Craig, G. (1996). Researching children: Methods and ethics. *Children and Society, 10,* 145–154.

Minichiello, V., Aroni, R., Timewell, E., & Alexander, L. (1995). *In-depth interviewing* (2nd ed.). Sydney, Australia: Longman.

Minkes, J., Robinson, C., & Weston, C. (1994). Consulting the children: Interviews with children using respite care services. *Disability and Society, 9*(1), 47–57.

Mishler, E. G. (1990). Validation in inquiry-guided research: The role of exemplars in

FOCUS ON AUTISM AND OTHER DEVELOPMENTAL DISABILITIES

narrative studies. *Harvard Educational Review, 60,* 415–441.

Morris, J. (1998). *Don't leave us out.* New York: Joseph Rowntree Foundation.

Myles, B. S., & Simpson, R. L. (1998). *Asperger syndrome: A guide for educators and practitioners.* Austin: PRO-ED.

Myles, B. L., & Southwick, J. (1999). *Asperger syndrome and difficult moments: Practical solutions for tantrums, rage and meltdown.* Shawnee Mission, KS: Autism Asperger Publishing.

Richards, T., & Richards, L. (1994). *QSR NUD*IST.* California: Alladin Systems.

Rogers, S. J. (2000). Interventions that facilitate socialization in children with autism. *Journal of Autism and Developmental Disorders, 30,* 399–409.

Simpson, R. L., & Myles, B. S. (1998). Aggression among children and youth who have Asperger's syndrome: A different population requiring different strategies. *Preventing School Failure, 42*(4), 149.

Strauss, A., & Corbin, J. (1994). Grounded theory methodology: An overview. In N. K. Denzin & Y. S. Lincoln (Eds.), *Handbook of qualitative research* (pp. 273–285). Thousand Oaks, CA: Sage.

Szatmari, P. (1991). Asperger syndrome: Diagnosis, treatment, and outcome. *Pervasive Developmental Disorders, 14,* 81–93.

Williams, K. (1995). Understanding the student with Asperger syndrome: Guidelines for teachers. *Focus on Autistic Behavior, 10*(2), 9–16.

APPENDIX
Interview Questions

Introduction

Introduce yourself. Welcome the student and thank him or her for coming.

Explain what the session is about: "We will be talking about friendships and how you get along with others. I will be asking you to tell me about your friendships and the things that are involved."

Explain that the identity of the students will be kept confidential and that the answers to the questions will be included in the results of the study, which will be used to help teachers and others understand how young people with Asperger syndrome get along with other people. Tell the student to ask if he or she does not understand anything. Let the student know that he or she does not have to answer every question and that he or she can stop the session at any time.

Questions

Those questions underlined should be asked of each student. Those questions in italics may be asked if more information and understanding is needed by the interviewer or the student.

- If someone could go out and organize friends for you, tell me what those friends would be like.
- *Tell me what you understand about people who are friends.*
- *Tell me what you understand about people who are acquaintances.*
- *Tell me what you understand about people who are not friends.*
- Tell me about your friends.
- *Who are your friends? Not just the people at school, but others at home, or somewhere else.*
- *Do you have friends who are younger or older than you? Tell me about these people. How are they different, and how are they the same?*

- *What sort of things do you like to do with your friends?*
- Tell me about the sort of things that work in your friendships.
- Tell me about the sort of things that don't work in your friendships.
- *What sort of things happen when you are with other people your age?*
- *Sometimes things with friends go well. Tell me about these things.*
- *Sometimes things with friends do not go so well. Tell me about these things.*
- *Tell me about things that didn't work with people who are no longer your friends.*
- *What sorts of things are difficult about your friendships and getting along with other kids?*
- What things are enjoyable and work well about your friendships?
- *What things are pleasant about your friendships?*
- *What things are enjoyable about your friendships?*
- *What things are important about your friendships?*
- *What things do you like doing with your friends?*
- If you could look into the future, how would you like your friendships to be?
- *What things would you like to keep the same with your friendships, those at school, those not at school?*
- *What things would you like to change about your friendships, those at school, those not at school?*
- What would you want your friends to know about you?
- What things do they need to know about you?
- What things should not be told to your friends about you?
- Tell me about how you would need help to change things with your friendships.
- *What help would you need from your teachers?*
- *What other help would you need?*

Thank the student for participating and tell him or her that if he or she has any questions to please contact the special needs teacher for the school.

Chapter 2

Quantitative and Qualitative Approaches

Learning Objectives

After completing your study of Chapter 2, you should be able to:

1. Define quantitative and qualitative research.

2. Explain the major ideas that have influenced the development of quantitative and qualitative research.

3. Identify characteristics that distinguish and are similar for quantitative and qualitative research in each of the six steps of research.

4. Identify the types of research designs used as procedures in quantitative, qualitative, or combined (or mixed) approaches.

5. Identify three factors useful in deciding whether quantitative or qualitative research is best for conducting a study.

Practice in Understanding Key Concepts

Important Terms and Concepts

The following items represent important concepts relating to quantitative and qualitative approaches. Using your own words, record definitions for the items in the space provided.

Quantitative research: _____

_____

_____

Qualitative research: _____

_____

_____

Research designs: _____

_____

_____

Applying the Concepts as a Consumer of Research

Carefully consider your definitions and descriptions of the key concepts for this chapter as you respond to the following items.

1. Summarize the major ideas that influenced the development of quantitative research. _____

_____

_____

_____

_____

2. Summarize the major ideas that influenced the development of qualitative research. _____

_____

_____

_____

_____

Now you should apply the characteristics of quantitative and qualitative research to two actual studies. Once again, read carefully the two articles at the end of Chapter 1: Sample Study #1 (SG pages 11–25) and Sample Study #2 (SG pages 26–33).

3. As you read each article, decide if it is an example of quantitative or qualitative research. Make annotated notes in the right-side margins indicating where the characteristics of the research approach (quantitative or qualitative) covered in this chapter appear to be addressed within the study.

Which approach did each study use and what evidence supports your answers?

Sample Study #1: _____

_____

_____

Sample Study #2: _____

_____

_____

Chapter 2

Activity Hint!

- See Chapter 2 section "*Useful Information for Consumers of Research*" and *Figure 2.1* for advice on distinguishing between quantitative and qualitative research approaches.

4. Consider Sample Study #1, "*The State of Music in the Elementary School: The Principal's Perspective*" (Abril & Gault, 2006). Briefly state how the authors implemented each step of the research process, highlighting characteristics that distinguish quantitative research.

Sample Study #1 (Abril & Gault, 2006):

Identifying a research problem: _____

_____

_____

Reviewing the literature: _____

_____

_____

Specifying a purpose for research: _____

_____

_____

Collecting data: _____

_____

_____

Analyzing and interpreting the data: _____

_____

_____

Reporting and evaluating research: _____

_____

_____

Activity Feedback!

- Note how Sample Study #1 is an example of quantitative research. This study identified a problem that called for describing trends in principals' perspectives about music education, reviewed a lot of literature to justify the importance of the problem, specified a narrow purpose that included seeking data on specific variables, collected numbered data on an instrument from a large number of participants, analyzed the data using statistical analyses, and reported the results in an objective and unbiased manner.

- Review Chapter 2 section "*What Characteristics Distinguish and Are Common to Quantitative and Qualitative Research in Each of the Six Steps?*" in the textbook for additional information.

5. Consider Sample Study #2, "*Adolescents with Asperger Syndrome and Perceptions of Friendship*" (Carrington, Templeton, & Papinczak, 2003). Briefly state how the authors implemented each step of the research process, highlighting characteristics that distinguish qualitative research.

Sample Study #2 (Carrington et al., 2003):

Identifying a research problem: _____

_____

_____

Reviewing the literature: _____

_____

_____

Specifying a purpose for research: _____

_____

_____

Collecting data: _____

_____

_____

Analyzing and interpreting the data: _____

_____

_____

Reporting and evaluating research: _____

_____

_____

Activity Feedback!

- Note how Sample Study #2 is an example of qualitative research. This study identified a problem that called for exploring the perceptions of friendship of adolescents who have Asperger syndrome in their own words, used the literature review in a minor role to justify the research problem, specified a broad purpose that included seeking to understand participants' experiences, collected word data from a small number of participants, analyzed the data using text analysis to develop description and themes, and reported the results in a subjective and reflexive manner.

Applying the Concepts as a Producer of Research

You will now practice applying the important concepts of this chapter to a new research problem relevant to you. Think of a potential research topic that interests you. This topic should be some kind of educational issue. You can use a topic of your own or one of the sample topics listed below.

Sample topics: Poor eating habits of college students
Disruptions of students in middle school classrooms
Use of testing in schools

6. My topic: _____

_____

_____

_____

      Suppose you have decided to conduct a **quantitative** study of this topic. Briefly describe how each of the following aspects of your study will reflect the quantitative approach.

7. What factor(s) will influence your decision to use a quantitative approach? _____

_____

_____

_____

8. What quantitative research problem will you identify? _____

_____

_____

_____

9. What will the role of the literature review be in your quantitative study? _____

_____

_____

_____

10. What quantitative purpose will you specify for your study? _____

_____

_____

_____

_____

11. Describe the quantitative data that you will collect: _____

_____

_____

_____

_____

12. Identify which quantitative research design you will use (experimental, correlational, or survey) and describe

why: _____

_____

_____

_____

Suppose you have decided to conduct a **qualitative** study of this topic. Briefly describe how each of the following aspects of your study will reflect the qualitative approach.

13. What factor(s) will influence your decision to use a qualitative approach? _____

_____

_____

_____

14. What qualitative research problem will you identify? _____

_____

_____

_____

15. What will the role of the literature review be in your qualitative study? _____

_____

_____

_____

16. What qualitative purpose will you specify for your study? _____

_____

_____

_____

_____

17. Describe the qualitative data that you will collect: _____

_____

_____

_____

_____

18. Identify which qualitative research design you will use (grounded theory, ethnographic, or narrative research)

and explain why: _____

_____

_____

_____

Practice Test Items

Answer the following items to check your understanding of the important concepts related to the quantitative and qualitative approaches. Once you have answered all of the items, you can check your ideas with the provided solutions.

1. Which of the following describes the qualitative approach to research? Circle the letter to the left of the correct response.

   a. An exploration of a central phenomenon
   b. A description of trends among variables
   c. Specific and narrow purpose
   d. Collecting information from a large number of individuals

2. Which of the following describes the quantitative research approach? Circle the letter to the left of the correct response.

   a. Seek to understand participants' experiences
   b. Collecting information from a small number of individuals
   c. An exploration of a central phenomenon
   d. Researchers take an unbiased approach

3. Which of the following approaches to educational research has been accepted the longest? Circle the letter to the left of the correct response.

   a. Mixed qualitative and quantitative approaches
   b. Qualitative approach
   c. Quantitative approach

4. Which of the following approaches to educational research emphasizes the collection of numbered data and statistical analyses? Circle the letter to the left of all correct responses.

   a. Qualitative approach
   b. Quantitative approach

5. Which of the following approaches to educational research uses a flexible reporting structure and researchers who take a biased and subjective approach? Circle the letter to the left of all correct responses.

    a. Qualitative approach
    b. Quantitative approach

6. Which of the following designs follow a quantitative approach? Circle the letter to the left of all correct responses.

    a. Action research   e. Grounded theory
    b. Correlational   f. Narrative research
    c. Ethnographic   g. Mixed methods
    d. Experimental   h. Survey

7. Which of the following designs follow a qualitative approach? Circle the letter to the left of all correct responses.

    a. Action research   e. Grounded theory
    b. Correlational   f. Narrative research
    c. Ethnographic   g. Mixed methods
    d. Experimental   h. Survey

8. Which of the following designs may combine both quantitative and qualitative approaches? Circle the letter to the left of all correct responses.

    a. Action research   e. Grounded theory
    b. Correlational   f. Narrative research
    c. Ethnographic   g. Mixed methods
    d. Experimental   h. Survey

9. Suppose a researcher studying adolescent tobacco use wants to describe the culture of the group of high school students who meet daily at the park adjacent to the school campus to smoke. Which research design would be best suited for this study? Circle the letter to the left of all correct responses.

    a. Action research   e. Grounded theory
    b. Correlational   f. Narrative research
    c. Ethnographic   g. Mixed methods
    d. Experimental   h. Survey

10. Suppose a researcher wants to measure the attitudes about tobacco use among high school students. Which research design would be best suited for this study? Circle the letter to the left of all correct responses.

    a. Action research   e. Grounded theory
    b. Correlational   f. Narrative research
    c. Ethnographic   g. Mixed methods
    d. Experimental   h. Survey

Chapter 2

1.   Which of the following describes the qualitative approach to research?

   a.   An exploration of a central phenomenon

   Review section "What Characteristics Distinguish and Are Common to Quantitative and Qualitative Research in Each of the Six Steps?" in the textbook

2.   Which of the following describes the quantitative research approach?

   d.   Researchers take an unbiased approach

   Review section "What Characteristics Distinguish and Are Common to Quantitative and Qualitative Research in Each of the Six Steps?" in the textbook

3.   Which of the following approaches to educational research has been accepted the longest?

   c.   Quantitative approach

   Review section "How Did Quantitative and Qualitative Research Develop?" in the textbook

4.   Which of the following approaches to educational research emphasizes the collection of numbered data and statistical analyses?

   b.   Quantitative approach

   Review section "What Characteristics Distinguish and Are Common to Quantitative and Qualitative Research in Each of the Six Steps?" in the textbook

5.   Which of the following approaches to educational research uses a flexible reporting structure and researchers who take a biased and subjective approach?

   a.   Qualitative approach

   Review section "What Characteristics Distinguish and Are Common to Quantitative and Qualitative Research in Each of the Six Steps?" in the textbook

6. Which of the following designs follow a quantitative approach?

    b. Correlational
    d. Experimental
    h. Survey

    Review section "What Are the Research Designs Associated with Quantitative and Qualitative Research?" in the textbook

7. Which of the following designs follow a qualitative approach?

    c. Ethnographic
    e. Grounded theory
    f. Narrative research

    Review section "What Are the Research Designs Associated with Quantitative and Qualitative Research?" in the textbook

8. Which of the following designs may combine both quantitative and qualitative approaches?

    a. Action research
    g. Mixed methods

    Review section "What Are the Research Designs Associated with Quantitative and Qualitative Research?" in the textbook

9. Suppose a researcher studying adolescent tobacco use wants to describe the culture of the group of high school students who meet daily at the park adjacent to the school campus to smoke. Which research design would be best suited for this study?

    c. Ethnographic

    Review section "What Are the Research Designs Associated with Quantitative and Qualitative Research?" in the textbook

10. Suppose a researcher wants to measure the attitudes about tobacco use among high school students. Which research design would be best suited for this study?

    h. Survey

    Review section "What Are the Research Designs Associated with Quantitative and Qualitative Research?" in the textbook

Chapter 3

Identifying a Research Problem

Learning Objectives

After completing your study of Chapter 3, you should be able to:

1. Define and identify a research problem and explain its importance to a study.

2. Distinguish between a research problem, the topic, the purpose, and the research questions.

3. Identify criteria for deciding whether you can or should study a research problem.

4. Describe how quantitative and qualitative research problems differ.

5. Describe the five elements that comprise a "statement of the problem" section.

6. Identify strategies useful in writing a "statement of the problem" section.

Practice in Understanding Key Concepts

Important Terms and Concepts

The following items represent important concepts relating to identifying a research problem. Using your own words, record definitions for the items in the space provided.

Research problems: _____

_____

_____

Statement of the problem: _____

_____

_____

_____

Educational topic: _____

_____

_____

Narrative hook: _____

_____

_____

Practical research problem: _____

_____

_____

Research-based research problem: _____

_____

_____

Justifying a research problem: _____

_____

_____

Deficiency in the evidence: _____

_____

_____

Audience: _____

_____

_____

Applying the Concepts as a Consumer of Research

Carefully re-read the introduction from Sample Study #2 on the next page. As you read this passage, identify the following features of the study's statement of the problem by making notes in the margin:

- Topic and narrative hook
- Research problem
- Justification of the problem
- Deficiencies in the existing knowledge
- Audiences that may benefit

Activity Hint!

- See Chapter 3 sections "*Useful Information for Consumers of Research*" and "*How Do You Write a 'Statement of the Problem' Section?*" for advice on reading the introduction to a study.

**Elements of a Statement
of the Problem**

Adolescents with Asperger Syndrome and Perceptions of Friendship
(Carrington, Templeton, & Papinczak, 2003, pp. 211–212)

Children who have been diagnosed with Asperger syndrome have difficulties in communicating with their peers and developing appropriate relationships with others at school. In spite of this, their intellectual ability can be within or above the normal range (Barnhill, Hagiwara, Myles, & Simpson, 2000). Researchers have agreed that difficulties communicating and learning unspoken social rules contribute to major challenges for children with Asperger syndrome as they develop (Church, Alisanki, & Amanullah, 2000; Frith, 1991; Koning & Magill-Evans, 2001). More specifically, idiosyncratic social skills present an enormous handicap in school, and continuing difficulties may result in aggressive behavior (Simpson & Myles, 1998) and depression (Barnhill, 2001). This is because these students frequently do not have the skills to engage in age-expected reciprocal social interactions (Simpson & Myles, 1998). Rather, these students could be described as socially awkward or self-centered with a lack of understanding of others. One reason social interactions are problematic for people with Asperger syndrome is that they experience difficulty in interpreting subtle social cues, particularly nonverbal body language (Koning & Magill-Evans, 2001). In addition, an inability to "mind read" means that these students will find it difficult to predict others' behavior, read the intentions of others, understand motives behind behavior, understand emotions, and understand how their behavior affects how others think or feel (Baron-Cohen, 1995; Baron-Cohen & Joliffe, 1997). These social and communication difficulties create additional stress for the developing adolescent at secondary school (Carrington & Graham, 2001).

Secondary students are required to cope with changes in routine and in behavioral expectations, engage in complex social interactions with peers and adults, and meet academic learning demands. In adolescence, when fitting in with peers is vitally important, complex, and stressful, students with Asperger syndrome have an increased need for social support and understanding. During their teens, these students generally become more aware of their differences. Carrington and Graham (1999) described how adolescents with Asperger syndrome have a need to fit in but do not know how to do so.

Little research has been conducted describing the perception of friendship and social experiences of adolescents who have Asperger syndrome, and there has been even less qualitative research incorporating children's own words. Church et al.'s (2000) study described characteristics of Asperger syndrome, including social skills and feelings about friends over time and during specific developmental stages. This article contains specific examples and illustrations provided by a group of students who have Asperger syndrome to support the findings in Church et al.'s article.

With this study, we aimed to advance understanding of the social difficulties that are characteristic of individuals with Asperger syndrome while providing a voice to this group of students. We asked the following research question: What are the perceptions of friendship for a group of secondary school students who have Asperger syndrome? Our professional knowledge of Asperger syndrome and the particular social difficulties experienced by this group of secondary school students can be expanded by listening to and reflecting on the voices of the participants in this study.

Using your margin notes, answer the following questions about this study's statement of the problem.

1. What was the study's topic? _____
_____
_____

2. What was the study's research problem? _____
_____
_____
_____

3. How did the authors justify this problem? _____
_____
_____
_____

4. What deficiency in the evidence did the authors identify? _____
_____
_____
_____
_____

5. For what audience(s) is this study important? _____
_____
_____
_____

6. Did the authors use a narrative hook? Was it effective? _____
_____
_____
_____

7. Is this research problem best suited for a quantitative or a qualitative study? Why? _____
_____
_____
_____

Chapter 3

Activity Feedback!

This introduction addresses the elements of a statement of the problem in the following ways:
- Topic: Children diagnosed with Asperger syndrome
- Research Problem: Children with Asperger syndrome experience challenges due to difficulties communicating and learning unspoken social rules
- Justification: Numerous references to the literature justifying the importance of communication
- Deficiency: Little research has described the perception of friendship and social experiences or included the voices of children with Asperger syndrome
- Audiences: Professionals working with and researching children with Asperger syndrome
- Narrative Hook: The first sentence of the passage presents a clear need for research
- Study approach: This research problem called for a qualitative study to explore the perceptions of friendship of a few adolescents who have Asperger syndrome in their own words.

Now apply the chapter content to a new study. Read the article at the end of this chapter (SG pages 55–59):

> **Sample Study #3:** Favaro, A., Zanetti, T., Huon, G., & Santonastaso, P. (2005). Engaging teachers in an eating disorder preventive intervention. *International Journal of Eating Disorders, 38*(1), 73–77.

Do the following as you read this study: (A) Note the major steps of the research process in the margins (Identifying the research problem; Reviewing literature; Specifying a purpose and research questions; Collecting data; Analyzing and interpreting data; and Reporting and evaluating research). (B) Focusing on the article's introduction, identify the following features of the study's statement of the problem with additional margin notes:
- Topic and narrative hook
- Research problem
- Justification of the problem
- Deficiencies in the existing knowledge
- Audiences that may benefit

Using your margin notes, answer the following questions about this study's statement of the problem.

8. What was the study's topic? _____

_____

9. What was the study's research problem? _____

_____

_____

_____

10. How did the authors justify this problem? _____

_____

_____

11. What deficiency in the evidence did the authors identify? _____

_____

_____

12. For what audience(s) is this study important? _____

_____

_____

13. Did the authors use a narrative hook? Was it effective? _____

_____

_____

_____

14. Is this research problem best suited for a quantitative or a qualitative study? Why? _____

_____

_____

_____

Applying the Concepts as a Producer of Research

You will now practice applying the important concepts to a new research problem of your choice. Assume that you are a researcher who is starting a new research project. Select a research topic by either picking one of interest to you or using one of the provided sample research topics. Develop the rationale for studying this topic by creating responses to the following items for this problem.

Sample topics: Providing effective counseling services to diverse students
                  Budgetary cutbacks for schools
                  High-stakes testing

15. The research topic: _____

16. The research problem: _____

_____

_____

_____

17. Can the problem be researched? Can you gain access to people and sites? What time, resources, and skills will

you need? _____

_____

_____

_____

_____

18. Should the problem be researched? In what way(s) will your study add to existing information? _____

_____

_____

_____

_____

19. Does the problem call for a quantitative or qualitative study? Why? _____

_____

_____

_____

_____

20. How will you justify the importance of studying this problem? _____

_____

_____

_____

_____

21. What deficiency exists in what is known about this problem? _____

_____

_____

_____

22. What audience(s) will benefit from the study? _____

_____

_____

_____

23. Write a narrative hook that you might use to start your study. _____

_____

_____

_____

_____

Practice Test Items

Answer the following items to check your understanding of the important concepts needed when identifying a research problem. Once you have answered all of the items, you can check your ideas with the provided solutions.

1. Which of the following lists of components of a research study is in order from the most general to the most specific? Circle the letter to the left of the correct response.

    a. Research problem, Purpose, Topic, Research questions
    b. Topic, Research questions, Purpose, Research problem
    c. Topic, Research problem, Purpose, Research questions
    d. Research questions, Topic, Research problem, Purpose

2. What are the five elements that comprise a "statement of the problem" section of a research study?

    a. _____

    b. _____

    c. _____

    d. _____

    e. _____

3. Consider how quantitative and qualitative research approaches differ. If a research problem requires you to do the following, would you choose a quantitative ("quan") approach or a qualitative ("qual") approach? Write "quan" or "qual" after each as appropriate.

    a. To obtain detailed information about a few people.   _____

    b. To test a theory.   _____

    c. To describe a process over time.   _____

    d. To assess the impact of variables on an outcome.   _____

    e. To generate a theory based on participant perspectives.   _____

    f. To apply results to a large number of people.   _____

4. Which of the following statements provide reasons why a problem should be researched? Circle the letter to the left of all correct responses.

    a. The study will fill a gap or void in the existing literature
    b. The study will examine people and sites to which access can be gained
    c. The study replicates a past study with different participants and sites
    d. The study gives voice to people not heard, silenced, or rejected in society

Read the following excerpts from the introduction from the study "*Predicting Asian Americans' Academic Performance in the First Year of College: An Approach Combining SAT Scores and Noncognitive Variables*."

[A] Asian Americans are the fastest growing minority group in universities in the United States (American Council on Education, 1998). [B] Between 1976 and 1996, the number of Asian American college students tripled from 2% to 6% of the total undergraduate student population (Snyder, 1999). ... [C] To match the needs of this increasing population, student affairs professionals and other educators must gain more information about Asian Americans, including factors (such as academic ability and coping strategies) affecting their academic performance and retention in universities.

[D] Asian Americans are often portrayed as a model minority because of their hard work and educational achievements, and for earning family incomes close to White Americans (Kao, 1995; Okutsu, 1989; Taylor & Stern, 1997). [E] Asian American students were found to spend significantly more time on homework and parents have higher educational expectations for their children than White Americans did (Mau, 1997). [F] In spite of their accomplishments, Asian Americans continue to face problems such as a discrepancy between education and income (Atkinson et al., 1993), insufficient mastery of English (Sue & Sue, 1990), racism (Delucchi & Do, 1996; Leung, 1990; Tan, 1994), and psychosocial and mental problems such as loneliness, isolation, and anxiety (Solberg, Ritsma, Davis, Tata, & Jolly, 1994). [G] Research studies show that, at colleges and universities, Asian Americans still face many challenges including inadequate services (Greene, 1987), challenge of affirmative action policy on admissions (Selingo, 1999), psychosocial problems when adjusting to universities (Abe & Zane, 1990), alcohol and substance abuse (Chi, Lubben, & Kitano, 1989), and less involvement than their White counterpart in student activities (Wang & Sedlacek, 1992). ...

[H] Owing to their minority status and cultural background, Asian American students face many challenges in universities. [I] Nonetheless, little has been found explaining academic performance of Asian Americans. (Ting, 2000, pp. 442–443)

Use this passage to answer questions 5–10. When answering the questions, refer to specific sentences in the passage by using the appropriate reference letter (e.g., [A]) given at the start of the sentence.

5. What is the research topic? _____ Sentence(s): _____

6. What is the research problem? _____

_____ Sentence(s): _____

7. Which sentence(s) serves to justify the research problem? _____

8. Identify the sentence where the author identifies a deficiency in the evidence. _____

9. Which sentence refers to potential audiences for this study? _____

10. (a) Do you think the author should adopt a quantitative or qualitative approach? _____

   (b) Explain why using specific sentences in the passage. _____

_____

_____

Practice Test Items - Answer Key

1. The following list of components of a research study is in order from the most general to the most specific:

    c. (Most general) Topic → Research problem → Purpose → Research questions (Most specific)

    Review section "How Does the Research Problem Differ from Other Parts of Research?" in the textbook

2. The five elements that comprise a "statement of the problem" section of a research study are:

    a. Introduction to the educational topic
    b. Statement of the research problem
    c. Justification of the research problem
    d. Identification of deficiencies in our existing knowledge
    e. Discussion of the audiences that will benefit from the study

    Review section "How Do You Write a 'Statement of the Problem' Section?" in the textbook

3. If a research problem requires you to do the following, would you choose a quantitative ("quan") approach or a qualitative ("qual") approach?

    a. To obtain detailed information about a few people.   qual

    b. To test a theory.   quan

    c. To describe a process over time.   qual

    d. To assess the impact of variables on an outcome.   quan

    e. To generate a theory based on participant perspectives.   qual

    f. To apply results to a large number of people.   quan

    Review section "How Does the Research Problem Differ in Quantitative and Qualitative Research?" in the textbook

4. Which of the following statements provide reasons why a problem should be researched?

    a. The study will fill a gap or void in the existing literature
    c. The study replicates a past study with different participants and sites
    d. The study gives voice to people not heard, silenced, or rejected in society

    Review section "Can and Should Problems Be Researched?" in the textbook

5. The research topic of the passage can be stated as: Asian American college students [A & B]

    Review section "How Do You Write a 'Statement of the Problem' Section?" in the textbook

6. The research problem can be summarized as: Asian Americans face many problems such as insufficient mastery of English [F] and as college students, they face challenges such as inadequate services [G].

    Review section "How Do You Write a 'Statement of the Problem' Section?" in the textbook

7. The research problem is justified by the literature in sentences [F & G].

    Review section "How Do You Write a 'Statement of the Problem' Section?" in the textbook

8. The author identified a deficiency in the evidence in the final sentence: [I] Nonetheless, little has been found explaining academic performance of Asian Americans.

    Review section "How Do You Write a 'Statement of the Problem' Section?" in the textbook

9. Potential audiences for this study are student affairs professionals and educators at colleges [C].

    Review section "How Do You Write a 'Statement of the Problem' Section?" in the textbook

10. (a) The author should adopt a quantitative approach
    (b) The author should adopt a quantitative approach since this passage discusses [C] the effect of variables ("the factors") on an outcome ("academic performance and retention") and refers to [I] "explaining" academic performance of Asian Americans.

    Review section "How Does the Research Problem Differ in Quantitative and Qualitative Research?" in the textbook

REGULAR ARTICLE

Engaging Teachers in an Eating Disorder Preventive Intervention

Angela Favaro, MD, PhD[1]
Tatiana Zanetti, MSc[1]
Gail Huon, PhD[2]
Paolo Santonastaso, MD[1]*

ABSTRACT

Objective: This study evaluated the effectiveness at 1-year follow-up of a psychoeducational eating disorders preventive intervention implemented by specifically trained teachers.

Method: Participating teachers participated in a 5-week training program. One hundred forty-one female students attending nine classes at a vocational training school in Mestre (Venice) were assessed via a structured clinical interview (Structured Clinical Interview for DSM-IV Axis I disorders) and via the 40-item Eating Attitudes Test (EAT-40). Three classes were randomly selected to participate in a 6-week prevention program conducted by the trained teachers.

Results: Our data show that a disturbing number of the girls who were asymptomatic at baseline had developed a full or partial eating disorder 1 year later. This was the case for 2 (5%) participants and 10 (11%) subjects in the control group. Subjects in the prevention group differed significantly from the control group at the 1-year follow-up. This was the case for their EAT Bulimia subscale scores, which showed a significant improvement. The intervention group also revealed a lower development of food restraint and pathologic body attitudes.

Discussion: Given the sample size, our findings must be considered cautiously. However, they suggest that students can benefit from participation in a preventive intervention program conducted by teachers, and the benefits appear to be particularly pronounced for bulimic symptoms. © 2005 by Wiley Periodicals, Inc.

Keywords: eating disorders prevention; teacher involvement; clinical assessment

(Int J Eat Disord 2005; 38:73–77)

Introduction

Given the incidence of eating disorders, their serious physical and psychological consequences, and the difficulties and high costs of treatment, it is not surprising that primary and secondary prevention programs for eating disorders are receiving attention in the scientific literature (Pearson, Goldklang, & Striegel-Moore, 2002).

Yet, prevention in this field continues to be controversial. Although some authors consider it to be an essential part of health promotion policy (Huon, 1996), and some countries have multilevel nationwide programs to decrease incidence and prevalence (e.g., Gresk & Karlsen, 1994), others have warned that our knowledge of etiology is inadequate, and that, in some cases, prevention is potentially dangerous (Carter, Stewart, Dunn, & Fairburn, 1997; Mann et al., 1997). Such discrepant views are not surprising, given that published accounts have yielded inconsistent findings (Pratt & Woolfenden, 2002; Stice & Shaw, 2004). Being able to demonstrate the effectiveness of cost-effective preventive interventions is, however, an important research objective.

Santonastaso et al. (1999) developed and evaluated the impact of a psychoeducational preventive intervention with a sample of 16-year-old schoolgirls in Italy. They found no significant prevention-control group differences for girls who, at baseline, were "high-risk" subjects (i.e., they scored more than 30 on the 40-item Eating Attitudes Test [EAT]). "Low-risk" girls, however, showed a significant reduction in body dissatisfaction and bulimic attitudes. The results concerning this particular issue are equivocal in the literature about eating disorders prevention, and seem to depend on the definition of "risk" status and, perhaps, also on the type of preventive intervention. So, although some studies have found that high-risk subjects show greater effects (Buddeberg-Fischer, Klaghofer, Gnam, & Buddeberg, 1998; Huon, Roncolato, & Ritchie, 1997; Stewart, Carter, Drinkwater, Hainsworth, & Fairburn, 2001),

Accepted 7 November 2004
[1] Psychiatric Clinic, Department of Neuroscience, University of Padua, Padova, Italy
[2] School of Psychology, University of New South Wales, Sydney, Australia
*Correspondence to: Paolo Santonastaso, MD, Psychiatric Clinic, Department of Neuroscience, Via Giustiniani 3, 35128 Padova, Italy. E-mail: paolo.santonastaso@unipd.it
Published online 21 June 2005 in Wiley InterScience (www.interscience.wiley.com). DOI: 10.1002/eat.20148
© 2005 Wiley Periodicals, Inc.

FAVARO ET AL.

others have found no differences (Killen et al., 1993), and still others have found results similar to ours (e.g., Neumark-Sztainer, Butler, & Palti, 1995). However, the results of Santonastaso et al. (1999) suggested that further reasearch was needed to see how robust the response of low-risk girls might be. Also, the program in Santonastaso et al. (1999) was conducted by professionals with specific eating disorders expertise. Such an approach to preventive intervention is hardly likely to be implemented on a large scale. It is costly, and school curricula have insufficient flexibility to include all topics that schools are expected to cover. Teachers and administrators are more likely to be sympathetic to preventive interventions if they can be integrated into the normal school curriculum.

The current study was designed, therefore, to determine the effectiveness of a prevention program implemented by teachers who were specifically trained for the role. We were particularly interested to observe the response to our intervention of low-risk girls. For that reason, our intervention was specifically targeted towards discouraging the use of unhealthy weight control practices, including strict dieting, and to developing the skills to deal with the media's overemphasis on thinness. The effectiveness of the intervention at the 1-year follow-up was, therefore, determined by considering the development of eating disorders and of specific symptoms addressed by the intervention.

Methods

Teacher Training

Three teachers who were interested in this project were taught about eating disorders in a training program devised by psychologists and psychiatrists with expertise in the field of eating disorders. The training provided information about adolescent health and development, the nature, clinical features of, and risk factors for, eating disorders, and critical reflection on prevention. Teachers also received training in conducting group sessions, and in utilizing students' existing knowledge in the discussions. Teachers were provided with all necessary didactic material, in the form of articles and books to read, as well as overheads and slides that they could use during the program.

Sample

Nine classes, comprising 141 girls, at a vocational training school in Mestre, an urbanized area near Venice, were identified for this research. Of these, 138 girls participated at the baseline assessment (98%) and 132 (including the

3 subjects who did not participate at baseline) participated at the 1-year follow-up. In total, 129 girls were assessed both at baseline and at the 1-year follow-up. Thus, the study had a 91.5% participation rate. The girls were 16–18 years old (mean age = 17.0 ± 1.1). We randomly selected three participation and six comparison classes. Randomization was done by class (rather than by individual subjects). For the three prevention classes, therefore, we included class as a possible source of variance in a within-subject analysis to test the possibility of intraclass dependence of responses. In contrast, control group subjects were included in the analysis as a single class.

Procedure and Outcome Measures

Formal permission was obtained from the local director of studies. The teachers conducted the program with classes that they did not teach. This was believed to be important to reduce the likelihood that students would feel that their participation was subject to any judgement or evaluation. The program consisted of six 2-hr weekly sessions. Participation was voluntary, and all participants gave informed consent for the data to be used in an anonymous way. The interviews were conducted by formally trained psychiatrists and psychologists with clinical experience in the field of eating disorders. All girls were assessed via a structured clinical interview (Structured Clinical Interview for DSM-IV Axis I disorders [SCID], section for eating disorders; First, Spitzer, Gibbon, & Williams, 1995) and the EAT-40 (Garner, Olmsted, Bohr, & Garfinkel, 1982) at baseline and 1 year later. The trained interviewers also collected information about sociodemographic data, eating habits, and weight history. On both occasions, the girls' heights and weights were also measured. Interviewers were blind to the treatment condition of subjects. The effectiveness of the preventive intervention was established by comparing the intervention and the control groups in terms of the development of eating disorders. The presence of both full and partial-syndrome eating disorders, as they were defined in Favaro, Ferrara, and Santonastaso (2003), was assessed by interviews. Partial anorexia nervosa is defined as all of the criteria for anorexia nervosa are met, except that either individuals have not developed amenorrhea, or, despite significant weight loss, their weight remains in the normal range. Partial bulimia nervosa is defined as all of the criteria for bulimia nervosa are met, except that either binge eating and inappropriate compensatory behavior occur less than twice a week or that recurrent compensatory behaviors are present and objective binge eating is not.

In addition, the development of specific symptoms addressed in the prevention program were compared between groups. The symptoms are strict dieting (i.e., eating less than 800–1,000 kcal per day), fasting (i.e., skipping one of the main meals at least 2 days per week), unhealthy weight control behaviors (self-induced vomiting, laxative/diuretics

74

abuse), and excessive importance of body weight/body shape on self-esteem. The presence or absence of these symptoms was determined according to the definitions of the Eating Disorders Examination (EDE; Fairburn & Cooper, 1993).

Program Contents

The content of the preventive intervention overlapped only partially with that employed in the Santonastaso et al. (1999) study.

First Session. Essentially, the first session dealt with adolescence, covering such issues as the relation between adolescents and their family, adolescents and their peers, and from the interpersonal to a more personal perspective, their relationship with themselves and their own body.

Second Session. A special session was developed to discuss the body during adolescence, with descriptions of normal growth and development processes, that moved from the morphologic changes of puberty to a more cognitive perspective on body image. Concepts like ideal body and body ideal, body acceptance, body dissatisfaction, and body denigration were also discussed.

Third Session. To facilitate the development of skills for dealing with the media's overemphasis on thinness, and to discourage the use of excessive caloric restriction, the focus in the third session was on the pressure to be thin, the different methods to lose weight, the advantages and disadvantages of the various forms of dieting, the effects on normal development, the reasons for the failure of excessive dieting, and the potential link with the development of eating disorders.

Fourth Session. The fourth session was about eating disorders, their diagnostic criteria, predisposing, precipitating, and perpetuating factors, clinical features (physical and psychological), and treatments.

Fifth Session. The girls were asked to suggest how eating disorders might be prevented, and whether they believed prevention was possible. This session also covered the different types and goals of prevention, their different strategies, target groups, and methods.

Sixth Session. The focus during the final session was on the media and its impact on their own beliefs about beauty, thinness, fitness, health, and well-being. Care was taken to help the girls distinguish between myth and fact, with the intention of encouraging the girls to be more skeptical and critical of what they are presented with in media images and messages.

At the beginning of each session, the teachers introduced the relevant topic and provided an overview for approximately 30–45 minutes. After that, the teacher facilitated a group discussion on the same topic (this lasted for approximately 1 hr 15 min). At the end of each session, the girls were asked to write a summary of the discussion and their reactions to it. After the completion of the 6 weeks of the intervention, there were two plenary sessions, attended also by the experts. During the first of these, the girls were encouraged to ask any questions, and to provide their comments about the program. The second was for the girls' parents, and a similar question-and-answer session took place.

Statistical Analyses

t Tests were performed to compare groups. Confidence intervals of incidence were calculated using the following formula: $p \pm 1.96[(p \times q)/N]^{1/2}$, where p is the prevalence (n/N), q is (1−p), n is the number of affected subjects, and N is the total number of subjects. The statistical significance of the differences between incidences was calculated using the formula indicated by Robins et al. (1984): $t = (p_1 \times p_2)/[((p_1 \times q_1)/N_1) + ((p_2 \times q_2)/N_2)]^{1/2}$. A nested analysis of variance (ANOVA) with intervention, classes within prevention group, and subjects within classes as the source of variance was conducted to determine the impact of the prevention program. SPSS software was used for the statistical analyses (SPSS, San Diego, CA).

Results

Initial Assessment

In the whole sample, the baseline prevalence rates for anorexia nervosa and bulimia nervosa were 0.7% and 2.1%, respectively. We found also some cases of partial anorexia nervosa (4.3%) and partial bulimia nervosa (6.4%). At the initial assessment, no differences were found between the prevention and control group in terms of age (16.7 ± 1.1 vs. 17.1 ± 1.0 years; $t = 1.82$; not significant [NS]), body mass index (BMI; 20.5 ± 2.5 vs. 20.8 ± 2.5 years; $t = 0.81$; NS), and EAT total scores (17.6 ± 9.7 vs. 15.1 ± 9.4 years; $t = 1.31$; NS).

One-Year Follow-Up

The rates of new cases of eating disorders in the two groups are presented in Table 1. Of those who participated in the prevention program, no new case of bulimia nervosa was found, whereas, in the control group, 3 new cases were present 1 year later. In the prevention group, 1 girl had developed a partial form of anorexia nervosa and 1, a partial form of bulimia nervosa. Considering the whole spectrum of eating disorders, there were 5.3% new cases in the prevention group and 11% new cases in the control group.

We then analyzed the development of key eating disorder symptoms in the two groups. Among subjects who did not restrict their food intake at the

FAVARO ET AL.

TABLE 1. Rates (with 95% confidence intervals) of development of ED in the two groups during the 1-year follow-up

Rate of New Cases	Prevention Group ($n = 38$)	Control Group ($n = 91$)	t	p
Anorexia nervosa	0.0 (0.0–0.0)	0.0 (0.0–0.0)		
Bulimia nervosa	0.0 (0.0–0.0)	3.3 (0.0–7.0)	1.74	<.05
Partial anorexia nervosa	2.6 (0.0–5.2)	2.2 (0.0–5.2)	0.14	NS
Partial bulimia nervosa	2.6 (0.0–5.2)	5.5 (3.1–7.9)	0.81	NS
Any ED	5.3 (1.7–8.9)	11.0 (7.7–14.3)	1.17	NS

Note: ED = eating disorders; NS = not significant.

baseline assessment (34 in the prevention group vs. 82 in the control group), 1 subject in the prevention group and 10 subjects in the control group had developed food restraint at the 1-year follow-up (3% vs. 12%; $t = 2.01$; $p < .03$). No significant difference was found for the development of other unhealthy weight control methods, such as fasting (5% vs. 7%) and self-induced vomiting and laxative/diuretics abuse (0% vs. 1%). Our next analysis focused on subjects for whom, at baseline, body weight and shape were not very important for their self-esteem (28 in the prevention group vs. 74 subjects in the control group). At the follow-up, we observed a significantly lower rate of prevention group girls reporting that "symptom" when compared with the control group (0% vs. 15%; $t = 3.60$; $p < .001$).

Table 2 shows the change in BMI and EAT scores in the two groups. We analyzed the effects of the preventive intervention using a nested ANOVA with intervention, classes within prevention group, and subjects within classes as the source of variance. The prevention and control groups did not differ in terms of the changes in BMI, total EAT scores, as well as in the Dieting and Oral Control subscales of the EAT. The prevention group showed a significant improvement in EAT Bulimia subscale scores (effect size = 0.55), whereas in the control group, no change was observed (Table 2). We performed

the same analyses excluding all the subjects with an eating disorder at baseline. The results were very similar. The between-group differences remained significant for the EAT Bulimia subscale (effect size = 0.70), $F(1,109) = 8.60$; $p < .005$. In both sets of analyses, no significant effect of classes within prevention group was observed.

Discussion

This study evaluated the effectiveness of an eating disorders preventive intervention for adolescent schoolgirls that was conducted by teachers. The data from our 1-year follow-up assessment showed that approximately 10% of the initially asymptomatic girls developed a full or partial-syndrome eating disorder, but that the rates were significantly lower among those who had taken part in the intervention. Among participants, there were no new cases of bulimia nervosa, and compared with the control group, the percentage of new eating disorder cases was substantially lower. The intervention that we evaluated targeted some specific symptoms considered by the literature to be very relevant in the development of new cases of eating disorders. These symptoms were the unhealthy weight control practices and the importance for self-esteem of body weight and shape. The intervention was found to be effective on some of these variables. Compared with the control group, fewer prevention group girls developed strict dieting or reported that weight and shape are very important for their self-esteem. In addition, the Bulimia subscale of the EAT improved for girls in the prevention program, but there was a slight worsening for the control group girls. These findings are noteworthy because concern was expressed not only about the lack of positive outcomes from prevention programs, but also, in some cases, the finding that prevention can do harm. Our findings indicate that prevention programs can yield positive results, and they can do so

TABLE 2. Body mass index and EAT at baseline and 1-year follow-up in the two groups

	Prevention Group ($n = 38$)		Control Group ($n = 91$)		
	Baseline M (SD)	Follow-Up M (SD)	Baseline M (SD)	Follow-Up M (SD)	ANOVA[a] $F(1,125)$
Body mass index	20.8 (2.6)	20.9 (2.7)	20.6 (2.4)	20.8 (2.3)	0.06
EAT	18.6 (10.3)	15.8 (9.9)	18.0 (13.0)	15.2 (12.4)	0.00
EAT Dieting	6.6 (5.9)	5.4 (5.8)	6.7 (6.9)	5.6 (6.3)	0.00
EAT Bulimia	1.1 (2.1)	0.1 (0.5)	0.8 (2.0)	0.8 (2.1)	8.46*
EAT Oral Control	2.5 (2.4)	2.2 (2.2)	3.1 (3.7)	2.1 (3.0)	1.92

Note: EAT = Eating Attitudes Test; ANOVA = analysis of variance.
[a]A nested ANOVA was used with prevention, classes within prevention group, and subjects within classes as source of variance. Only the Time × Group effect was reported. The Time × Class effect was not significant for all the measures.
*Significant at $p < .005$ at ANOVA for repeated measures.

PREVENTIVE INTERVENTION

without doing harm. Although it is difficult to compare this study with our previous one (Santonastaso et al., 1996), because of the differences in the assessment methods (interview vs. self-report), the findings of the current study confirm the importance of assessing the impact of the preventive intervention only in low-risk subjects. In the current study, we deliberately removed from most of the analyses all the girls who showed any symptoms of eating disorders at baseline so that we could determine the effectiveness of our intervention with the girls who were assumed to be lower in risk at the outset.

Our study findings highlight three additional important points. First, the initial eating disorders prevalence rates were high. It is perhaps worth noting that our study was conducted in a recently industrialized region, where, our interviews revealed, girls uncharacteristically (for Italy) eat lunch and spend most of the day in the absence of both parents. For that reason, they can be considered, in the Italian context, to be at high risk for the development of an eating problem. Second, a major strength of our study is the clinical assessment of the whole sample both at the baseline and at the 1-year follow-up, by interviewers who were blind to the intervention condition of their interviewees. The latter might be regarded as the gold standard for the evaluation of a prevention program. Third, and most importantly, our findings suggest that prevention can be implemented successfully by teachers, at least if they have been provided with specific and detailed training. Engaging teachers in prevention is efficient and likely to be viewed positively by school administrators. Also, teachers are in close contact with adolescents and are likely to be among the first to recognize when problems exist.

Although some might argue that a possible limitation of this study is the use of the EAT, the agreement between interview and EAT score results should be noted. The main limitation of the current study is the small sample size. Our study has yielded some important and statistically significant findings, largely attributable to the high incidence of some bulimic symptoms in what might be considered a high-risk sample. These findings are encouraging. However, the replication of the study with a larger sample size is needed so that the generalization of our findings can be established.

References

Buddeberg-Fischer, B., Klaghofer, R., Gnam, G., & Buddeberg, C. (1998). Prevention of disturbed eating behaviour: A prospective intervention study in 14- to 19-year-old Swiss students. Acta Psychiatrica Scandinavica, 98, 146–155.

Carter, J.C., Stewart, A., Dunn, N.V.J., & Fairburn, C.G. (1997). Primary prevention of eating disorders: Might it do more harm than good? International Journal of Eating Disorders, 22, 167–172.

Fairburn, C.G., & Cooper, Z. (1993). The Eating Disorder Examination (12th ed.). In C.G. Fairburn & G.T. Wilson (Eds.), Binge eating: Nature, assessment, and treatment (pp. 123–143). New York: Guilford Press.

Favaro, A., Ferrara, S., & Santonastaso, P. (2003). The spectrum of eating disorders in young women: A prevalence study in a general population sample. Psychosomatic Medicine, 65, 701–708.

First, M.B., Spitzer, R.L., Gibbon, M., & Williams, J.B.W. (1995). Structured Clinical Interview for DSM-IV axis I disorders. Washington DC: American Psychiatric Press.

Garner, D.M., Olmsted, M.P., Bohr, Y., & Garfinkel, P.E. (1982). The Eating Attitude Test: Psychometric features and clinical correlates. Psychological Medicine, 12, 871–878.

Gresk, O.R.B., & Karlsen, A. (1994). Norwegian program for the primary, secondary and tertiary prevention of eating disorders. Eating Disorders, 2, 1, 57–63.

Huon, G.F. (1996). Health promotion and the prevention of dieting-induced disorders. Eating Disorders, 4, 27–32.

Huon, G.F., Roncolato, W.G., Ritchie, J.E., & Braganza, C. (1997). Prevention of dieting-induced disorders: Findings and implications of a pilot study. Eating Disorders, Treatment and Prevention, 5, 280–293.

Killen, J.D., Taylor, C.B., Hammer, L., Litt, I., Wilson, D.M., Rich, T., Hayward C., Simmonds, B., Kraemer, H., & Varady, A. (1993). An attempt to modify unhealthful eating attitudes and weight regulation practices of young adolescent girls. International Journal of Eating Disorders, 13, 369–384.

Mann, T., Nolen-Hoeksema, S., Huang, K., Burgard, D., Wright, A., & Hanson, K. (1997). Are two interventions worse than none: Joint primary and secondary prevention of eating disorders in college females. Health Psychology, 16, 215–225.

Neumark-Sztainer, D., Butler, R., & Palti, H. (1995). Eating disturbances among adolescent girls: Evaluation of a school-based primary prevention program. Journal of Nutritional Education, 27, 24–31.

Pearson, J., Goldklang, D., & Striegel-Moore, R.H. (2002). Prevention of eating disorders: Challenges and opportunities. International Journal of Eating Disorders, 31, 233–239.

Pratt, B.M., & Woolfenden, S.R. (2002). Interventions for preventing eating disorders in children and adolescents. The Cochrane Database of Systematic Reviews, CD002891.

Robins, L.N., Helzer, J.E., Weissman, M.M., Orvaschel, H., Gruenberg, E., Burke, J.D., & Regier, D.A. (1984). Lifetime prevalence of specific psychiatric disorders in three sites. Archives of General Psychiatry, 41, 949–958.

Santonastaso, P., Zanetti, T., Sala, A., Favaretto, G., Vidotto, G., & Favaro, A. (1996). Prevalence of eating disorders in Italy: A survey on a sample of 16-year-old female students. Psychotherapy and Psychosomatics, 65, 158–162.

Santonastaso, P., Zanetti, T., Ferrara, S., Olivotto, M.C., Magnavita, N., & Favaro, A. (1999). A preventive intervention program in adolescent schoolgirls: A longitudinal study. Psychotherapy and Psychosomatics, 68, 46–50.

Stewart, D.A., Carter, J.C., Drinkwater, J., Hainsworth, J., & Fairburn, C.G. (2001). Modification of eating attitudes and behavior in adolescent girls: A controlled study. International Journal of Eating Disorders, 29, 107–118.

Stice, E., & Shaw, H. (2004). Eating disorder prevention programs: A meta-analytic review. Psychological Bulletin, 130, 206–227.

Int J Eat Disord 38:1 73–77 2005

77

Chapter 4

Reviewing the Literature

Learning Objectives

After completing your study of Chapter 4, you should be able to:

1. Define what it means to review the literature and explain its importance.

2. List the differences in a literature review for quantitative and qualitative research.

3. Identify the five steps in conducting a literature review.

4. Write a literature review.

Practice in Understanding Key Concepts

Important Terms and Concepts

The following items represent important concepts relating to reviewing the literature. Using your own words, record definitions for the items in the space provided.

Literature review: _____

_____

_____

ERIC database: _____

_____

_____

Primary source literature: _____

_____

_____

Secondary source literature: _____

_____

Meta-analysis: _____

_____

_____

Summaries: _____

_____

_____

Encyclopedias: _____

_____

_____

Dictionaries and glossaries: _____

_____

_____

Handbooks: _____

_____

_____

Statistical indexes: _____

_____

_____

Reviews and syntheses: _____

_____

_____

Abstract: _____

_____

_____

Literature map: _____

_____

_____

Style manual: _____

_____

_____

End-of-text references: _____

_____

_____

Chapter 4

Within-text references: _____

_____

_____

Levels of headings: _____

_____

_____

Thematic review of the literature: _____

_____

_____

Study-by-study review of the literature: _____

_____

_____

Applying the Concepts as a Consumer of Research

Carefully consider your definitions and descriptions of the key concepts for this chapter. Using your own words, briefly elaborate on these concepts by comparing and contrasting the following ideas.

1. Compare and contrast how literature is typically used in quantitative and qualitative studies. _____

_____

_____

_____

_____

2. Compare and contrast the use of primary sources and secondary sources for a literature review. _____

_____

_____

_____

_____

3. Compare and contrast the use of published journal articles and web postings for a literature review. _____

_____

_____

_____

Now you will practice abstracting the elements of a quantitative study by completing the following five items for Sample Study #3 "*Engaging Teachers in an Eating Disorder Preventive Intervention*" (SG pages 55–59).

Activity Hint!

- See Chapter 4 section "***Taking Notes and Abstracting Studies***" and *Figure 4.6* for advice on writing an abstract for a quantitative study.

4. Write out the complete reference for this article in APA (5th Edition) form:

_____

_____

_____

_____

5. Research Problem: _____

_____

_____

_____

_____

_____

6. Research Questions or Hypotheses: _____

_____

_____

_____

_____

_____

_____

7. Data Collection Procedure: _____

_____

_____

_____

_____

_____

_____

8. Results: _____

_____

_____

_____

_____

_____

_____

_____

_____

Now you will practice abstracting the elements of a qualitative study by completing the following five items for Sample Study #2 "*Adolescents with Asperger Syndrome and Perceptions of Friendship*" (SG pages 26–33).

Activity Hint!

- See Chapter 4 section "***Taking Notes and Abstracting Studies***" and ***Figure 4.7*** for advice on writing an abstract for a qualitative study.

9. Write out the complete reference for this article in APA (5th Edition) form:

_____

_____

_____

_____

10. Research Problem: _____

_____

_____

_____

11. Research Questions: _____

_____

_____

_____

_____

12. Data Collection Procedure: _____

_____

_____

_____

_____

_____

_____

13. Findings: _____

_____

_____

_____

_____

_____

_____

_____

_____

_____

Activity Feedback!
- You can find complete end-of-text references for these studies in APA form in the References list at the end of this Study Guide (SG page 295).
- Review Chapter 4 section "***Using a Style Manual***" in the textbook for additional information.

Applying the Concepts as a Producer of Research

You will now practice applying the important concepts to a new research problem of your choice. Assume that you are a researcher who is starting a new research project. Select a research topic by either picking one of interest to you or using one of the provided sample research topics.

Sample research topics: Strategies for reading instruction
Teacher preparation and training
Behavior problems

14. My research topic: _____

_____

_____

Chapter 4

Apply the five-step process explained in this chapter for designing and conducting a literature review.

15. Step 1 – Identify Key Terms: Write a working title for your study or a short general question that you hope to answer. Select two to three keywords that capture the central idea.

Working title/General question: _____

_____

Key terms: _____

_____

16. Step 2 – Locate literature: Using the keywords you identified, conduct a search in one of the databases discussed in the textbook. Refine your search until you successfully locate some research studies on your topic.

Description of my search: _____

_____

_____

_____

_____

17. Step 3 – Critically evaluate and select the literature for your review.

What criteria will you use to decide if a study in the literature is relevant? _____

_____

_____

_____

_____

18. Step 4 – Organize the literature. Describe how you will organize the literature that you find on your topic. ____

_____

_____

_____

19. Step 5 – Write a review: What type of review will you write (thematic or study-by-study)? What style manual

will you use? _____

_____

_____

_____

_____

20. Describe the importance of this literature review for your study: _____

_____

_____

_____

_____

Practice Test Items

Answer the following items to check your understanding of the important concepts needed when reviewing the literature. Once you have answered all of the items, you can check your ideas with the provided solutions.

1. Which of the following sources is most appropriate and desirable to use in a literature review? Circle the letter to the left of the correct response.

    a. An essay
    b. A meta-analysis study
    c. A primary source
    d. A secondary source

2. Which of the following kinds of literature is most appropriate and desirable to use in a literature review? Circle the letter to the left of the correct response.

    a. Research handbooks
    b. Refereed journal articles
    c. Professional association newsletters
    d. Conference papers

3. Which of the following represent appropriate uses of the literature in a typical qualitative research study? Circle all that apply.

    a. Used to document the importance of the research problem
    b. Used to support the theory used in the study
    c. Used to foreshadow the research questions
    d. Used to compare and contrast the study with other studies
    e. Used to explain the results of the study

4. Which of the following represent appropriate uses of the literature in a typical quantitative research study? Circle all that apply.

    a. Used to document the importance of the research problem
    b. Used to support the theory used in the study
    c. Used to foreshadow the research questions
    d. Used to compare and contrast the study with other studies
    e. Used to explain the results of the study

5. Which of the following represent appropriate ways for an author to use literature in a typical qualitative research study? Circle all that apply.

    a. Used at the beginning of the study
    b. Used at the end of a study
    c. Used a minimal amount
    d. Used a substantial amount

6. Which of the following represent appropriate ways for an author to use literature in a typical quantitative research study? Circle all that apply.

    a. Used at the beginning of the study
    b. Used at the end of a study
    c. Used a minimal amount
    d. Used a substantial amount

7. A friend wants to find articles that study research problems similar to the Gunman Incident study (Asmussen & Creswell, 1995) in the textbook. This friend plans to search the ERIC database using the following three key terms: "Gunman," "Incident," and "Study."

    a. Are these key terms good to use? Yes or no? _____

    b. If not, what three might you suggest? _____

    _____

    _____

8. Which of the following is an advantage of using the Internet to locate resources for a literature review in a research study? Circle the letter to the left of the correct response.

    a. Research studies may be difficult to find.
    b. Research posted to a web site is not reviewed for quality by "experts."
    c. Research posted on a web site may be plagiarized.
    d. Research posted on a web site is typically current information.

9. List two types of criteria you could use to determine whether a resource is relevant to your study.

    a. _____

    b. _____

10. Briefly describe the difference between a thematic literature review and a study-by-study literature review.

    _____

    _____

    _____

    _____

    _____

Practice Test Items - Answer Key

1. Which of the following sources is most appropriate and desirable to use in a literature review?

    c. A primary source

    Review section "Locate Literature" in the textbook

2. Which of the following kinds of literature is most appropriate and desirable to use in a literature review?

    b. Refereed journal articles

    Review section "Locate Literature" and Figure 4.2 in the textbook

3. Which of the following represent appropriate uses of the literature in a typical qualitative research study?

    a. Used to document the importance of the research problem
    d. Used to compare and contrast the study with other studies

    Review section "What Are the Differences between a Literature Review for a Quantitative Study and for a Qualitative Study?" and Table 4.1 in the textbook

4. Which of the following represent appropriate uses of the literature in a typical quantitative research study?

    a. Used to document the importance of the research problem
    b. Used to support the theory used in the study
    c. Used to foreshadow the research questions
    d. Used to compare and contrast the study with other studies
    e. Used to explain the results of the study

    Review section "What Are the Differences between a Literature Review for a Quantitative Study and for a Qualitative Study?" and Table 4.1 in the textbook

5. Which of the following represent appropriate ways for an author to use literature in a typical qualitative research study?

   a. Used at the beginning of the study
   b. Used at the end of a study
   c. Used a minimal amount

   Review section "What Are the Differences between a Literature Review for a Quantitative Study and for a Qualitative Study?" and Table 4.1 in the textbook

6. Which of the following represent appropriate ways for an author to use literature in a typical quantitative research study?

   a. Used at the beginning of the study
   b. Used at the end of a study
   d. Used a substantial amount

   Review section "What Are the Differences between a Literature Review for a Quantitative Study and for a Qualitative Study?" and Table 4.1 in the textbook

7. A friend wants to find articles that study research problems similar to the Gunman Incident study. This friend plans to search the ERIC database using the following three key terms: "Gunman," "Incident," and "Study."

   a. These are not good key terms to use because they do not address the key issues and content of the study
   b. The following might be suggested (although others would be possible):

   <u>   Violence   </u>   <u>   Guns   </u>   <u>   College   </u>

   Review section "Identify Key Terms" in the textbook

8. Which of the following is an advantage of using the Internet to locate resources for a literature review in a research study?

   d. Research posted on a web site is typically current information.

   Review section "Early Stage Literature" and Table 4.4 in the textbook

9. List two types of criteria you could use to determine whether a resource is relevant to your study.

   Possibilities include topic relevance, individual and site relevance, problem relevance, and accessibility relevance.

   Review section "Critically Evaluate and Select the Literature" in the textbook

10. Briefly describe the difference between a thematic literature review and a study-by-study literature review.

    In a thematic literature review, the author identifies a theme and discusses it. This discussion includes brief references to literature that documents the theme. No single study is discussed in detail. In a study-by-study literature review, the author summarizes each cited study in detail. The studies are discussed under a broad topic theme.

    Review section "Write a Literature Review" in the textbook

Chapter 5

Specifying a Purpose and Research Questions or Hypotheses

After completing your study of Chapter 5, you should be able to:

1. Distinguish among purpose statements, research questions, hypotheses, and objectives.

2. Define the nature of a variable and the types of variables in quantitative research.

3. Define a theory and its test using variables.

4. Write quantitative purpose statements, research questions, and hypotheses.

5. Identify similarities and differences between quantitative and qualitative purpose statements and research questions.

6. Define a central phenomenon in qualitative research.

7. Describe the emerging design process in qualitative research.

8. Write qualitative purpose statements and research questions.

Practice in Understanding Key Concepts

Important Terms and Concepts

The following items represent important concepts relating to purpose statements, research questions, and hypotheses. Using your own words, record definitions for the items in the space provided.

Purpose statement: _____

_____

_____

Research questions: _____

_____

_____

Chapter 5

Hypotheses: _____

_____

_____

Research objectives: _____

_____

_____

Quantitative research terms and concepts

Variable: _____

_____

_____

Measurement: _____

_____

_____

Variable measured in categories: _____

_____

_____

Variable measured as continuous: _____

_____

_____

Construct: _____

_____

_____

Dependent variable: _____

_____

_____

Independent variable: _____

_____

_____

Measured variable: _____

_____

_____

Control variable: _____

_____

Treatment variable: _____
_____
_____

Moderating variable: _____
_____
_____

Intervening variable: _____
_____
_____

Confounding variable: _____
_____
_____

Probable causation: _____
_____
_____

Theory in quantitative research: _____
_____
_____

Quantitative purpose statement: _____
_____
_____

Descriptive question: _____
_____
_____

Relationship question: _____
_____
_____

Comparison question: _____
_____
_____

Null hypothesis: _____
_____
_____

Chapter 5

Directional alternative hypothesis: _____

_____

_____

Nondirectional alternative hypothesis: _____

_____

_____

Qualitative research terms and concepts

Central phenomenon: _____

_____

_____

Emerging process: _____

_____

_____

Qualitative purpose statement: _____

_____

_____

Qualitative research questions: _____

_____

_____

Central question: _____

_____

_____

Subquestions: _____

_____

_____

Issue subquestions: _____

_____

_____

Procedural subquestions: _____

_____

_____

Applying the Concepts as a Consumer of Research

Carefully consider your definitions and descriptions of the key concepts for this chapter as you read each of the following passages. Analyze each of the passages by completing the questions that immediately follow.

Passage from Sample Study #1:

> The purpose of this study was to investigate principals' perceptions of the elementary general music curriculum. The following questions guided the study: (1) What are elementary school principals' perceptions of music learning outcomes as they are currently being met and as they should be met under ideal conditions? (2) Is there a difference between principals' perceptions of current and ideal conditions? (3) What are elementary school principals' perceptions of broad educational goals as they are currently met and as they should be met under ideal conditions? (4) Is there a difference between principals' perceptions of current and ideal conditions? And (5) What are principals' perceptions about the degree to which certain variables affect music education in their respective schools? (Abril & Gault, 2006, p. 10)

1. Underline the major variables named in this passage and list three of them here: _____

_____

_____

2. Who are the participants and where are the research sites? _____

_____

_____

3. Write a descriptive quantitative purpose statement for this study using the script from the textbook: _____

_____

_____

_____

_____

Passage from Sample Study #2:

> With this study, we aimed to advance understanding of the social difficulties that are characteristic of individuals with Asperger syndrome while providing a voice to this group of students. We asked the following research question: What are the perceptions of friendship for a group of secondary school students who have Asperger syndrome? (Carrington, Templeton, & Papinczak, 2003, p. 212)

4. What is the central phenomenon of this study? _____

_____

_____

5. Who are the participants and where are the research sites? _____

_____

_____

6. Write a qualitative purpose statement for this study using the script from the textbook: _____

_____

_____

_____

_____

Activity Feedback!

- A possible purpose statement for Sample Study #1 is: The purpose of this quantitative study is to describe attitudes about music learning outcomes, broad educational goals, and the degree to which certain variables affect music education under current and ideal conditions for principals at U.S. elementary schools.

- A possible purpose statement for Sample Study #2 is: The purpose of this qualitative study is to describe the perceptions of friendship for a group of adolescents who have Asperger syndrome at a large secondary school in Australia.

- Review Chapter 5 sections "***Writing Quantitative Purpose Statements***" and "***Writing Qualitative Purpose Statements***" in the textbook for additional information.

Review your margin notes for Sample Study #3 (SG pp. 55–59), including the passage you identified as the purpose statement for this study. Use this study to answer the following questions.

Activity Hint!

- See Chapter 5 section "***Useful Information for Consumers of Research***" for advice on identifying and interpreting a study's purpose statement.
- Sometimes you also need to examine the results to see the names of the variables used in a study.

7. What outcome(s) is (are) being predicted in this study? _____

_____

_____

8. What factor(s) is (are) advanced that might explain the outcome(s)? _____

_____

_____

9. Does the purpose of this study seem to be to relate variables, compare groups, or describe variables? _____

_____

_____

_____

10. What is the major independent variable in this study? _____

_____

_____

11. Is the independent variable measured in categories or as continuous? _____

_____

12. What are the major dependent variables in this study? List two examples. _____

_____

_____

13. Are the dependent variables measured in categories or as continuous? _____

_____

_____

14. Write a quantitative purpose statement for this study using the script from the textbook: _____

_____

_____

_____

_____

_____

15. Write a research question for one independent and one dependent variable in this study. _____

_____

_____

_____

16. Rewrite your question in #15 as a null hypothesis statement. _____

_____

_____

_____

17. Rewrite your question in #15 as a directional alternative hypothesis statement. _____

_____

_____

_____

18. Rewrite your question in #15 as a nondirectional alternative hypothesis statement. _____

_____

_____

_____

Activity Feedback!

- A possible purpose statement for Sample Study #3 is: The purpose of this quantitative study is to test the effectiveness of the prevention program by comparing the prevention group and control group in terms of the development of eating disorders and eating disorder symptoms for adolescent girls at one Italian school.

- Review Chapter 5 section "***Writing Qualitative Purpose Statements***" in the textbook for the elements that go into a quantitative purpose statement.

Now apply the chapter content to a new study. Read the article at the end of this chapter (SG pages 85–103):

> **Sample Study #4:** Rushton, S. P. (2004). Using narrative inquiry to understand a student-teacher's practical knowledge while teaching in an inner-city school. *The Urban Review, 36*(1), 61–79.

Note that "Julie" and "July" are both referring to the same individual in this article. Do the following as you read this study: (A) Note the six major steps of the research process in the margins. (B) Focus on the article's overall purpose, research questions, and emerging process to answer the following questions.

19. Identify the central phenomenon of this study. _____

_____

_____

20. Identify the participant(s) and research site(s). _____

_____

_____

21. Write a qualitative purpose statement for this study using the script from the textbook: _____

_____

_____

_____

_____

22. Is there evidence that this study underwent an emerging process? Explain why or why not. _____

_____

_____

_____

23. Write an issue subquestion that could be appropriate for this study. _____

_____

_____

_____

Applying the Concepts as a Producer of Research

You will now practice applying the important concepts of this chapter to a new research problem of your choice. Assume that you are a researcher who is working on a research project. Select a research topic by either picking one of interest to you or using one of the sample research topics identified in earlier chapters.

24. My research topic: _____

_____

Answer questions 25–30 assuming that you will use a quantitative research approach to study your topic.

25. What dependent variable do you want to explain or predict? _____

_____

_____

26. What independent variable do you think will influence or explain the outcome? _____

_____

_____

27. Who will your participants be and where is the research site? _____

_____

_____

28. Write a purpose statement for your quantitative study. _____

_____

_____

_____

_____

29. Write a research question for this study. _____

_____

_____

30. Write a hypothesis statement for this study. What type did you choose to write? _____

_____

_____

_____

_____

Answer questions 31–36 assuming that you will use a qualitative research approach to study your topic.

31. What central phenomenon do you want to study? _____

_____

_____

_____

32. Who will your participants be and where is the research site? _____

_____

_____

33. Write a purpose statement for this qualitative study. _____

_____

_____

_____

_____

_____

34. Write a central research question for this study. _____

_____

_____

_____

_____

35. Write issue subquestions for this study. _____

_____

_____

_____

_____

36. Write procedural subquestions for this study. _____

_____

_____

_____

_____

Practice Test Items

Answer the following items to check your understanding of the important concepts needed when specifying a purpose and research questions or hypotheses. Once you have answered all of the items, you can check your ideas with the provided solutions.

Questions 1–3 represent statements about the content of this chapter. Read each statement carefully and decide if it represents a true or false statement. Circle the word (true or false) to designate your answer. If the statement is false, rewrite the statement in a way to make it true.

1. Hypothesis statements are used when an author wants to state a prediction for the outcome
   of a study.   True   False

   _____

   _____

2. Research questions should be used only when taking a quantitative research approach.   True   False

   _____

   _____

3. Independent variables are attributes or characteristics that influence or affect the outcome
   of a study.   True   False

   _____

   _____

4. Consider the following terms used in the study on the eating disorders prevention program (Sample Study #3). Which of these terms are variables in this study? Circle the letter to the left of all correct responses.

   a. Girls
   b. Prevention group
   c. Eating Attitudes Test (EAT) scores

5. What type of research question is best addressed with an emerging process? Circle the letter to the left of all correct responses.

   a. Central research question
   b. Comparison question
   c. Descriptive question
   d. Relationship question

Read the following passage (Ting, 2000, p. 444). You will use it to answer questions 6–8.

> The purpose of the current study was to use SAT scores and Tracey and Sedlacek's psychosocial variables to predict Asian American students' GPA and retention in the first year of college.

6. Which of the following best describes the role of "SAT scores" in this passage? Circle the letter to the left of the correct response.

   a. Independent variable
   b. Intervening variable
   c. Dependent variable
   d. Confounding variable
   e. Treatment variable

7. Which of the following best describes the role of "retention in the first year of college" in this passage? Circle the letter to the left of the correct response.

   a. Independent variable
   b. Intervening variable
   c. Dependent variable
   d. Confounding variable
   e. Moderating variable

8. What type of research question would you write for this study? Circle the letter to the left of the correct response.

   a. Central research question
   b. Comparison question
   c. Descriptive question
   d. Issue subquestion
   e. Relationship question

Read the following passage (Feen-Calligan, 1999, pp. 138–139). You will use it to answer questions 9–10.

> The aim of this study is to generate theory about art therapy in recovery from addiction, 'grounded in,' or based upon the interviews of art therapists, psychiatrists, and individuals in recovery. The study sought to answer the following question: What is the theory that explains the process of art therapy in addiction treatment?

9. Identify the central phenomenon of this study.

   _____

   _____

10. What type of research question would you write for this study? Circle the letter to the left of all correct responses.

    a. Central research question
    b. Comparison question
    c. Descriptive question
    d. Relationship question

Practice Test Items - Answer Key

1. Hypothesis statements are used when an author wants to state a prediction for the outcome of a study.   True

   Review section "Writing Quantitative Hypotheses" in the textbook

2. Research questions should only be used when taking a quantitative research approach.   False

   Research questions are appropriate for both quantitative and qualitative approaches.

   Review section "Writing Qualitative Research Questions" in the textbook

3. Independent variables are attributes or characteristics that influence or affect the outcome of a study.   True

   Review section "The Family of Variables" in the textbook

4. Consider the following terms used in the study on the eating disorders prevention program (Sample Study #3). Which of these terms are variables in this study?

   c. Eating Attitudes Test (EAT) scores

   Review section "Specify Variables" and Figure 5.2 in the textbook

Chapter 5

5. What type of research question is best addressed with an emerging process?

a. Central research question

Review section "How Do You Design Qualitative Purpose Statements and Research Questions?" in the textbook

6. Which of the following best describes the role of "SAT scores" in this passage?

a. Independent variable

Review section "The Family of Variables" in the textbook

7. Which of the following best describes the role of "retention in the first year of college" in this passage?

c. Dependent variable

Review section "The Family of Variables" in the textbook

8. What type of research question would you write for this study?

e. Relationship question

Review section "Writing Quantitative Research Questions" in the textbook

9. Identify the central phenomenon of this study: Possible answer would be the process of art therapy in addiction treatment.

Review section "The Central Phenomenon in Qualitative Research" in the textbook

10. What type of research question would you write for this study?

a. Central research question

Review section "Writing Qualitative Research Questions" in the textbook

The Urban Review, Vol. 36, No. 1, March 2004 (© 2004)

Using Narrative Inquiry to Understand a Student–Teacher's Practical Knowledge While Teaching in an Inner-City School

Stephen P. Rushton

The present study uses narrative inquiry to follow, July, a preservice teacher's journey through her yearlong placement in an inner-city school. A qualitative analysis of four interviews, 12 written reflections, and seven transcribed group discussions revealed a sense of culture shock felt by Julie. In particular, her sense of conflict focused around self as she interacted with her mentoring teachers, her students, and coping with doubts about her own abilities and self-worth. Julie's story suggests clear ways of avoiding similar situations in the future and improving preservice teaching generally.

KEY WORDS: narrative inquiry; inner-city; preservice teaching.

"What do I teach a child who knows fatal?
What do I teach the child who knows 'fatal'
as a bullet that pierced a loved one on the porch?
What do I teach the 12-year-old child that sucks her thumb
all day at her desk?
What do I teach the child who wiped up his father's death-
blood off the bathroom floor?
What do I teach the child whose teeth are rotted to the gums,
but neglected puppies bring authorities to their door?
What do I teach the child who learns persuasive language
by begging her father not to shoot Momma?
What do I teach the child who knows a meal only as it is
served on a school tray?
Suggestions please".
Written Reflection #8

Stephen P. Rushton is an associate professor of education at the University of South Florida at Sarasota. Address correspondence to Stephen P. Rushton, Department of Education, University of South Florida, 5700 N. Tamiami Trail, PMC 217, Sarasota, FL, USA; e-mail: srushton@sar.usf.edu.

61

0042-0972/04/0300-0061/0 © 2004 Springer Science+Business Media, Inc.

62   THE URBAN REVIEW

Narrative inquiry provides a means to help preservice teachers entering the field of education reflect upon their prior constructions and beliefs of what it means to be a teacher. Olson (2000) asserts that preservice teachers already have developed an understanding and knowledge of what good teaching looks like and have an image of the type of teacher they want to be. These images of what it means to be a teacher are implicit, unexamined and instilled prior to entering teacher's college. Connelly and Clandinin (2000) examine both the personal and contextual elements of the narrative understanding, particularly in the area of teacher knowledge. They maintain the importance of understanding the stories of what happens when the teacher and student meet in the teaching–learning environment. In relation to preservice teachers, they assert that the students are "exposed to professional knowledge, issues, and views that are not yet part of or that contradict their present narrative knowledge of teaching and learning" (p. 110). Previous works by the same authors, Connelly and Clandinin (1990) indicate that the teachers stories can take the shape of a metaphor for the teaching–learning relationship; indicating that "Life's narratives are the context for making meaning of school situations" (p. 2). The introductory narrative above provides insight into the preservice student's practical knowledge and experiences of working in the inner-city context.

Lived experiences can be translated into rich narrative stories useful for both teaching and research. In the early 1990s, several educational researchers turned their attention to the value of collected stories based on diaries, interviews, group discussions, and other reflective procedures. According to Carter (1993), the purpose was to "capture the richness and indeterminacy of our experiences as a central focus for conducting research in the field" (p. 5).

Narrative stories provide a rich backdrop for understanding the contextualized situations in which teachers come to know what they know and make the decisions that they do. Using narrative stories, Rushton (2001) observed Mary, a student-teacher, grow in self-efficacy during her year-long internship while teaching in an inner-city school. Additionally, Rushton (2003) shared the stories of two African-American's experience of teaching in the inner-city school as they revealed their progression from dissonance to empowerment. Clandinin (1989) followed the process by which a first year kindergarten teacher gained practical knowledge of how the classroom worked. Further, Craig (1995, 1998) tracked a teacher's career over a 5-year period as it developed from "preservice teacher," to "substitute teacher," to "long-term replacement substitute teacher," to "full-time teacher," and illustrated how the particularities of placement can influence a professional life. Collier (1999) observed that reflective practices enabled educators, particularly preservice teachers still in the process of forming their ideas, to

STUDENT–TEACHER'S PRACTICAL KNOWLEDGE   63

better understand the learner and adapt their planning accordingly. She also found that reflecting during these experiences helped in the discovery and synthesis of personal philosophies. Finally, Brindley and Emminger (2000) used the diary of a preservice teacher to tell of "one thoroughly discouraging placement and a second excellent experience" (p. 110), from which they derived recommendations for improved teacher supervision.

There have been many calls for improvement in teacher preparation (Holmes Group, 1995; National Commission, 1996; The Project Alliance 30, 1991). One issue is the growing ethnic diversity in schools. Preservice teachers should know that pupils today are about 35% non-White, a percentage predicted to grow substantially in the next decade (National Center for Educational Statistics, 1998). Preservice teachers need to acquire the background knowledge and skills necessary for handling cultural diversity, along with an awareness of any stereotypes they bring to the situation (Kea & Bacon, 1999; Peterson, Cross, Johnson & Howell, 2000).

Cochran-Smith and Lytle (1990) and later, Rushton (2001, 2003), both indicate that research on student-teaching has been negligent in establishing the perspective and the student's voice working in the inner-cities schools. Hynes and Socoski (1991) also reviewed the literature and concluded similarly, i.e., "effort to assess preservice teachers' individual attitudes about teaching in urban schools" are not sustained. What they discovered was that students entering a teacher preparation program generally held negative attitudes toward teaching in inner-city schools. A recent search conducted by this author on the ERIC and Education Abstracts data bases revealed that the situation is beginning to change slightly in the past 2–3 years (Rushton, 2003).

Early studies on the observation of student teaching were typically limited to 13–20 weeks in suburban, white, middle-class environments (Fuller, 1969; McDermott et al., 1995; Nettle, 1998). With respect to inner-city schools, although studies have been conducted on how teachers manage (Kozol, 1991; Kretovics and Nussel, 1994; Weiner, 1993), information is scarce about how preservice teachers fare (Rushton, 2001). Recent studies, however, have begun to explore this topic. For example, Kea and Bacon (1999) used reflective journal writing from 69 preservice education majors (40 of whom were African-American) to open a dialogue on cross-cultural awareness. Rushton (2000, 2003) analyzed interviews, written reflections, and transcribed group discussions to follow the life experiences of five preservice teachers as they grew in self-efficacy in an inner-city school. These findings suggest that preservice teachers experienced a culture shock when they entered the schools. Aggravating their concerns were the normal worries about getting along with their mentoring teachers and pupils, as well as coping with self-doubts about their abilities and values that maybe unique

64   THE URBAN REVIEW

to the inner-city school context. Eventually, the preservice teachers began to manage their problems, take risks, and grow in self-efficacy. The great majority opted to pursue a career in teaching. Rushton (2003) also described the two African-American student-teacher's journey as preservice interns also in an inner-city school environment. Jillian and Mia moved from initial shock, eliciting both emotional and cognitive dissonance, to cultural assimilation as they adapted to their concerns about their students, their worries about getting along with their mentoring teacher and their doubts about their own abilities to teach.

Recently, studies (Calderhead, 1991; Clandinin, 1989; Joram and Gabriele, 1998; Tillema, 1994) are also beginning to look at practical knowledge and beliefs about learning and teaching that preservice students bring to their teaching practicum's and how prior beliefs influence (1) their understanding of children's learning, (2) the social context of learning environment, and (3) their own ability to process new information. Anderson et al. (1995) suggest that the student's practical knowledge and established belief systems will restrain the preservice teacher's ability to learn and be open to different perspectives. Further, Kagan (1992) indicates that some students' beliefs relating to how schools work and are so well-established that they are unable to change those beliefs. This is particularly so, when the environmental cues and learning/teaching environment is significantly different from that in of the preservice teachers.

The present study uses a narrative inquiry to follow Julie, a preservice teacher, as she journeys through a special 1-year teaching placement in an inner-city school to an unfavorable outcome and a decision not to pursue teaching as a career. Julie came to the program at the University of Tennessee at Knoxville because it had been specially designed to deal with urban/multicultural issues. Resulting in a Master's degree, it provided an additional fifth year of teacher's college with a wider range of experiences regarding the way inner-city schools worked. Julie wanted "to make a difference in the lives of these children." By using Julie's oral and written accounts of her interactions with her mentoring teachers and pupils, we watch her struggle to make a career decision as she is torn between wanting to "minister" to these children as she had previously experienced working with church's urban ministry program, and finding her own self as a teacher.

METHODOLOGY

Theoretical Framework

This research study incorporated a blending of symbolic interactionism and narrative inquiry in order to better understand Julie's journey as she

STUDENT–TEACHER'S PRACTICAL KNOWLEDGE   **65**

completed her fifth year of teacher's college. Symbolic interactionists explore the functional relationship between how people perceive themselves, how they see others, and how they believe others perceive them (Blumer, 1969; Van Manen, 1991). Blumer (1969, p. 12) described the interactions of individuals as lines of actions which, collectively must be recognized as the inter-linkage of separate acts by the various participants.

Lived experiences can be translated into rich narrative stories. Narrative in the form of stories has become a powerful tool for researchers. As Noddings (1991) claimed, "stories have the power to direct and change our lives" (p. 157). In the early 1990s, educational researchers such as Carter (1993), Connelly and Clandinin (1990), and Van Manen (1991) turned their attention to the benefits of collecting stories. Carter (1993) stated that the purpose was to "capture the richness and indeterminacy of our experiences" resulting in narrative stories as "a central focus for conducting research in the field" (p. 5).

An in depth, semistructured approach was used to gather three separate sources of text (Denzin and Lincoln, 1994; Fraenkel and Wallen, 1996; Seidman, 1991). The first source of data consisted of interviews conducted with Julie throughout the course of the 1996–1997 school year, in September, November, February, and April. During the interviews, Julie described her experiences and perceptions. To guide the interview, Julie answered questions such as, "What experiences stood out for you the most?", "Tell me a story about what has happened to you or one of your students during the past month?" and "What has impacted you the most?" The second source of data consisted of 12 weekly reflections that Julie wrote about her experiences during the year. In these I asked Julie to reflect on and write about a particular incident she had observed that stood out for her. The third source of data consisted of transcriptions from weekly taped discussions in which Julie and the other preservice teachers from her cohort discussed their previous week's experiences.

Data Analysis

The initial analysis of Julie's stories and interviews began with a complete reading of all interviews, weekly narratives, and discussions she had had with the other student teachers in her cohort. During this initial set of readings, it became apparent that several themes were consistent throughout her narratives (written or oral). At this point, I began to index these themes with various highlighted colors and with notes in the margins. For example, conversations relating to her mentoring teachers were coded in one color and filed separately, discussions she had with her relationship with God in another, and her beliefs about working with the inner-city children yet a

66   THE URBAN REVIEW

third and so on. From here, I created new folders for each of these separate narratives and re-read them looking for new themes. Several categories emerged covering three basic areas and yet one main theme prevailed throughout. The main issue facing Julie was that of conflict and discontentment between her previous beliefs regarding working with inner-city children, from an Urban/ministry perspective and her desire and subsequent conflict with those beliefs in becoming an elementary school teacher. The three areas of discussion that persisted were her interactions with her two mentoring teachers, her belief in not being supported by the university supervisor, and her own lack of confidence in handling classroom management. Her faith in God was also a dominant theme throughout all the interviews, discussions and narratives. Indeed, it was Julie's faith in God, and her inability to pursue this in an educational context that finally had July decide not to teach.

My Role

Prior to becoming a doctoral student and instructor for the Urban/Multicultural program at the University of Tennessee, I had supervised several student teachers in the program and was interested in their experiences and transitions into becoming teachers. Later, as a graduate teaching assistant, I both taught and supervised these students in the semester prior to their final internship. In this semester, each of the students was required to spend several half-days a week, for 4 months (January–April), in an inner-city school classroom so as to become familiar with the school and its environment. As part of their course requirements the preservice teachers were required to write journals about their initial experiences. Also, at the end of each week, we would discuss what their experiences had been during that particular week. I became both concerned and interested in their experiences as many of the students became intrigued with the issues facing them in the inner-city and discovered that their beliefs about teaching were challenged. This led me to decide to study the experiences of these preservice teachers more fully as they moved into their year-long internship. Julie was a participant in this study (Rushton, 1997). Before the beginning of their final year-long internship, I stepped down from serving as her supervisor and instructor so as to minimize biasing her responses during the interviews.

Setting

The elementary school in which Julie was placed was located in downtown Knoxville, about 5 miles from the campus of the University of

STUDENT–TEACHER'S PRACTICAL KNOWLEDGE 67

Tennessee. The school had been chosen along with three other inner-city schools to participate in the Urban/multi-cultural program established by the university to train preservice teachers. There were approximately 500 kindergarten to sixth grade students, of whom 90% were African-American. Of the 500 students, 95% were on a subsidized lunch program. The school was within walking distance of the public housing estates known as "The Projects."

The Participant: Julie

Julie described herself as an optimistic 23-year-old single white woman who had lived most of her life in Knoxville, the same city where she attended the university. Julie expressed herself freely on the intimate details of her life. She described her up-bringing as "somewhat unstable," as her parents had divorced when she was 10. Following the divorce, her mother took Julie and her two brothers to another state; but, after a bankruptcy and a broken engagement, the family returned to the mother's hometown. After living in a trailer park with dwindling financial resources, Julie and her brothers moved back to live with their father. When Julie was 16 her father re-married and life changed again. After living "with my Dad and younger brother in the bachelor's pad in which we stayed up late and hung out," her life incorporated a step-brother and sister and a more "Beaver-Cleaver type of environment." Julie continued to live with her father and stepfamily until she entered the university where she lived with a roommate, Mary, who was also in the program.

Julie completed her internship at Washington Pike Elementary School along with Mary (see Rushton, 2001). She described Washington Pike Elementary as one of the most difficult inner-city schools in the city. Nonetheless, she also claimed to have loved it (at least at the beginning of the interviews). From the very first interview, it was obvious that Julie's passion in life was to do "the Lord's" work. She was candid about her Christian beliefs stating:

> ...probably my strongest desire is to be a light in people's lives. You know, if I had the opportunity and if someone wants to hear me talk about the Lord, to talk to them what my hope is, I would. I don't know what I would do without God.

In early adolescence, Julie became a Christian. "Finding God" gave Julie comfort during the disruptions in her home life and "saved her from temptation during her teenage years." She said, "I see now that God has protected me from all these things [drugs and teenage sex], and I'm very

68   THE URBAN REVIEW

thankful." Julie s faith played a major role in leading her to become a teacher. It was part of how she defined herself. Prior to enrolling in teachers college she had taught in an "Urban, inner-city ministry," and really enjoyed "hanging out with black kids in the projects." She stated, "probably my strongest desire is to be a light in people s lives."

FINDINGS

Julie's internship revolved around a series of interrelated conflicts dealing with her mentoring teachers, the university and beliefs about her own inadequate teaching. Julie began her intern year with a somewhat naïve belief that she was going to be a "sort of savior" in the lives of the students she was to encounter. Difficulties in teaching philosophies with her mentoring teachers, a perceived lack of support from her university professor and her awakening perceptions of the lives of the inner-city children led to conclude that she was not "called" to be a classroom teacher. Julie's personal and practical knowledge was challenged and shifted during this year-long internship. Although she had previously worked with inner-city children with a local ministry organization, her experiences with the culture of the students at this school was far more drastic than what she was used to. She also felt dismay over the lives led by the inner-city children and the inadequate training she had received to handle disruptive behavior. Three areas of discontent were identified in Julie's narratives.

Mentoring Teachers

Most of Julie's stories and discussion centered on her mentoring teachers. Her first mentor was Mrs Sanders, of whom Julie had a favorable initial impression. "I think she respects me, and I'm real honest with her," Julie said. She discussed how she could learn from her and believed that this was a profitable learning situation. However, Julie soon came to perceive Mrs Sanders as much too stern, during the second interview Julie states:

> I struggle with my teacher. She's a real drill sergeant. I want to learn strengths from her, but I don't want to learn her weaknesses. I'm scared that I would learn her weaknesses and learn her discipline style and end up doing it her way. She screams at the kids all day long. It's really mean.

Julie believed her mentoring teacher lacked sympathy. Caught between trying to please Mrs Sanders and wanting to embrace the upset children, she did not know which way to turn. When relating a story about a first grader

STUDENT–TEACHER'S PRACTICAL KNOWLEDGE **69**

whose cat had been killed the night before, Julie wrote in her reflective journal, "As Kari walked into class today struggling with Blackie's death, she [the teacher] showed no compassion. Mrs. Sanders just saw Kari's sluggishness as disobedience, she sarcastically announced, 'Why are you so slow today Kari? Get on the ball!'" In another story, Julie wrote,

> Chris looked up and saw the dreaded stare of Mrs Sanders. He knew her wrath was on him, and there was no escaping it. 'Have you done your chalk plate!' Mrs Sanders said very sternly. 'No,' Chris replied. 'Why not young man? You know the routine. This is the 12th day of school. What is wrong with you? Did you hear me? Hello [she knocks on his head], is anyone in there?'

These examples of her mentor's unyielding attitude took place during the first months of school and Julie at first attributed them to the teacher's need to gain control. Julie described how unpleasant the teacher was to her too, and in front of the pupils. She said, "I do feel like she treats me like one of the kids at times like, 'I told you to do that!' or 'Turn the page!'" During the third interview, after Julie had changed classrooms, she continued to describe her former mentor in the same way:

> The teacher was mean and hateful... 'I feel like she was a dictator...' Didn't give me any control. Would yell at me in front of the principal. She could be nice, but she had such a control thing that we didn't go well together.

For the second half of the year Julie was given a younger grade of student and her mentor proved to be at the opposite extreme from her first. Julie described the differences between the two teachers as, "my first teacher was so hard on them, and I didn't want to be like that and the second teacher was so lenient on them and I didn't want to be like that either." At first, Julie described Ms. Mallory as "the teacher next door... we have a lot of the same morals, seems like we have a lot in common. She is a Christian." But Julie was soon alienated by Ms. Mallory's lack of planning, disorganized behavior, and ineffective management style, all of which compounded the serious behavior problems in this fourth grade class. Recognizing that this "is probably the worst class in the school... and the attitudes of the students are REAL bad," Julie had hoped to discover management techniques to deal with disruptive behavior. Julie found that the main method Ms. Mallory employed was to send pupils to the office. She said, "We have the most discipline problems in the school because Ms. Mallory just won't handle a situation on her own. She is like, 'I am sick of you, go to the office.' You know... 'I am angry. Go to the office.'

70   THE URBAN REVIEW

At first, there was a positive outcome for Julie from Ms. Mallory's "hands off" approach in that Julie was given full reign over what she could do. Julie began a variety of new activities in the classroom. "I started journals, started 'read alouds', and hands-on projects, and did... like... fun games like, 'spelling basketball.'" However, as time passed, Julie would ask, "Ms. Mallory, what is your plan for this afternoon?" and Ms Mallory would say, "We will just wing it for today." Julie said, "She just didn't even know what we were doing the next day. There was never a plan. I think it is great to be flexible and have a place for structure, but they need to go together."

After 5 months of what Julie perceived to be poor mentoring from two different teachers, she began to question whether to continue in the program. Aggravating Julie's difficulties with her mentors was her view that they lacked sympathy for many problems in the pupils' lives. Some of her writings reflected how she imagined the children felt. Her written reflections focused on the children's perspective of what they felt, and why they felt it, and how the teachers perceived the children. For example, Julie wrote the following reflections in which she blended the experiences of her student' lives into a story format:

Hi my name is Tina and I am nine years old. I live with my mom and step-daddy and three brothers and sisters. I had a brother that died, but I don't think about him anymore. My sister died when she was a baby. One day, I can't wait to go to heaven. Maybe I will get to see my real daddy again. He got shot when I was four. My step daddy just got out of prison and my mom just went in. I don't see how they ever have time to get together, if one of them is in jail all of the time. I live in Washington Pike Elementary Homes and am in Ms. Mallory's forth grade class. They say I have an attitude.

Hi, my name is Duane and I am nine years old. I live with my mom in Washington Pike Elementary Homes. She drinks every night, but I am used to it. Last night she got drunk again, and came home with a man that I had never seen before. She gets drunk a lot. Somebody told me that she is addicted to alcohol and can't get off of it. She falls down a lot and tells me to go to my room. I am in fourth grade. They also say that I can have an attitude too. I get in trouble a lot.

Hi my name is Eric and I am nine years old. I am a mixed kid from Washington Pike Elementary Home. My mama is white and my daddy is black. I never get to see my daddy too much, but my mamma does have men over all the time. Today I found out how my mom gets money beside what we get from welfare. When men come to our house, almost every night, they go to her bedroom. Then once I saw one of them give her money. Someone told me my mamma was a prostitute. I called them a liar and hit them. Men yell at my mama and always have their hands on her. It makes me mad, but she doesn't stop them. People tell me my

94

STUDENT–TEACHER'S PRACTICAL KNOWLEDGE   71

mama is a Whore, but I love her very much. I wish she wouldn't let men be mean to her. I am in fourth grade. I recently got suspended for three days for pinching Ms. Mary (an intern at Washington Pike Elementary) on the butt. I saw my mama's friend do it to her, so I thought it was okay. I also get in trouble a lot.

In each of the above cases a child's life is described as though the child was telling the story. Julie had captured both the child's voice and the impact the environment had played. The punch line, "I also get in trouble a lot" is indicative of Mary's beliefs of the teacher's seeming lack of insight and understanding of the child's life. Julie's wish to "save these children" ran deep and she could not understand why her mentoring teacher and other teachers were not equally as compassionate.

Conflict with Self

Julie had begun her intern year believing that teaching in a school would be similar to her earlier experience working in an urban ministry, a belief that was disconfirmed. In the urban ministry she had enjoyed being spontaneous with the children, but she felt the culture of the school, and the behavior problems and issues of control that plagued teaching there, made this inappropriate. Julie's prior experience of working with inner-city children had allowed her to show a "more natural, creative, joyful self," whereas at school, "dancing and playing with children on the playground" was unacceptable. The contradictions between her expectations and reality led Julie to doubt her career choice. During her first interview she said,

I don't know what the future holds. I don't know if I'm supposed to be a teacher. I mean, hopefully that is what I will do for the next couple of years. But I love what I did in [the inner-city ministry]. That would be more my job, I think.

In her second interview, Julie again expressed frustration at not being able to be as friendly to the pupils as she desired to be. Julie's initial belief that being friendly to the children would also gain their respect, gave way to needing to exert control.

I tried to bring balance. I found myself just not having any respect. You know why? Cause in the beginning I was this fun teacher that would dance with them on the playground. Then I had to take more control, and they didn't understand.

By the third interview, Julie was still struggling with how to be a friend to the children while maintaining a professional demeanor. Julie continued

72   THE URBAN REVIEW

to feel frustrated about having to restrain her natural spontaneity. She stated,

> I am silly, and I like to be silly and do kid stuff. But I think when I teach, especially in the inner-city school, I feel like I turn into something I don't want to be because when you do the kid things, these children don't see me being a kid and an adult. They can't associate the two. They don't know what that is like. You know... most teachers here scream, and I mean scream, at them to get them to do things.

By the fourth interview, Julie reviewed her progression over the year from being the children's friend to being a professional teacher. She said,

> I started the year out being these children's friend, and all I knew was ministry and hanging out with black kids in the projects and I loved it. And I wish I had been told to start out tough. Don't give second chances in the beginning cause they will walk all over you. And they did.

Julie remained confused and uncertain throughout the year. Toward the end of her last interview, Julie compared herself to the other interns in her cohort, emphasizing the differences between their goals and her own:

> I am just very confused about what I am supposed to do with my life. I know that I have a heart for the poor, and I see myself working best one on one with kids, and that is just why I don't know if teaching is for me. Maybe the difference between me and the other interns is that I went into this with a total 'ministry mind set' rather than a 'teaching mind set.' The reason I chose [this school] is because I knew [this school's] kids. I had done two years of inner-city ministry, and I loved it. But as I got into teaching, I was like, 'this is not exactly what I was looking for.

Julie found her internal conflict over preservice teaching very stressful. At one point she had to leave the classroom, go into the bathroom, get on her hands and knees, and pray to God to help her get through the day. Julie claims that that was a turning point for her:

> It wasn't like this big breakdown, but it was like my turning point. I went to the bathroom in the teacher's lounge, literally got down on my knees and I was like 'God, I can't do this alone.' And I think that is when my attitude started changing. I had been doing everything on my own... 'I can do this. I can do this. I

STUDENT–TEACHER'S PRACTICAL KNOWLEDGE   73

can be a good teacher'. Finally, when I got down on my knees and said, 'I can't do this, but You can,' is when I felt like I had more strength, more peace and more 'you know I messed up, but I am OK.'

Conflict with the University

Julie felt that the university had not taken proper care of her. Her supervising professor had dropped by only twice throughout the year to indicate, in an offhand manner that everything was going well. He had not taken the time to ask her how things were going from her perspective. She said, "There are times when I may really need to talk. My advice in the future would be just to watch out for the intern and really be there for them."

In her last reflection, Julie also stated that the university had not prepared her enough for coping with inner-city issues. She concluded that she had "learned more about poverty-stricken environments and poor children than I've ever known before." All she could think of to do at this point was to "cry a lot and pray a lot" because nothing else seemed to work. Even though she desired to "take my kids home with me everyday," she seriously questioned her ability to teach, saying, "I definitely have had more doubts this year than I ever had about teaching and about working with inner-city youth." Even though Julie had experienced working with inner-city children, the intense exposure to their lives as well as the responsibilities involved in teaching appeared to contradict her earlier experiences.

During her very last interview, Julie made a more specific assessment of what was missing in her university courses. She expressed frustration at the university for not training her in techniques of classroom discipline, stating that "pretty much all the inner-city interns that I have talked to feel that [the university] did not prepare us whatsoever about working in the inner-city schools." Julie even claimed the brochure for the Multi-Cultural Studies Unit misled when it stated that one of its goals was "to teach future teachers to educate in low socio-economic areas and with poverty children." As Julie pointed out, "one of the biggest things we have to deal with is problem behavior and classroom management, and we did not have one class on that, which I don't understand." Instead, Julie felt she was taught a "bunch of theories" and "cute ideas" that did not apply to typical school events: "What do you do with children who will not do their work, and every time someone even brushes them, they [explode in anger], but yet you know that their daddy is a drug dealer and they probably only get two hours of sleep a night?"

Julie described her frustration with a program that had failed to give her the structure she needed. She believed that a bit more structure, or better mentors, or a more interested supervisor could have tipped the balance

74   THE URBAN REVIEW

against her decision to leave. She especially regretted that her mentoring teachers had not supported her need to be friendly while giving her practical advice on how to deal with disruptive behavior:

> I feel like I had no structure through this entire intern process. I am not telling you this to complain. But I am trying to tell you my situation. I have tried to have a good attitude and I can do this... I am not saying that if I had this great mentor teacher, I would want to teach... but I mean, I struggle so much now with wanting to teach. I don't know if that is because my internship has been so hard or if I am not supposed to be a teacher. Do you know what I mean?

DISCUSSION

Julie spent a year student teaching with children in the inner-city school. In her narratives she describes a powerful journey in which her original intention of becoming an elementary school teacher with disadvantaged children changed. After 5 years working toward a Master's degree, in a program designed specifically to train teachers to work with the intricate complexities of working in the context of the inner-city, Julie decided not to become a teacher, but rather work with Urban/missionary youths. Had Julie's experiences been different, i.e. had she been in a more supportive environment would she have come to this same conclusion? How much of her decision was influenced by the circumstances and experiences she encountered during her internship? And, to what degree could this have been prevented with more supportive mentoring teachers?

From the first interview, Julie shared openly her passion and faith in God and "being the light in people's life." She also talked about wanting to become a teacher and her passion for working with inner-city children in an educational setting. Julie's journey and subsequent stories indicated a difficult path. Other researchers have alluded to the preservice experiences as being one that attests to many difficulties and uncertainties (Fuller & Brown, 1975; Pilard, 1992; Rushton, 2001, 2003; Sitter, 1982) faced by student teachers. However, in all of these cases, the preservice teacher was student-teaching from 13 to 20 weeks in suburban, middle class environment. Julie student taught for a year in an urban setting. It is also evident that preservice teachers often undergo a period of time in their student-teaching placements in which they experience periods of self-doubt (Rushton, 2001, 2003). Julie clearly had demonstrated her concerns, doubts and moments of fear to the degree of changing her occupation.

The results of this study supported earlier work on preservice students. Lantz's study (1964) indicated that students of education ought to be placed in "non-threatening classrooms" in order to better develop their self-

STUDENT–TEACHER'S PRACTICAL KNOWLEDGE   **75**

efficacy. In light of Julie's experiences, one could conclude that a more nurturing mentoring teacher and classroom may have provided her with a more solid foundation. Walberg (1968) indicated that often the student teacher finds themselves caught between wanting to befriend the children in their class and maintaining classroom discipline. For Julie, her entire year was a juggling act between "ministering" and "dancing with the students" and maintaining a setting in which her students respected her as the teacher. Similarly, Glassberg and Sprinthall (1980) indicated in their work that "student teachers often become more authoritarian, rigid, impersonal, restrictive, arbitrary, bureaucratic and custodial by the end of their student-teaching" (p. 14). However, for Julie, this was not the case. She maintained throughout her internship an inner quality of support and compassion for these students.

By the end of her intern year, Julie decided that teaching was not what she had expected. She had entered teacher training with a view to helping disadvantaged children. She came with positive expectations based on prior experience working with children as a religious missionary in the inner-city. Despite her knowledge of these children's life-situations and her obvious sympathy for them, after 5 years studying to be a teacher and earning her Master's degree, she realized that formal teaching was not for her.

The inner-city school poses special challenges to preservice teachers. To what extent are teacher preparation programs adequately preparing them for such adverse conditions? The Urban/Multicultural Education program that Julie participated in had been uniquely designed to help preservice teachers understand the socio-economic, cultural, and political issues involved. Julie was one of 23 students in this cohort and the only student that chose not to continue teaching.

Connelly and Clandinin (2000) discuss the nature of teacher knowledge through the use of narrative inquiry in terms of three-dimensional space, these being temporal (past, present, and future), personal/existential, and place. They state, "We imagine a teacher's knowledge to be positioned along each of these dimensions and, therefore, to inhabit a three-dimensional space." (p. 317) They connect 'Temporal' with Dewey's belief that experience is continuous. Each experience we have—an event, situation, or feeling—is cultivated from a prior experience and becomes part of the next one. Julie described her confrontations, joys, and moments of truth in relationship to what her prior understanding was (i.e., missionary work) and what she hoped to achieve. As I watched and listened to her experiences, I saw a student whose mounting experiences clearly lead her to her decision not to teach. For Julie, her past imprints and reference points of working with the Urban/ministry, at times, appeared to be a detriment in her developing her teacher stance. She continually compared her not connecting with her stu-

76   THE URBAN REVIEW

dents at the same level she had in prior circumstances. Julie often discussed what it was like for her working with former children with a "missionary mind-set."

Again, Connelly and Clandinin (2000) discuss the second criteria, personal/existential, of teacher knowledge and narrative inquiry in terms of Dewey' beliefs that exchange takes place between a person's inner self and the surrounding world. They elaborate on this further by stating that teacher's knowledge is the combination of personal and existential, inner and outer, qualities. Few teachers, and even fewer student teachers, have the opportunities to experience the kind of incidents that Julie had. Her story is rich, one that involved a dilemma between her faith in God and wanting to teach inner-city ministry and her personal goal of becoming a teacher. For Julie, the year was about how her mentoring teacher, the students, her interaction with others in inner-city environment and her lack of support from the university shaped her story and her knowledge of becoming a teacher. Her existential faith and the nature of her beliefs regarding her role in "being a light to people" clearly shone in all of her discussions. It is interesting to note that in the earlier study (Rushton, 2000) all of the interns had a strong religious component and view. Further study of the role of one's religious beliefs and faith in God and how that impacts becoming a teacher might be warranted.

The third dimension Connelly and Clandinin (2000) discuss in terms of teacher knowledge is that of "place." They state that place has a special influence on teacher knowledge, such that, "we think of it as a third dimension in our narrative inquire space. Virtually everything changes in some significant measure as teacher narratives unfold in different places." (p. 318) Certainly the interaction and impact that teaching in the inner-city in Knoxville, Tennessee, had on Julie was important in shaping her views of teaching. Had Julie taught in a middle class suburban setting with supportive mentors, she may indeed still have wanted to be a teacher. The inner-city environment poses special challenges to teachers and preservice teachers alike. Of particular concern is whether teacher preparation programs are adequately preparing student teachers to teach in such adverse conditions? The Urban/Multicultural Education program Julie participated in was unique in that it was designed to help student teachers understand the socio-economic, cultural, and political issues that face teachers who work in the inner-city.

Julie believed her mentors had curtailed her natural enthusiasm, her supervisor had not been there to discuss the situation with her, and the university had failed to train her adequately. Julie was a well-motivated, warm-hearted person, and the program should have been able to rectify the situation and find better solutions for the difficulties she encountered. Julie's narratives show the importance and impact that a mentoring teacher can have on a preservice teacher's aspirations and how a university supervisor's position of power can influence a student-teacher's willingness to step forward and discuss what is happening to them.

Unfortunately Julie's experience is not all that unusual. Another adverse experience by a preservice teacher was described by Brindley and Emminger (2000), who made suggestions about how to prevent such events in the future. They pointed out that whoever determines the intern's placement, whether university or local school personnel, it is important that the needs of the intern be prioritized. Brindley and Emminger's (2000) suggested that one way to minimize such adverse experiences for preservice teachers was to make greater use of the Professional Development School (PDS) model that has emerged as a leading university–school partnership model in the United States where as many as 1043 exist (Abdul-Haqq, 1998). While individual PDS vary, they typically include: (1) placing interns as a cohort on the school site; (2) building co-teaching teams of pre- and inservice teachers; and (3) utilizing site-based delivery of university courses incorporating applied assignments and school teachers as instructors. PDS models are reported to produce lower attrition rates once the teacher has entered the profession versus those students that experience typical teacher preparation programs (Abdul-Haqq, 1998).

Understandably, this is one case study, and generalizations are inappropriate. However, further research could be conducted to explore the impact of preparing teachers in the inner city. Using Julie's example, several questions arise. "How are we screening mentoring teachers, epically those that teach in urban schools, i.e. what criteria is used to determine quality mentoring teachers?", "How do we teach preservice teachers to deal effectively with the unique situations and circumstances that arise in inner-city schools?", "What is the long range impact of this year on Julie's career and life?" and, "What role does one's religion, spiritual or existential beliefs have on the teacher?"

In the end, Julie's story reminds us of how challenging an internship can be. Teacher educator's need to remember that fieldwork can lead to a miserable experience and leave a sense of abject failure, destroying both the trust felt toward the university program and the preservice teacher's commitment to the profession. Julie's experience reminds us all that there is much room for improvement on all sides. Mentoring teachers might learn from Julie's experiences to remind themselves of just how much influence they have on aspiring young teachers. Future interns might learn from Julie's experiences and build upon them to create richer experiences for themselves. Colleges of Education might become more aware of the

78   THE URBAN REVIEW

dynamics between mentoring teachers and preservice teachers in terms of placement and support.

REFERENCES

Anderson, L. M., Blumenfeld, P., Pintrich, P. R., Clark, M., Marx, R. W., and Peterson, P. (1995). Educational psychology for teachers: Reforming our courses, rethinking our roles. *Educational Psychologist* 30:143–157.

Abdul-Haqq, I. (1998). *Professional Development Schools: Weighing the Evidence.* Thousand Oaks, CA: Corwin Press.

Blumer, H. (1969). Symbolic Interactionism. New York: Prentice Hall Inc.

Brindley, R., and Emminger, P. (2000). Betrayal and redemption: Lessons to be learned from the diary of an intern. *Action in Teacher Education* 21(4):110–126.

Calderhead, J. (1991). Images of teaching: Preservice teachers' early conceptions of classroom practice. *Teaching and Teacher Education* 7:1–8.

Carter, K. (1993). Teachers' knowledge and learning to teach. In W. R. Houston (Ed.), *Handbook of Research on Teacher Education* (pp. 291–310). New York: Macmillan.

Clandinin, D. J. (1989). *Personal Practical Knowledge: A Study of Teacher's Classroom Images.* Toronto, Canada: Wiley.

Cochran-Smith, M., and Lytle, S. (1990). Research on teaching and teacher research: The issues that divided. *Educational Researcher* 2(11):24–29.

Connelly, M. F., and Clandinin, D. J. (2000). Narrative understanding of teacher knowledge. *Journal of Curriculum and Supervision* 15(4):315–31.

Connelly, M. F., and Clandinin, D. J. (1990). Stories of experiences and narrative inquiry. *Educational Researcher* 19(5):2–14.

Collier, S. T. (1999). Characteristics of reflective thought during the student teaching experience. *Journal of Teacher Education* 50(3):173–181.

Craig, C. J. (1995). Knowledge communities: A way of making sense of how beginning teachers come to know. *Curriculum Inquiry* 25(2):151–175.

Craig, C. J. (1998). The influence of context on one teacher s interpretive knowledge of team teaching. *Teaching and Teacher Education* 14(4):371–383.

Craig, C. J. (2000). Stories of schools/teacher stories: A two part invention on the walls theme. *Curriculum Inquiry* 30(1):11–41.

Denzin, K., and Lincoln, N. (1994). *Handbook of Qualitative Research.* New York: Sage.

Fraenkel, J. R., and Wallen, N. E. (1996). *How to Design and Evaluate Research in Education.* New York: McGraw-Hill.

Fuller, F. F. (1969). Concerns of teachers: A developmental conceptualization. *American Educational Research Journal* 6(2):207–226.

Fuller, F., and Brown, O. (1975). Becoming a Teacher. In K. Ryan (Ed.), *Teacher Education: 74th Yearbook of the National Society for the Study of Education.* (Part II, pp. 25–52). Chicago: University of Chicago Press.

Glassberg, S., and Sprinthall, N. A. (1980). A developmental approach. *Journal of Teacher Education* 31–38.

The Holmes Group (1995). *Tomorrow's schools of education: A report of the Holmes group.* East Lansing, MI.: The Holmes Group.

Hynes, J., and Socoski, P. (1991). Undergraduates' attitudes towards teaching in urban and non-urban schools. *Paper presented at the Annual Meeting of the Eastern Educational Research Association:* Boston. ERIC, ED 362 498.

STUDENT–TEACHER'S PRACTICAL KNOWLEDGE   79

Joram, E., and Gabriele, A. (1998). Preservice teachers' prior beliefs: Transforming obstacles into opportunities. *Teaching and Teacher Education* 32:175–189.

Kagan, M. (1992). Professional growth among preservice and beginning teachers. *Review of Educational Research* 62:129–169.

Kea, C. D., and Bacon, E. H. (1999). Journal reflections of preservice education students on multicultural experiences. Action *in Teacher Education* 21(2):34–50.

Kozol, J. (1991). Savage inequalities: Children in America's schools. New York: Harper.

Kretovics, J., and Nussel, E. (1994). *Transforming Urban Education*. Boston: Allyn and Bacon.

Lantz, D. L. (1964). Changes in student teacher's concept of self and others. *Teacher Education* 15(2):200–203.

McDermott, P., Gormley, K., Rothenberg, J., and Hammer, J. (1995). The influence of classroom practice experiences on students teachers' thoughts about teaching. *Journal of Teacher Education* 46(3):184–191.

National Center for Education Statistics (1998). Public High School Dropouts and Completors from the Common Core of Data. Washington, D.C.

National Commission on Teaching and America' s Future (1996). *What Matters Most: Teaching for America's Future*. Washington, DC: U.S. Government Printing Office.

Nettle, E. (1998). Stability and change in the beliefs of student teachers during practice teaching. *Teaching and Teacher Education* 14(2):193–204.

Noddings, N. (1991). Stories in dialogue: Caring and interpersonal reasoning. In C. Witherell and N. Noddings (Eds), Stories Lives Tell: Narrative and Dialogue in Education. (pp. 157–170). New York: Teachers College Press.

Olson, M. R. (2000). Linking personal and professional knowledge of teaching practice through narrative inquiry. *The Teacher Educator* 35(4):109–127.

Peterson, K. M., Cross, L. F., Johnson, E. J., and Howell, G. L. (2000). Diversity education for preservice teachers: Strategies and attitude outcomes. *Action in Teacher Education* 22(2):33–38.

Pilard, D. (1992). *The Socialization Process of Student Teaching: A Descriptive Study*. East Lansing, MI: National Center for Research on Teacher Learning, ERIC No. 479 865.

The Project Alliance 30 (1991). *Project 30 year Two Report: Institutional Accomplishments*. Newark, Delaware: University of Delaware.

Rushton, S. (1997). *The experiences of five inner-city student teachers*. Unpublished doctoral dissertation, University of Tennessee. TN, Knoxville.

Rushton, S. (2000). Student teacher efficacy in inner-city schools. *Urban Review* 32(4): 365–383.

Rushton, S. (2001). Cultural assimilation: A narrative case study of student-teaching in an inner-city school. *Teacher and Teacher Education* 17:147–160.

Rushton, S. (2003). Two preservice teachers growth in self-efficacy while teaching in an inner-city school. *Urban Review* 35(3):167–189.

Seidman, I. E. (1991). *Interviewing as Qualitative Research*. New York: Teachers College.

Sitter, J. P. (1982). *The student teaching experience from the perspective of the student teacher: A descriptive study*. Unpublished doctoral dissertation, Michigan State University.

Tillema, H. H. (1994). Training and professional expertise: Bridging the gap between new information and pre-existing beliefs of teachers. *Teaching and Teacher Education* 10:601–615.

Van Manen, M. (1991). *Researching Lived Experiences: Human Science for an Action Sensitive Pedagogy*. London, Ontario: The State University of New York.

Walberg, H. (1968). Personality-role conflict and self-conception in urban practice teaching. *School Review* 79:41–49

Weiner, L. (1993). *Preparing Teachers for Urban Schools: Lessons from Thirty years of School Reform*. New York: Teachers College.

Chapter 6

Collecting Quantitative Data

After completing your study of Chapter 6, you should be able to:

1. Identify five steps in the process of quantitative data collection.

2. Define different approaches used to sample participants for a quantitative study.

3. Describe the process of obtaining permissions to study individuals and research sites.

4. List different options for types of data often collected in quantitative research.

5. Identify how to locate, select, and assess an instrument(s) for use in data collection.

6. Describe procedures for administering quantitative data collection.

Practice in Understanding Key Concepts

Important Terms and Concepts

The following items represent important concepts relating to collecting quantitative data. Using your own words, record definitions for the items in the space provided.

Unit of analysis: _____

_____

_____

Representative: _____

_____

_____

Population: _____

_____

_____

Target population (Sampling frame): _____

_____

_____

Sample: _____

_____

_____

Probability sampling: _____

_____

_____

Simple random sampling: _____

_____

_____

Systematic sampling: _____

_____

_____

Stratified sampling: _____

_____

_____

Multistage cluster sampling: _____

_____

_____

Nonprobability sampling: _____

_____

_____

Convenience sampling: _____

_____

_____

Snowball sampling: _____

_____

_____

Chapter 6

Sampling error: _____

_____

_____

Sample size formulas: _____

_____

_____

Institutional review board: _____

_____

_____

Informed consent form: _____

_____

_____

Operational definition: _____

_____

_____

Instrument: _____

_____

_____

Performance measure: _____

_____

_____

Attitudinal measure: _____

_____

_____

Behavioral observation: _____

_____

_____

Factual information or personal documents: _____

_____

_____

Modifying an instrument: _____

_____

_____

Reliability: _____

_____

_____

Validity: _____

_____

_____

Test-retest reliability: _____

_____

_____

Alternative forms reliability: _____

_____

_____

Alternative forms and test-retest reliability: _____

_____

_____

Interrater reliability: _____

_____

_____

Internally consistent: _____

_____

_____

Coefficient alpha: _____

_____

_____

Content validity: _____

_____

_____

Chapter 6

Criterion-related validity: _____

_____

_____

Construct validity: _____

_____

_____

Scales of measurement: _____

_____

_____

Nominal scale (categorical scale): _____

_____

_____

Ordinal scale (ranking scale): _____

_____

_____

Interval scale (rating scale): _____

_____

_____

Ratio scale (true zero scale): _____

_____

_____

Applying the Concepts as a Consumer of Research

Carefully consider your descriptions of the key concepts for this chapter as you read the following passage.

Passage from Sample Study #1:

> A random sample of 350 was drawn from a list of 8,506 active elementary public school principals enrolled as members of the National Association of Elementary School Principals. An initial mailing, a follow-up, and two reminders yielded a 61% response rate. Surveys were returned from principals representing various regions of the United States: Midwest (32%), Northeast (27%), South (26%), and West (15%). These proportions closely reflected the membership of the population from which the sample was drawn. Respondents ($N = 214$) reported... (Abril & Gault, 2006, p. 11)

Analyze this passage by answering the following questions about the process of quantitative data collection.

Identifying who will be studied

1. What is the unit of analysis for this study? _____

_____

2. What is the population for this study? _____

_____

3. What is the target population for this study? _____

_____

4. What is the sample used in this study? _____

_____

5. What type of sampling strategy did the authors use in this study? _____

_____

6. Do you think this study used an adequate sample size? _____

_____

_____

Activity Feedback!

This study selected individuals to study in the following ways:
- Unit of analysis: Individual principals
- Population: All U.S. elementary public school principals
- Target Population: All active elementary public school principals enrolled as members of the National Association of Elementary School Principals
- Sample: 214 principals who responded
- Sampling Strategy: Probability sampling—simple random sampling
- Sample Size: Large sample used, but would prefer at least 350 participants for a survey study

    o See Chapter 6 section "***Whom Will You Study?***" for additional information on selecting a sample.

Now apply the chapter content to a new study. Read the article at the end of this chapter (SG pages 117–130):

Sample Study #5: Kim, R. I., & Goldstein, S. B. (2005). Intercultural attitudes predict favorable study abroad expectations of U.S. college students. *Journal of Studies in International Education, 9*(3), 265–278.

Do the following as you read this study: (A) Note the six major steps of the research process in the margins. (B) Focus on the article's discussion of data collection to complete the following questions.

Activity Hint!

- See Chapter 6 section "***Useful Information for Consumers of Research***" for advice on evaluating a study's data collection.

Chapter 6

Analyze the process of quantitative data collection in Sample Study #5 (Kim & Goldstein, 2005) by answering the following questions.

Who was studied?

7. What type of sampling strategy did the authors use in this study? _____

_____

8. Describe the sample used in this study. _____

_____

_____

What permissions were needed?

9. What type(s) of permissions needed to be obtained in this study? Were these permissions discussed in the

article? _____

_____

_____

What information needed to be collected?

10. List the major independent variable(s) in this study. _____

_____

_____

11. List the major dependent variable(s) in this study. _____

_____

_____

12. Consider one independent variable. What type of measure was used? _____

_____

13. Consider one dependent variable. What type of measure was used? _____

_____

What instruments were used?

14. Did the authors provide evidence that the scores from past use of the instruments were reliable? If so, give an

example of the evidence and type(s) of reliability discussed. _____

_____

_____

_____

15. Did the authors provide evidence that the scores from past use of the instruments were valid? If so, give an example of the evidence and type(s) of validity discussed. _____

_____

_____

_____

_____

16. For the independent and dependent variables you listed in questions 12 and 13, what scales of measurement (categorical or continuous) were used? _____

_____

_____

How were the data collected?

17. Do you think standard procedures were used to collect the data? Why or why not? _____

_____

_____

_____

18. Were any ethical issues addressed in the article? _____

_____

_____

Applying the Concepts as a Producer of Research

You will now practice applying the important concepts of this chapter to a new research problem of your choice. Assume that you are a researcher who is working on a quantitative research project. Select a research topic by either picking one of interest to you or using one of the sample research topics identified in earlier chapters.

19. My research topic: _____

_____

Selecting participants

20. Describe the population for your study. _____

_____

_____

Chapter 6

21. Describe the sample for your study, including how you will select the participants. _____

_____

_____

_____

Obtaining permissions

22. List the different types of permissions you will need to obtain to conduct this study. _____

_____

_____

_____

Selecting types of data

23. What are the major variables you will want to measure in this study? _____

_____

_____

_____

24. What types of measures (performance, attitudinal, etc.) will you need to use? _____

_____

_____

_____

Identifying instruments

25. Why will it be important to consider reliability when choosing your instruments? _____

_____

_____

_____

_____

26. Why will it be important to consider validity when choosing your instruments? _____

_____

_____

_____

_____

27. Give one example of a nominal scale (e.g., gender) that you might use in this study. _____

_____

_____

28. Give one example of an interval or ratio scale (e.g., age in years) that you might use in this study. _____

_____

_____

Administering data collection

29. What kind(s) of standard procedures will you use for your data collection? Explain. _____

_____

_____

_____

30. What kind(s) of ethical issues will you consider in designing this study? Explain. _____

_____

_____

_____

Practice Test Items

Answer the following items to check your understanding of the important concepts related to collecting quantitative data. Once you have answered all of the items, you can check your ideas with the provided solutions.

1. A child's age is measured as "25 months." This is an example of what kind of measurement scale? Circle the letter to the left of the correct response.

   a. Nominal scale
   b. Ordinal scale
   c. Interval scale
   d. Ratio scale

2. A participant's age is measured as "senior citizen." This is an example of what kind of measurement scale? Circle the letter to the left of the correct response.

   a. Nominal scale
   b. Ordinal scale
   c. Interval scale
   d. Ratio scale

Chapter 6

3. A researcher measures the age of all of the participants by ranking them from oldest to youngest. This is an example of what kind of measurement scale? Circle the letter to the left of the correct response.

   a. Nominal scale
   b. Ordinal scale
   c. Interval scale
   d. Ratio scale

4. Which of the following groups in a single study typically has the largest number of members? Circle the letter to the left of the correct response.

   a. Population
   b. Sample
   c. Target population

5. Which of the following sampling strategies is considered to be the least rigorous in quantitative research? Circle the letter to the left of the correct response.

   a. Multistage cluster sampling
   b. Simple random sampling
   c. Snowball sampling
   d. Stratified sampling
   e. Systematic sampling

6. A researcher is conducting a study to compare two different teaching strategies for middle school mathematics. She collects student attendance information from the principal's office. This is an example of what kind of instrument? Circle the letter to the left of the correct response.

   a. Performance measure
   b. Attitudinal measure
   c. Behavioral observation
   d. Factual information

7. A researcher is conducting a study to compare two different teaching strategies for middle school mathematics. She collects time-on-task data for students during math class. This is an example of what kind of instrument? Circle the letter to the left of the correct response.

   a. Performance measure
   b. Attitudinal measure
   c. Behavioral observation
   d. Factual information

8. A researcher is conducting a study to compare two different teaching strategies for middle school mathematics. She collects student scores on an in-class math test. This is an example of what kind of instrument? Circle the letter to the left of the correct response.

   a. Performance measure
   b. Attitudinal measure
   c. Behavioral observation
   d. Factual information

9. Which of the following would provide you with the best evidence that the scores from a particular attitudinal measure are consistent? Circle the letter to the left of the correct response.

    a. Test-retest reliability
    b. Alternative forms reliability
    c. Interrater reliability
    d. Construct validity
    e. Criterion-related validity

10. Which of the following would provide you with the best evidence that the scores from one particular attitudinal measure can be used to draw meaningful and useful inferences? Circle the letter to the left of the correct response.

    a. Test-retest reliability
    b. Alternative forms reliability
    c. Interrater reliability
    d. Construct validity
    e. Criterion-related validity

Practice Test Items - Answer Key

1. A child's age is measured as "25 months." This is an example of what kind of measurement scale?

    d. Ratio scale

    Review section "Are Adequate Scales of Measurement Used?" in the textbook

2. A participant's age is measured as "senior citizen." This is an example of what kind of measurement scale?

    a. Nominal scale

    Review section "Are Adequate Scales of Measurement Used?" in the textbook

Chapter 6

3. A researcher measures the age of all of the participants by ranking them from oldest to youngest. This is an example of what kind of measurement scale?

    b. Ordinal scale

    Review section "Are Adequate Scales of Measurement Used?" in the textbook

4. Which of the following groups in a single study typically has the largest number of members?

    a. Population

    Review section "Specify the Population and Sample" in the textbook

5. Which of the following sampling strategies is considered to be the least rigorous in quantitative research?

    c. Snowball sampling

    Review section "Probabilistic and Nonprobabilistic Sampling" in the textbook

6. A researcher is conducting a study to compare two different teaching strategies for middle school mathematics. She collects student attendance information from the principal's office. This is an example of what kind of instrument?

    d. Factual information

    Review section "Choose Types of Data and Measures" in the textbook

7. A researcher is conducting a study to compare two different teaching strategies for middle school mathematics. She collects time-on-task data for students during math class. This is an example of what kind of instrument?

    c. Behavioral observation

    Review section "Choose Types of Data and Measures" in the textbook

8. A researcher is conducting a study to compare two different teaching strategies for middle school mathematics. She collects student scores on an in-class math test. This is an example of what kind of instrument?

    a. Performance measure

    Review section "Choose Types of Data and Measures" in the textbook

9. Which of the following would provide you with the best evidence that the scores from a particular attitudinal measure are consistent?

    a. Test-retest reliability

    Review section "Criteria for Choosing a Good Instrument" in the textbook

10. Which of the following would provide you with the best evidence that the scores from one particular attitudinal measure can be used to draw meaningful and useful inferences?

    d. Construct validity

    Review section "Criteria for Choosing a Good Instrument" in the textbook

Intercultural Attitudes Predict Favorable Study Abroad Expectations of U.S. College Students

Randi I. Kim
Susan B. Goldstein

This study focused on identifying intercultural attitudes associated with favorable expectations about participation in study abroad programs. A total of 282 U.S. 1st-year college students completed a questionnaire that included measures of ethnocentrism, intercultural communication apprehension, language interest and competence, prejudice, intolerance of ambiguity, and expectations about study abroad. Stepwise multiple regression analysis indicated that favorable expectations about study abroad were best predicted by levels of language interest, followed by low ethnocentrism and low intercultural communication apprehension. Female participants were significantly more likely than male participants to have positive expectations of study abroad and indicated significantly less ethnocentrism and intercultural communication apprehension and greater language interest. These findings suggest that interest in international study programs may be facilitated in part by interventions addressing intergroup attitudes as well as programs that help students understand the value of language study.

Keywords: study abroad; intercultural attitudes; college students; sojourn experience

During the past decade, the number of undergraduates in the United States who study abroad has increased significantly (Institute of International Education, 2003). Empirical research on such sojourners has focused almost exclusively on identifying the factors that impact adjustment to the host culture and difficulties upon reentry (Ward, Bochner, & Furnham, 2001). Few studies have investigated characteristics of students who study abroad as compared with those who remain in their home country.

Authors' Note: This study was supported by a Hewlett Foundation Grant for the Improvement of Academic Programs through the University of Redlands.

Journal of Studies in International Education, Vol. 9 No. 3, Fall 2005 265-278
DOI: 10.1177/1028315305277684

266 *Journal of Studies in International Education*   *Fall 2005*

Documented benefits of participating in a study abroad program include increased international political concern (Carlson & Widaman, 1988); greater interest in the arts, language, history, and architecture of countries outside of one's own (Carsello & Creaser, 1976); increased foreign language competency (Opper, Teichler, & Carlson, 1990); and the ability to see members of different national groups as individuals rather than in association with nonpersonal attributes such as food or geographical characteristics (Drews, Meyer, & Peregrine, 1996). Given the benefits and opportunities afforded by study abroad, researchers and practitioners have expressed concern about the degree to which students have equal access to such programs (Hembroff & Rusz, 1993). Demographic data indicate that U.S. participants in study abroad programs are more likely to be women than men, to be majoring in humanities and social sciences rather than business or natural sciences, and to be White rather than students of color (Hembroff & Rusz, 1993; Martin & Rohrlich, 1991).

Research attempting to predict participation in study abroad (e.g., Carlson, Burn, Useem, & Yachimowicz, 1990) has focused primarily on student perceptions about the relevance of international study to academic and career goals. U.S. students who participate in study abroad programs generally do so with the expectation that this experience will cultivate cross-cultural skills and knowledge, enhance personal growth and self-confidence, and allow them to be more competitive in an increasingly diverse and globally oriented job market (Carlson et al., 1990). Carlson and colleagues (1990) reported that U.S. students intending to study abroad were significantly more open with regard to career choice than those staying home and viewed study abroad as "almost essential to their career development" (p. 16). In contrast, the nonparticipating students viewed study abroad as unnecessary or inappropriate for their major and expressed concern that study abroad would delay their graduation.

Varying perceptions of the relevance of study abroad to academic programs and career goals may only partially explain the likelihood of student participation. The present study focused on specific intercultural attitudes that have not been systematically applied to the context of study abroad in previous research. It was our intent to identify specific predictors of students' expectations of study abroad and perhaps facilitate the development of strategies for attracting a broader segment of the student population to study abroad opportunities.

As indicated earlier, studies have consistently shown that in the United States, significantly more female than male students participate in study abroad programs (Hembroff & Rusz, 1993; Martin & Rohrlich, 1991). The overrepresentation of women in study abroad programs has been attributed to decision making that is less career driven than that of men, yet this gender imbalance in study abroad participation has continued over time despite the increasing career orientation of female students. Because little attention has been given to alternative explanations for the overrepresentation of women in study abroad programs, we were interested in exploring gender differences with respect to the intercultural attitudes addressed in the present study.

Ethnocentrism

Neuliep and McCroskey (1997b) identified ethnocentrism as "one of the central concepts in understanding outgroup attitudes and intergroup relations" (p. 385). Definitions of ethnocentrism focus on a universal tendency to evaluate other cultures using standards from one's own value system. In one of the earlier definitions, Sumner (1906) described ethnocentrism as the "view of things in which one's own group is the center of everything, and all others are scaled and rated with reference to it" (p. 13). Ethnocentrism may diminish intercultural communication competence by reducing culture-specific and culture-general understanding (Wiseman, Hammer, & Nishida, 1989) and creating misperceptions about the behavior of culturally different individuals (Gudykunst & Kim, 1997). Neuliep (2002) suggested that one result of ethnocentrism is the tendency to "intentionally circumvent communication with persons of different cultures" (p. 203). Thus, it seems likely that greater ethnocentrism would be associated with diminished interest in travel and intercultural interaction.

Intercultural Communication Apprehension

Neuliep and McCroskey (1997a) used the term *intercultural communication apprehension* to describe anxiety associated with real or anticipated interaction with others of different cultural backgrounds from oneself. Neuliep and Ryan (1998) suggested that the novelty and dissimilarity associated with intercultural contact situations creates significant potential for anxiety. Intercultural communication apprehension consistently correlates with ethnocentrism (Lin & Rancer, 2003; Neuliep & McCroskey, 1997a). Lin and Rancer (2003) also found intercultural communication apprehension to be inversely correlated with a measure of "intercultural willingness-to-communicate." It seems then that individuals with a high level of intercultural communication apprehension would be more likely to have negative expectations of intercultural contact situations and thus of a study abroad experience.

Prejudice

Sampson (1999) defined prejudice as "an unjustified, usually negative attitude directed towards others because of their social category or group member-

268   *Journal of Studies in International Education*   *Fall 2005*

ship" (p. 4). It is clear that prejudice impacts expectancies about intergroup interaction. Spencer-Rodgers and McGovern (2002) reported that high levels of prejudice are associated with more negative emotions regarding communication with international students. Plant and Devine (2003) suggested that a lack of positive previous experiences with outgroup members creates negative expectancies about interracial interactions, which result in intergroup anxiety and thus greater hostility toward and avoidance of members of an outgroup. We expect that higher levels of prejudice will be associated with a desire to avoid intercultural interaction and thus more negative expectations of study abroad.

Language Interest and Competence

Hembroff and Rusz (1993) reported that interest in foreign languages is associated with attending international programs on campus and discussing international issues inside and outside of the classroom. We suggest that interest in foreign languages may be linked with intergroup attitudes in terms of interest in and respect for other cultures. Thus, we predict that higher levels of interest in foreign languages would be associated with more positive expectations of study abroad.

Language competence is a critical component of intercultural communication competence (G.-M. Chen & Starosta, 1996; Redmond & Bunyi, 1991; Sercu, 2002) and intercultural sensitivity (Olson & Kroeger, 2001) and has been found to be one predictor of successful cross-cultural adjustment (Ward & Kennedy, 1993). We suggest that individuals with greater competence in nonnative languages may have more positive expectations of a study abroad experience.

Intolerance of Ambiguity

Budner (1962) defined intolerance of ambiguity as a tendency to perceive ambiguous situations as a source of threat. Tolerance for ambiguity is consistently reported to be a correlate of favorable intergroup attitudes and support for diversity programs (C. C. Chen & Hooijberg, 2000; Sinha & Hassan, 1975; Strauss, Connerley, & Ammermann, 2003) and a component of intercultural competence and adaptation (Cui & Awa, 1992; Leong & Ward, 2000). Neuliep and Ryan (1998) found that the anxiety associated with interacting with a culturally different individual creates greater uncertainty about one's own and one's partner's future behavior. We thus predict that those with greater tolerance for ambiguity would have more positive expectations for intercultural encounters and thus more positive expectations of a study abroad experience.

Kim, Goldstein / Study Abroad Expectations   269

Travel Experience

The few investigations of the impact of travel experience on participation in study abroad have reported inconsistent results. Whereas previous travel experience was not a predictor of participation in the Carlson et al. (1990) study, other studies found travel experience to be associated with study abroad (Opper et al., 1990) as well as sojourners' greater perceived intercultural competence (Martin, 1987). Yet Hembroff and Rusz (1993) found previous travel experience within the United States to be inversely correlated with U.S. students' participation in study abroad. Thus, previous travel experience was included as an exploratory variable in the present study.

Hypotheses

Based on the previous rationales, we hypothesized that positive expectations of study abroad would be associated with lower levels of ethnocentrism, intercultural communication apprehension, prejudice, and ambiguity intolerance and higher levels of language interest and competence. We also expected to find female research participants would be more likely than male participants to have intercultural attitude scores that support positive expectations of study abroad. Specifically, we hypothesized that women when compared with men would score lower in ethnocentrism, intercultural communication apprehension, prejudice, and ambiguity intolerance and score higher in language interest. Finally, in an exploratory analysis, we investigated the relationship between previous travel experience and expectations of study abroad.

METHOD

Participants

Questionnaires were administered to 282 undergraduate volunteers enrolled in a required 1st-year seminar course at a small liberal arts college in the Southwestern United States. Approximately two thirds of the 1st-year seminar instructors contacted agreed to have the questionnaire administered to their class. Very few students within these classes declined to participate, resulting in recruitment of the majority of all 1st-year students. This college places students in a wide variety of international education programs, and approximately 40% to 50% of each graduating class participates in study abroad programs, generally for a semester in duration.

270   *Journal of Studies in International Education*   *Fall 2005*

Instruments

The questionnaire used in this study took approximately 20 minutes to complete and consisted of intercultural measures as well as items on basic demographics and travel experience. Brief, exploratory items on academic and career concerns related to study abroad were also included. The independent measures included assessments of ethnocentrism, intercultural communication apprehension, cognitive and affective prejudice, language interest and competence, intolerance of ambiguity, and travel experience. The dependent measure assessed expectations about study abroad. Scales were selected based on evidence of reliability and validity as well as previous use in conjunction with research on intergroup attitudes. The wording and numbering of the Likert anchor labels on some of the original scales were modified slightly to create greater consistency across measures.

Ethnocentrism. Neuliep and McCroskey's (1997b) Generalized Ethnocentrism Scale (GENE) is a 22-item measure that assesses individual differences in ethnocentrism regardless of cultural background. High scores on this measure reflect the view that one's own culture is superior to others and should be used as the standard by which other cultures are judged (e.g., "Other cultures should try to be more like my culture" and the reverse scored "People in my culture could learn a lot from people in other cultures"). Several studies using this measure have reported strong reliability estimates for the GENE, with Cronbach's alphas ranging from .82 to .92 (Neuliep, 2002). Neuliep (2002) reported that the validity of the GENE is supported by correlations with a variety of intergroup attitude measures, including the Patriotism Scale (Adorno, Frenkel-Brunswik, Levinson, & Sanford, 1950) and the Traveling to Other Countries and Working With Foreigners scales (Neuliep, 2002).

Intercultural communication apprehension. Neuliep and McCroskey's (1997a) Personal Report of Intercultural Communication Apprehension (PRICA) was used to assess anxiety associated with real or anticipated intercultural interaction. The higher the score on this 14-item scale, the greater apprehension indicated. In two studies using this scale with U.S. samples, good internal consistency was obtained, with Cronbach's alpha equal to .92 (Lin & Rancer, 2003; Neuliep & Ryan, 1998). Neuliep and McCroskey (1997a) reported support for the construct and discriminant validity of the PRICA. Lin and Rancer (2003) found significant correlations between the PRICA and a measure of intercultural willingness to communicate.

Cognitive and affective subscales of Quick Discrimination Index. The cognitive and affective subscales of Quick Discrimination Index (QDI; Ponterotto et al., 1995) were used to assess attitudes toward racial equality and intergroup contact. Ponterotto et al. (1995) reported test-retest reliabilities of .90 and .82 for the 9-item cognitive subscale and 7-item affective subscale, respectively. Coefficient alphas for both subscales exceeded .80 across several samples. Ponterotto et al. (1995) also provided factor analytic confirmation of the subscale structure of this measure and evidence for a lack of social desirability response bias.

Language interest and competence. Hembroff and Rusz's (1993) Interest in Foreign Languages Scale, adapted from Barrows et al. (1981), was used to assess language interest. This measure consists of six statements regarding the usefulness of studying foreign languages (e.g., "Studying a foreign language can be important because it allows one to meet and converse with more and varied people"). Hembroff and Rusz reported strong internal consistency (Cronbach's alpha = .94) for this measure. Students were also asked to indicate their native language(s) as well as competence in nonnative languages in terms of ability to speak, read, and/or write each language.

Intolerance of ambiguity. Intolerance of ambiguity was assessed by Yellen's (1992) Ambiguity Intolerance Measure. People who score high on this 14-item scale are those who are uncomfortable when problems, responsibilities, social situations, or the reactions of others are unfamiliar, complex, or uncertain. Yellen reported split-half reliability of .81 for this scale. Additional evidence for the reliability of this measure was reported by Myers, Henderson-King, and Henderson-King (1997) and Goldstein, Dudley, Erickson, and Richer (2002) with Cronbach's alphas of .86 and .91, respectively.

Travel experience. Based on methodology used in previous research (Hembroff & Rusz, 1993; Martin & Rohrlich, 1991), several aspects of travel experience were assessed. These include the number of trips outside of the student's home country, the length of these trips, the purpose of these trips, and geographic regions visited.

Academic/career orientation. Three additional Likert-scaled items were used to explore possible gender differences in the impact of academic/career orientation on study abroad. These items assessed the degree to which students perceived study abroad as (a) affecting the likelihood of completing their major, (b) affecting the likelihood of graduating on time, and (c) influencing the perceptions of future employers.

Expectations of international study. The dependent measure, the International Study Expectancies Scale (ISES), is a 10-item inventory constructed by the authors to assess students' attitudes and concerns about studying abroad. These items address expectations of international studies in relation to social and personal domains (see Table 1) and were drawn from previous studies indicating the salience of these concerns for students considering study abroad (e.g., Carlson et al., 1990; Hembroff & Rusz, 1993; Martin & Rohrlich, 1991). Higher scores on the ISES indicate more positive expectations about studying abroad.

272   *Journal of Studies in International Education*   *Fall 2005*

Table 1   Sample International Study Expectancies Scale (ISES) Items

---

1. Participating in an international study program would build my self-confidence.
2. International study will be stressful (reverse score).
3. I will enjoy studying in a country other than my own.
4. Experiences in my own country can teach me many of the same things one learns through international study (reverse score).
5. Participating in an international study program would allow me to meet interesting people.

Procedure

Between mid–October and mid–November 2000, 1st-year seminar students completed an extensive survey packet during a class period. Volunteer participants were read instructions for completing the questionnaire and then did so at their own pace during the survey administration session.

RESULTS

Of the 282 students who completed the questionnaire, there were 146 women and 120 men (16 unidentified), with an average age of 18 years. The participants self-identified as 71% European American, 11% Latino/a, 7% Asian/Pacific Islander, 7% multiracial, 2% African American, and 2% other racial/ethnic identification. Nearly all participants (97%) reported that they were aware of the availability of study abroad programs. Approximately 75% of the participants reported having traveled outside of the United States prior to attending college, including countries in North America (48%), Europe (34%), Central America (28%), and Asia (11%). One fourth of the students reported speaking a language other than English at home.

The reliability analysis of the primary measures resulted in Cronbach's alphas meeting or exceeding Nunnally's (1978) standard of .80 for each of the measures, with the exception of the QDI affective subscale, which was eliminated from further analyses. The reliability analysis of the independent measures resulted in Cronbach's alphas of .89, .91, .80, .86, and .87 for the ethnocentrism, intercultural communication apprehension (ICA), QDI cognitive, language interest, and intolerance of ambiguity scales, respectively. An alpha of .80 was obtained for the newly designed ISES.

Participants' scores on the ISES were significantly correlated ($p < .001$) with their scores on language interest ($r = .49$), ethnocentrism ($r = -.45$), intercultural communication apprehension ($r = -.37$), and the Cognitive subscale of the QDI ($r = -.40$). Table 2 presents interscale correlations for these variables and the intolerance of ambiguity measure.

Kim, Goldstein / Study Abroad Expectations   273

Table 2   Interscale Correlations

	1	2	3	4	5
1. Ethnocentrism	1.00	.42*	.54*	−.34*	.10
2. Intercultural communication apprehension		1.00	.23*	−.31*	.25*
3. Quick Discrimination Index cognitive			1.00	−.39*	.04
4. Language interest				1.00	.01
5. Intolerance of ambiguity					1.00

*$p < .001$.

Table 3   Predictors of Favorable Expectations of Study Abroad

Predictors	Beta	p
Language interest (high)	.35	.000
Ethnocentrism (low)	−.26	.000
Intercultural communication apprehension (low)	−.16	.004

Table 4   Analysis of Variance for Intercultural Variables by Gender

Intercultural Variable	Women		Men		F	p
	M	SD	M	SD		
Language interest	33.4	6.02	29.2	8.4	22.9	.000
Ethnocentrism	62.7	14.1	76.9	17.9	48.9	.000
Intercultural communication apprehension	38.1	15.1	43.7	14.7	8.9	.003
Quick Discrimination Index cognitive	31.4	8.1	35.4	9.0	13.5	.000

Stepwise multiple regression analysis (see Table 3) indicated that scores on the ISES were best predicted by levels of language interest, followed by low ethnocentrism and low intercultural communication apprehension. These three variables account for 34% of variance ($F = 48$, $p < .000$).

Female participants were more likely than male participants to have intercultural attitude scores that support positive expectations of study abroad. Specifically, one-way analyses of variance indicated that women scored significantly lower on ethnocentrism, intercultural communication apprehension, and cognitive prejudice and higher on the measure of language interest (see Table 4). Exploratory analysis of variance of the three single-item academic/career measures indicated no significant gender differences in concerns about completing the major, graduating on time, or perceptions of future employers.

Sample Study #5

274   *Journal of Studies in International Education*   *Fall 2005*

None of the indices of travel experience or self-assessed language competence were significantly correlated with the ISES. Students who spoke a language other than English at home were not significantly different in terms of the ISES from those who spoke English as their primary language.

DISCUSSION

This study investigated the role of intercultural attitudes in expectations of study abroad. Consistent with the hypotheses, favorable expectations of study abroad were predicted by low levels of ethnocentrism and intercultural communication apprehension and high levels of language interest. Students who had unfavorable expectations of study abroad may believe they have little to gain from experiencing another culture (ethnocentrism) and may feel anxious about the prospect of intercultural interaction (intercultural communication apprehension).

Not surprisingly, students who viewed language study to be beneficial were also more inclined toward a favorable perception of study abroad. Although language learning and study abroad were not explicitly linked in our questionnaire, students seem to have made that connection, viewing study abroad as perhaps requiring additional language skills. Surprisingly, language competence was not a predictor of positive expectations. Future research might investigate the role of language competence in study abroad expectations by using more refined assessment tools than the self-rating measure used in this study. In addition, it may be helpful to consider whether the student is competent in a language relevant to available study abroad opportunities.

Contrary to our hypothesis, intolerance of ambiguity was not a predictor of study abroad expectancies. Given the consistency with which previous research has associated tolerance of ambiguity with favorable intergroup attitudes, we suspect that this finding may be due to the more global nature of the Ambiguity Intolerance Measure, which addresses ambiguous situations in a variety of domains (academic, work, social, and personal). We suggest that because the intercultural communication apprehension measure, which implicitly addresses the ambiguity of intercultural interaction, was a predictor of the ISES, aspects of ambiguity intolerance specific to intercultural situations may in fact be relevant to study abroad expectations.

The study abroad literature generally attributes gender differences in participation rates to the assumption that men are more concerned than women with the potential career and academic implications of study abroad. In this study however, we found no significant gender differences in exploratory measures of career or academic concerns. However, male and female participants were significantly different in terms of the intercultural attitudes associated with positive expectations of study abroad in that the scores of female students indicated significantly greater language interest as well as lower ethnocentrism, intercultural communication apprehension, and prejudice than the male students. These findings are consistent with previous research in which men expressed more negative intercultural and intergroup attitudes than women. As compared with women, men generally score higher on measures of ethnocentrism (Neuliep, Chaudoir, & McCroskey, 2001; Wrench & McCroskey, 2003) and on measures of various forms of prejudice, including racism (e.g., Mills, McGrath, Sobkoviak, Stupec, & Welsh, 1995), sexism (e.g., Frieze et al., 2003), and heterosexism (e.g., Qualls, Cox, & Schehr, 1992; Wrench & McCroskey, 2003). The present findings suggest that intercultural attitudes may be a key direction for future research on gender differences in study abroad program participation.

Finally, our exploratory analysis indicated that previous travel experience was not significantly correlated with expectations of study abroad. It is possible that had we asked students to evaluate those prior experiences, we may have found that more positive travel experiences contribute to favorable expectations of study abroad.

Previous research focusing on academic and career variables as predictors of study abroad have resulted in academically oriented recommendations for increased participation, such as offering required courses more frequently, asking students to plan for the application of their study abroad experience to their coursework once they return, and providing faculty with information about the relevance of coursework abroad for specific majors (Burn, 1991). Our research suggests that interest in international study programs may be additionally facilitated in part by interventions that seek to reduce ethnocentrism and apprehension about communicating with culturally different others as well as programs that assist students in understanding the value of language study.

REFERENCES

Adorno, T. W., Frenkel-Brunswik, E., Levinson, D. J., & Sanford, R. N. (1950). *The authoritarian personality.* New York: Harper.

Barrows, T. S., Bennett, M. F., Braun, H. I., Clark, J. L. D., Harris, L. G., & Klein, S. F. (1981). *College students' knowledge and beliefs: A survey of global understanding the final report of the Global Understanding Project.* New Rochelle, NY: Change Magazine Press.

Budner, S. (1962). Intolerance of ambiguity as a personality variable. *Journal of Personality, 30,* 29-50.

Burn, B. B. (1991). *Integrating study abroad into the undergraduate liberal arts curriculum: Eight institutional case studies.* Westport, CT: Greenwood.

276   *Journal of Studies in International Education*   *Fall 2005*

Carlson, J. S., Burn, B. B., Useem, J., & Yachimowicz, D. (1990). *Study abroad: The experience of American undergraduates.* Westport, CT: Greenwood.

Carlson, J. S., & Widaman, K. F. (1988). The effects of study abroad during college on attitudes toward other cultures. *International Journal of Intercultural Relations, 12*, 1-17.

Carsello, C., & Creaser, J. (1976). How college students change during study abroad. *College Student Journal, 10*, 276-278.

Chen, C. C., & Hooijberg, R. (2000). Ambiguity intolerance and support for valuing-diversity interventions. *Journal of Applied Social Psychology, 30*, 2392-2408.

Chen, G.-M., & Starosta, W. J. (1996). Intercultural communication competence: A synthesis. *Communication Yearbook, 19*, 353-383.

Cui, G., & Awa, N. E. (1992). Measuring intercultural effectiveness: An integrative approach. *International Journal of Intercultural Relations, 16*, 311-328.

Drews, D. R., Meyer, L. L., & Peregrine, P. N. (1996). Effects of study abroad on conceptualizations of national groups. *College Student Journal, 30*, 452-461.

Frieze, I. H., Ferligoj, A., Kogovsek, T., Rener, T., Horvat, J., & Sarlija, N. (2003). Gender-role attitudes in university students in the United States, Slovenia and Croatia. *Psychology of Women Quarterly, 27*, 256-261.

Goldstein, S. B., Dudley, E. A., Erickson, C. M., & Richer, N. L. (2002). Personality traits and computer anxiety as predictors of Y2K anxiety. *Computers in Human Behavior, 18*, 271-284.

Gudykunst, W. B., & Kim, Y. Y. (1997). *Communicating with strangers: An approach to intercultural communication.* New York: McGraw-Hill.

Hembroff, L. A., & Rusz, D. L. (1993). *Minorities and overseas studies programs: Correlates of differential participation* (Occasional Papers on International Educational Exchange: Research Series 30). New York: Council on International Educational Exchange.

Institute of International Education. (2003). *Open doors: Report on international educational exchange.* Annapolis Junction, MD: IIE Books.

Leong, C.-H., & Ward, C. (2000). Identity conflict in sojourners. *International Journal of Intercultural Relations, 24*, 763-776.

Lin, Y., & Rancer, A. S. (2003). Ethnocentrism, intercultural communication apprehension, intercultural willingness-to-communicate, and intentions to participate in an intercultural dialogue program: Testing a proposed model. *Communication Research Reports, 20*, 62-72.

Martin, J. N. (1987). The relationship between student sojourner perceptions of intercultural competencies and previous sojourn experience. *International Journal of Intercultural Relations, 11*, 337-355.

Martin, J. N., & Rohrlich, B. (1991). The relationship between study-abroad student expectations and selected student characteristics. *Journal of College Student Development, 32,* 39-46.

Mills, J. K., McGrath, D., Sobkoviak, P., Stupec, S., & Welsh, S. (1995). Differences in expressed racial prejudice and acceptance of others. *Journal of Psychology, 129,* 357-359.

Myers, J. R., Henderson-King, D. H., & Henderson-King, E. I. (1997). Facing technological risks: The importance of individual differences. *Journal of Research in Personality, 31,* 1-20.

Neuliep, J. W. (2002). Assessing the reliability and validity of the Generalized Ethnocentrism Scale. *Journal of Intercultural Communication Research, 31,* 201-215.

Neuliep, J. W., Chaudoir, M., & McCroskey, J. C. (2001). A cross-cultural comparison of ethnocentrism among Japanese and United States college students. *Communication Research Reports, 18,* 137-146.

Neuliep, J. W., & McCroskey, J. C. (1997a). The development of intercultural and interethnic communication apprehension scales. *Communication Research Reports, 14,* 145-156.

Neuliep, J. W., & McCroskey, J. C. (1997b). The development of a U.S. and generalized ethnocentrism scale. *Communication Research Reports, 14,* 385-398.

Neuliep, J. W., & Ryan, D. J. (1998). The influence of intercultural communication apprehension and socio-communicative orientation on uncertainty reduction during initial cross-cultural interaction. *Communication Quarterly, 46,* 88-99.

Nunnally, J. C. (1978). *Psychometric theory* (2nd ed.). New York: McGraw-Hill.

Olson, C. L., & Kroeger, K. R. (2001). Global competency and intercultural sensitivity. *Journal of Studies in International Education, 5,* 116-137.

Opper, S., Teichler, U., & Carlson, J. (1990). *Impacts of study abroad programs on students and graduates.* London: Jessica Kingsley Publishers.

Plant, E. A., & Devine, P. G. (2003). The antecedents and implications of interracial anxiety. *Personality & Social Psychology Bulletin, 29,* 790-801.

Ponterotto, J. G., Burkard, A., Rieger, B. P., Grieger, I., D'Onofrio, A., Dubuisson, A., et al. (1995). Development and initial validation of the Quick Discriminatory Index (QDI). *Educational and Psychological Measurement, 55,* 1016-1031.

Qualls, R. C., Cox, M. B., & Schehr, T. L. (1992). Racial attitudes on campus: Are there gender differences? *Journal of College Student Development, 33,* 524-530.

278 *Journal of Studies in International Education*   *Fall 2005*

Redmond, M. V., & Bunyi, J. M. (1991). The relationship of intercultural communication competence with stress and the handling of stress as reported by international students. *International Journal of Intercultural Relations, 17,* 235-254.

Sampson, E. E. (1999). *Dealing with differences.* Fort Worth, TX: Harcourt Brace.

Sercu, L. (2002). Autonomous learning and the acquisition of intercultural communicative competence: Some implications for course development. *Language, Culture & Curriculum, 15,* 61-74.

Sinha, R. R., & Hassan, M. K. (1975). Some personality correlates of social prejudice. *Journal of Social and Economic Studies, 3,* 225-231.

Spencer-Rodgers, J., & McGovern, T. (2002). Attitudes toward the culturally different: The role of intercultural communication barriers, affective responses, consensual stereotypes, and perceived threat. *International Journal of Intercultural Relations, 26,* 609-631.

Strauss, J. P., Connerley, M. L., & Ammermann, P. A. (2003). The "threat hypothesis," personality, and attitudes toward diversity. *Journal of Applied Behavioral Science, 39,* 32-52.

Sumner, W. G. (1906). *Folkways.* Boston: Ginn.

Ward, C., Bochner, S., & Furnham, A. (2001). *The psychology of culture shock.* New York: Routledge.

Ward, C., & Kennedy, A. (1993). Where's the "culture" in cross-cultural transition? *Journal of Cross-Cultural Psychology, 24,* 221-249.

Wiseman, R. L., Hammer, M. R., & Nishida, H. (1989). Predictors of intercultural communication competence. *International Journal of Intercultural Relations, 13,* 349-370.

Wrench, J. S., & McCroskey, J. C. (2003). A communibiological examination of ethnocentrism and homophobia. *Communication Research Reports, 20,* 24-33.

Yellen, S. B. (1992). *The Ambiguity Intolerance Measure: Development and initial construction validation.* Unpublished manuscript, Rush Medical College, Departments of Psychology and Social Sciences and Medicine, Chicago.

Randi I. Kim is assistant professor of psychology at Rhode Island College. She received her PhD in counseling psychology at Michigan State University. Her research interests are in cross-cultural issues, health risk behaviors, and career development.

Susan B. Goldstein is professor of psychology at the University of Redlands in Southern California. She received her PhD in psychology from the University of Hawaii while a grantee of the East West Center. Her research has focused on stigma, cross-cultural conflict resolution, and intercultural attitudes.

Chapter 7

Analyzing and Interpreting Quantitative Data

Learning Objectives

After completing your study of Chapter 7, you should be able to:

1. Describe the process of preparing and organizing your data for analysis.

2. Identify the procedures for analyzing your descriptive research questions.

3. Identify the procedures for analyzing your inferential research questions or hypotheses.

4. Recognize how to design and present results in tables, figures, and a results section.

5. Describe a discussion section of a research report that interprets the results.

Practice in Understanding Key Concepts

Important Terms and Concepts

The following items represent important concepts relating to analyzing and interpreting quantitative data. Using your own words, record definitions for the items in the space provided.

Preparing and organizing data for analysis: _____

_____

_____

Scoring data: _____

_____

_____

Codebook: _____

_____

_____

Chapter 7

Single-item score: _____

_____

_____

Summed score: _____

_____

_____

Net (or difference) score: _____

_____

_____

Inputting the data: _____

_____

_____

Values: _____

_____

_____

Cleaning the data: _____

_____

_____

Missing data: _____

_____

_____

Descriptive statistics: _____

_____

_____

Inferential statistics: _____

_____

_____

Statistics: _____

_____

_____

Measures of central tendency: _____

_____

_____

Mean (*M*): _____

_____

_____

Median: _____

_____

_____

Mode: _____

_____

_____

Range of scores: _____

_____

_____

Variance: _____

_____

_____

Standard deviation (*SD*): _____

_____

_____

Normal distribution (or normal probability curve): _____

_____

_____

Measures of relative standing: _____

_____

_____

Percentile rank: _____

_____

_____

Standard score: _____

_____

_____

z-score: _____

_____

_____

Chapter 7

Hypothesis testing: _____

_____

_____

Confidence interval (or interval estimate): _____

_____

_____

Effect size: _____

_____

_____

Significance level (or alpha level): _____

_____

_____

Critical region: _____

_____

_____

Two-tailed test of significance: _____

_____

_____

One-tailed test of significance: _____

_____

_____

p value: _____

_____

_____

Degrees of freedom (*df*): _____

_____

_____

Statistical significance: _____

_____

_____

Type I error: _____

_____

_____

Type II error: _____

_____

_____

Power: _____

_____

_____

Table: _____

_____

_____

Figure: _____

_____

_____

Presentation of results: _____

_____

_____

Summary: _____

_____

_____

Implications: _____

_____

_____

Limitations: _____

_____

_____

Future research directions: _____

_____

_____

Chapter 7

Applying the Concepts as a Consumer of Research

Carefully re-read Sample Study #5, paying close attention to the Results and Discussion sections (SG pages 124–127). As you read these sections, identify the following features of the study's data analysis and interpretation by making notes in the margins:

- Descriptive analysis results
- Inferential analysis results
- Reporting results in tables or figures
- Presenting results

- Summary of major results & implications
- Explanation why results occurred
- Advance limitations
- Suggest future research

Activity Hint!

- See Chapter 7 sections "*How Do You Report the Results?*" and "*How Do You Discuss the Results?*" for discussion of how researchers report and discuss their quantitative data analysis.

Now carefully consider your definitions and descriptions of the key concepts for this chapter as you read the following passage. Analyze this passage by answering questions 1–9.

Passage #1 from Sample Study #5:

Table 4   Analysis of Variance for Intercultural Variables by Gender

Intercultural Variable	Women		Men			
	M	SD	M	SD	F	p
Language interest	33.4	6.02	29.2	8.4	22.9	.000
Ethnocentrism	62.7	14.1	76.9	17.9	48.9	.000
Intercultural communication apprehension	38.1	15.1	43.7	14.7	8.9	.003
Quick Discrimination Index cognitive	31.4	8.1	35.4	9.0	13.5	.000

(Kim & Goldstein, 2005, p. 273)

Analyzing data to address descriptive research questions

1. Considering these results, what is an example of a descriptive research question that the authors sought to

answer? _____

_____

_____

2. Did the authors report a measure of central tendency that answers the question you stated in #1? What was the

measure and what does it tell you? _____

_____

_____

3. Did the authors report a measure of variability related to the question you stated in #1? What was the measure and what does it tell you? _____

_____

_____

Analyzing data to address comparison research questions

4. Considering these results, what is an example of a comparison research question that the authors sought to answer? _____

_____

_____

_____

5. Consider the question you stated in #4. (a) What are the independent variable(s)? _____

_____

(b) How many independent variable(s) do you have in the question? _____

(c) Are they categorical or continuous? _____

6. Consider the question you stated in #4. (a) What are the dependent variable(s)? _____

_____

(b) How many dependent variable(s) do you have in the question? _____

(c) Are they categorical or continuous? _____

_____

7. Are any covariates being controlled in the question you stated in #4? _____

_____

8. Did the authors report a test statistic related to the question you stated in #4? What test statistic was reported, what was its value, and what was its associated *p value*? _____

_____

_____

9. Did the authors find a significant difference between groups for the question you stated in #4? How do you know? _____

_____

_____

Chapter 7

Analyzing data to address descriptive research questions:
- Sample research question: What is the average level of language interest for women?
- Measure of central tendency: Mean values for women and men for each variable are indicated by *M.*
- Measure of variability: Standard deviation values are indicated by *SD.*

Analyzing data to address comparison research questions:
- Sample research question: Do women differ from men in terms of language interest?
- Independent variable: Gender; One independent variable (with two levels); Categorical
- Dependent variable: Language interest; One dependent variable; Continuous
- Test statistic: F statistic; $F = 22.9$; $p = .000$
- Conclusion: p is less than .05 and, therefore, the data indicate that there is a significant difference in language interest between men and women.

   o Review Chapter 5 section "***Writing Quantitative Research Questions***" for additional information on identifying variables and writing research questions.
   o Review Chapter 7 sections "***Conduct Descriptive Analysis***" and "***Conduct Inferential Analysis***" for additional information on conducting and reporting quantitative data analyses.

Passage #2 from Sample Study #5:

Participants' scores on the ISES were significantly correlated ($p < .001$) with their scores on language interest ($r = .49$), ethnocentrism ($r = -.45$), intercultural communication apprehension ($r = -.37$), and the Cognitive subscale of the QDI ($r = -.40$). (Kim & Goldstein, 2005, p. 272)

Analyzing data to address relationship research questions

10. Considering the results in Passage #2, what is an example of a relationship research question that the authors sought to answer? _____

_____

_____

_____

11. Did the authors report a test statistic related to the question you stated in #10? What test statistic was reported, what was its value, and what was its associated *p value*? _____

_____

_____

12. Did the authors find a significant relationship among the variables for the question you stated in #10? How do you know? _____

_____

_____

_____

138

Applying the Concepts as a Producer of Research

You will now practice applying the important concepts of this chapter to a new research problem of your choice. Assume that you are a researcher who is working on a quantitative research project. Select a research topic by either picking one of interest to you or using one of the sample research topics identified in earlier chapters.

13. My research topic: _____

_____

_____

14. How will you prepare your data for analysis? _____

_____

_____

_____

15. What is a descriptive question that you would like to answer? _____

_____

_____

_____

16. What descriptive statistics will you use to answer this question? _____

_____

_____

17. What is a comparison or relationship question that you would like to answer? _____

_____

_____

_____

_____

18. How many independent variables do you have? _____

19. How many dependent variables do you have? _____

20. Are there any covariates being controlled? _____

_____

21. Is the independent variable(s) categorical or continuous? _____

22. Is the dependent variable(s) categorical or continuous? _____

23. Assume that the scores are normally distributed. What statistical test do you think is appropriate for this situation? _____

_____

_____

24. Identify the null hypothesis for this study. _____

_____

_____

_____

_____

25. Identify the alternative hypothesis for this study. _____

_____

_____

_____

_____

26. Choose the level of significance (or alpha level) for rejecting the null hypothesis. _____

Suppose that your study resulted in a statistically significant result and you therefore reject the null hypothesis.

27. Write a summary that might be appropriate for this study. _____

_____

_____

_____

28. What limitations might there be with your study? _____

_____

_____

_____

_____

29. What future research directions might be suggested by your study? _____

_____

_____

_____

Practice Test Items

Answer the following items to check your understanding of the important concepts related to analyzing and interpreting quantitative data. Once you have answered all of the items, you can check your ideas with the provided solutions.

1. Suppose you have a quantitative data set to be analyzed to test a given hypothesis. Put the following five steps in the order that you would complete them, starting with the first step. Use the letters found to the left of the choices to designate each step in the provided blanks.

    a. Calculate descriptive statistics
    b. Clean the data
    c. Conduct a hypothesis test
    d. Input the data
    e. Score the data

    First step _____   _____   _____   _____   _____   Last step

2. If you want to know the most common response given to an item, which statistic would you choose? Circle the letter to the left of the correct response.

    a. Mean
    b. Median
    c. Mode
    d. Variance
    e. Percentile rank

3. Percentile rank is an example of what kind of statistic? Circle the letter to the left of the correct response.

    a. Measure of central tendency
    b. Measure of variability
    c. Measure of relative standing
    d. Inferential statistic

4. Which of the following is an example of a measure of variability? Circle the letter to the left of the correct response.

    a. Mean
    b. Mode
    c. Percentile rank
    d. Standard deviation
    e. z-score

5. Read the following two hypothesis statements and decide which of the following statistical procedures would be most appropriate. Circle the letter to the left of the correct response.

    Null hypothesis: There is no difference in attitudes toward the use of group activities for males and females.
    Alternative hypothesis: Females have more positive attitudes toward the use of group activities than males.

    a. One-tail hypothesis test
    b. Two-tail hypothesis test
    c. Effect size calculation
    d. Standard score

6. Consider a scenario where a person has been charged with a crime. You can think of the null hypothesis as "the person is innocent" and the alternative hypothesis as "the person is guilty." Suppose the person is found guilty in court, even though in reality, the person was innocent. This is an example of which of the following? Circle the letter to the left of the correct response.

    a. Type I error
    b. Type II error
    c. Power
    d. Effect size

7. Which of the following probabilities would you prefer to have a large value in a study using hypothesis testing? Circle the letter to the left of the correct response.

    a. *p value*
    b. Alpha (probability of a Type I error)
    c. Beta (probability of a Type II error)
    d. Power

8. List four elements that a researcher should include when writing a conclusion to a study.

    _____

    _____

    _____

    _____

Four different studies (a, b, c, and d) were conducted and a summary of the results is given in the following table. Use these results to answer questions 9 and 10.

Study	df	t-value	p value	Effect size
a	8	2.306	0.05	1.8
b	12	1.356	0.20	0.3
c	20	2.528	0.02	0.6
d	30	1.697	0.10	0.6

9. Which of the studies (a, b, c, or d) had the most statistically significant difference between the two groups? Circle the letter to the left of the correct response.

    a. Study a
    b. Study b
    c. Study c
    d. Study d

10. Which of the studies (a, b, c, or d) had the most practically significant difference between the two groups? Circle the letter to the left of the correct response.

    a. Study a
    b. Study b
    c. Study c
    d. Study d

Practice Test Items - Answer Key

1. Suppose you have a quantitative data set to be analyzed to test a given hypothesis. Put the following five steps in the order that you would do them, starting with the first step.

   First step: e. Score the data
               d. Input the data
               b. Clean the data
               a. Calculate descriptive statistics
   Last step: c. Conduct a hypothesis test

   Review section "How Do You Prepare the Data for Analysis?" in the textbook

2. If you want to know the most common response given to an item, which statistic would you choose?

   c. Mode

   Review section "Conduct Descriptive Analysis" in the textbook

3. Percentile rank is an example of what kind of statistic?

   c. Measure of relative standing

   Review section "Conduct Descriptive Analysis" in the textbook

4. Which of the following is an example of a measure of variability?

   d. Standard deviation

   Review section "Conduct Descriptive Analysis" in the textbook

5. Read the following two hypothesis statements and decide which of the following statistical procedures would be most appropriate.

   Null hypothesis: There is no difference in attitudes toward the use of group activities for males and females. Alternative hypothesis: Females have more positive attitudes toward the use of group activities than males.

   a. One-tail hypothesis test

   Review section "Conduct Inferential Analysis" in the textbook

6. Consider a scenario where a person has been charged with a crime. You can think of the null hypothesis as "the person is innocent" and the alternative hypothesis as "the person is guilty." Suppose the person is found guilty in court, even though in reality, the person was innocent. This is an example of which of the following?

   a. Type I error

   Review section "Potential Errors in Outcomes" and Table 7.8 in the textbook

7. Which of the following probabilities would you prefer to have a large value in a study using hypothesis testing?

   d. Power

   Review section "Potential Errors in Outcomes" and Table 7.8 in the textbook

8. List four elements that a researcher should include when writing a conclusion to a study. Possible elements include:

   A summary of major conclusions to each research question.
   Implications of the study for different audiences.
   Explanations of why the results occurred.
   Advance limitations of the study.
   Suggest future research.

   Review section "How Do You Report the Results?" in the textbook

9. Which of the studies (a, b, c, or d) had the most statistically significant difference between the two groups?

   c. Study c $(p = 0.02)$

   Review section "Conduct Inferential Analysis" in the textbook

10. Which of the studies (a, b, c, or d) had the most practically significant difference between the two groups?

    a. Study a $(p \leq 0.05,$ effect size $= 1.8)$

    Review section "Conduct Inferential Analysis" in the textbook

Chapter 8

Collecting Qualitative Data

Learning Objectives

After completing your study of Chapter 8, you should be able to:

1. Identify different approaches to selecting participants and sites.

2. Know the levels of permissions required to gain access to participants and sites.

3. Identify and weigh the alternative types of qualitative data you can collect.

4. Identify the procedures for recording qualitative data.

5. Recognize the administrative and ethical considerations involved in collecting qualitative data.

Practice in Understanding Key Concepts

Important Terms and Concepts

The following items represent important concepts relating to collecting qualitative data. Using your own words, record definitions for the items in the space provided.

Purposeful sampling: _____

_____

_____

Maximal variation sampling: _____

_____

_____

Extreme case sampling: _____

_____

_____

Chapter 8

Typical sampling: _____

_____

_____

Theory or concept sampling: _____

_____

_____

Homogeneous sampling: _____

_____

_____

Critical sampling: _____

_____

_____

Opportunistic sampling: _____

_____

_____

Confirming and disconfirming sampling: _____

_____

_____

Gatekeeper: _____

_____

_____

Observation: _____

_____

_____

Participant observer: _____

_____

_____

Nonparticipant observer: _____

_____

_____

Changing observational role: _____

_____

_____

Fieldnotes: _____

_____

_____

Descriptive fieldnotes: _____

_____

_____

Reflective fieldnotes: _____

_____

_____

Interview: _____

_____

_____

Open-ended questions: _____

_____

_____

Open-ended response: _____

_____

_____

One-on-one interview: _____

_____

_____

Focus group interview: _____

_____

_____

Telephone interview: _____

_____

_____

E-mail interview: _____

_____

_____

Probes: _____

_____

_____

Documents: _____

_____

_____

Audiovisual materials: _____

_____

_____

Data recording protocol: _____

_____

_____

Interview protocol: _____

_____

_____

Observational protocol: _____

_____

_____

Ethical issues: _____

_____

_____

Applying the Concepts as a Consumer of Research

Carefully re-read the "Data Collection" section of Sample Study #2 (SG page 27). As you read, look for the following features of the study's data collection and make corresponding notes in the margins:

- Selecting participants
- Gaining permissions
- Selecting data types
- Using data recording protocols

Now carefully consider your definitions and descriptions of the key concepts for this chapter as you answer questions 1–5 for Sample Study #2.

1. What kind of sampling strategy was used? How do you know? _____

_____

_____

2. What was the sample size and who were the participants? _____

_____

_____

3. What kinds of permissions do you think were necessary to obtain for this study? _____

_____

_____

_____

4. What types of data did the authors collect and how did they record the qualitative data? _____

_____

_____

_____

5. What field issues and ethical issues may have arisen during this study? _____

_____

_____

_____

_____

Activity Feedback!

This study implemented data collection in the following ways:

- Sampling Strategy: Purposeful sampling—homogenous sampling
- Sample Size and Participants: Five secondary students who have Asperger syndrome
- Needed Permissions: These permissions could include (a) the institutional review board of the researchers' institution, (b) the school's principal, (c) the special education teacher (the gatekeeper), (d) the adolescents, and (e) their parents.
- Data Type(s) and How Recorded: Semistructured one-on-one interviews using the protocol and questions found in the article's appendix.
- Field and Ethical Issues: These issues could include (a) Gaining access to the adolescents; (b) Providing the questions to the students in advance; (c) Preparing the interview equipment; (d) Conveying the purpose of the study; (e) Not disrupting the participants' school day; and (f) Protecting confidentiality

Chapter 8

Now apply the chapter content to a new study. Read the article at the end of this chapter (SG pages 157–175):

> **Sample Study #6**: Komives, S. R., Owen, J. E., Longerbeam, S. D., Mainella, F. C., & Osteen, L. (2005). Developing a leadership identity: A grounded theory. *Journal of College Student Development, 46*(6), 593–611.

Do the following as you read this study: (A) Note the six major steps of the research process in the margins. (B) Focus on the article's discussion of data collection to answer questions 6–10.

Activity Hint!

- See Chapter 8 section "*Useful Information for Consumers of Research*" for advice on evaluating a study's data collection.

6. What kind of sampling strategy was used? How do you know? _____

_____

_____

_____

7. What was the sample size and who were the participants? _____

_____

_____

8. What kinds of permissions do you think were necessary to gain for this study? _____

_____

_____

_____

_____

9. What types of data did the authors collect and how did they record the qualitative data? _____

_____

_____

_____

10. What field issues and ethical issues may have arisen during this study? _____

_____

_____

_____

_____

_____

Applying the Concepts as a Producer of Research

You will now practice applying the important concepts of this chapter to a new research problem of your choice. Assume that you are a researcher who is working on a qualitative research project. Select a research topic by either picking one of interest to you or using one of the sample research topics identified in earlier chapters.

11. Identify the central phenomenon of your qualitative study. _____

_____

_____

Selecting participants

12. Identify the participants for your qualitative study. _____

_____

_____

13. Describe the purposeful sampling strategy that you will use. _____

_____

_____

_____

_____

14. How many participants or research sites do you expect to have? _____

_____

_____

Gaining permissions

15. What permissions will you need to gain? _____

_____

_____

_____

_____

16. Who might serve as a gatekeeper for this study? Why might this person serve this role? _____

_____

_____

_____

Chapter 8

Selecting the data type(s)

17. What type(s) of data will you collect to address your research question? _____

_____

_____

_____

Recording the data

18. How will you record the data? _____

_____

_____

_____

19. Write a sample open-ended question you might use in an interview during this study. _____

_____

_____

_____

20. Write a sample probe question you might use with the above interview question. _____

_____

_____

_____

Administering data collection

21. What field issues do you anticipate arising in this study? _____

_____

_____

_____

_____

22. What ethical issues do you anticipate arising in this study? _____

_____

_____

_____

_____

Practice Test Items

Answer the following items to check your understanding of the important concepts related to collecting qualitative data. Once you have answered all of the items, you can check your ideas with the provided solutions.

Read the following passages (Way, Stauber, Nakkula, & London, 1994, pp. 343–344). You will use these passages to answer questions 1–6.

[A] Our qualitative analyses were conducted on interview data from the 19 students across both schools who scored in the top 10% of our sample on the CDI [Children's Depression Inventory], with depression scores ranging from 19 to 30.

[B] The interview is semi-structured, and designed to explore the extent, nature, and quality of the participants' thoughts and feelings about a range of personal, interpersonal, and behavioral phenomena. [C] The interview process is guided by open-ended questions that lead into topical areas including substance use. [D] Initial responses to interview questions (such as "How often do you drink?" "What is it that you like about drinking?" "Why don't you drink more than you do?") were probed by the interviewer to invite increasingly detailed and thoughtful reports of students' self-perspectives on their substance use or nonuse. [E] These kinds of questions were asked for each substance (e.g., "Why do you think you haven't tried marijuana?" "Why do you smoke cigarettes?" etc.). [F] The goal of the interview is to explore the meaning and attributions that the students assign to their behavior.

[G] Interviews were conducted by advanced doctoral students in counseling or developmental psychology. [H] Participants were interviewed in one-on-one meetings held in private rooms at the respective school sites. [I] We assured all participating students of full confidentiality.

When answering questions 1–6, you may be asked to refer to specific sentences in the passage. If this is the case, you should refer to each individual sentence by the reference letter (e.g., [A]) given at the start of each sentence.

1. What type of sampling strategy was used in this passage? Circle the letter to the left of the correct response.

    a. Snowball
    b. Extreme case
    c. Typical
    d. Opportunistic

2. Suppose this study was redone using maximal variation sampling. Which of the following groups would be likely participants? Circle the letter to the left of the correct response.

    a. Students with very low depression scores
    b. Students with typical depression scores
    c. Students with high, typical, and low depression scores
    d. Random sample of students from the selected high schools

3. What interview type was used in this study? Circle the letter to the left of the correct response.

    a. Telephone interview
    b. Email interview
    c. Focus group interview
    d. One-on-one interview

4. Which sentence from the passage ([A] - [I]) gives evidence that the authors considered the ethical concerns of their study? Write the letter in the provided space.

    Sentence: _____

5. Which sentence from the passage ([A] - [I]) gives an example of a probe that was used during the interview? Write the letter in the provided space.

    Sentence: _____

6. Suppose this study was redone with a new group of participants. After the start of the study, a group of students at a high school were caught with an illegal substance and required to attend a 6-month substance abuse education program. The researchers decide to study the meaning of substance abuse for this group as they go through the program. Which of the following describes this new sampling strategy? Circle the letter to the left of the correct response.

    a. Snowball
    b. Extreme case
    c. Typical
    d. Opportunistic

7. Which of the following sampling strategies occurs after data collection has started? Circle the letter to the left of the correct response.

    a. Homogeneous sampling
    b. Confirming/disconfirming sampling
    c. Theory of concept sampling
    d. Random sampling
    e. Critical sampling

8. Which of the following sampling strategies is typically not appropriate to use in a qualitative study? Circle the letter to the left of the correct response.

    a. Homogeneous sampling
    b. Confirming/disconfirming sampling
    c. Theory or concept sampling
    d. Random sampling
    e. Critical sampling

9. Briefly describe the difference between the intention of using probabilistic sampling and using purposeful sampling.

_____

_____

_____

_____

_____

10. Briefly describe the difference between descriptive fieldnotes and reflective fieldnotes.

_____

_____

_____

_____

_____

Practice Test Items - Answer Key

1. What type of sampling strategy was used in this passage?

    b.   Extreme case

    Review section "Purposeful Sampling" in the textbook

2. Suppose this study was redone using maximal variation sampling. Which of the following groups would be likely participants?

    c.   Students with high, typical, and low depression scores

    Review section "Purposeful Sampling" in the textbook

Chapter 8

3. What interview type was used in this study?

    d. One-on-one interview

    Review section "Interviews" in the textbook

4. Which sentence from the passage ([A] - [I]) gives evidence that the authors considered the ethical concerns of their study?

    Sentence: [I] We assured all participating students of full confidentiality.

    Review section "Ethical Issues in Data Collection" in the textbook

5. Which sentence from the passage ([A] - [I]) gives an example of a probe that was used during the interview?

    Sentence: [E] These kinds of questions (the probes) were asked for each substance (e.g., "Why do you think you haven't tried marijuana?" "Why do you smoke cigarettes?" etc.).

    Review section "Interviews" in the textbook

6. Suppose this study was redone with a new group of participants. After the start of the study, a group of students at a high school were caught with an illegal substance and required to attend a 6-month substance abuse education program. The researchers decide to study the meaning of substance abuse for this group as they go through the program. Which of the following describes this new sampling strategy?

    d. Opportunistic

    Review section "Purposeful Sampling" in the textbook

7. Which of the following sampling strategies occurs after data collection has started?

    b. Confirming/disconfirming sampling

    Review section "Purposeful Sampling" and Figure 8.2 in the textbook

8. Which of the following sampling strategies is typically not appropriate to use in a qualitative study?

    d. Random sampling

    Review section "What Participants and Sites Will You Study?" and Figure 8.1 in the textbook

9. Briefly describe the difference between the intention of using probabilistic sampling and using purposeful sampling.

    Probabilistic sampling is used when the intention of a study is to generalize from a sample to a population. Purposeful sampling is used when the intention of a study is to develop a detailed understanding of a central phenomenon.

    Review section "What Participants and Sites Will You Study?" and Figure 8.1 in the textbook

10. Briefly describe the difference between descriptive fieldnotes and reflective fieldnotes.

    Descriptive fieldnotes record the events and activities taking place during an observation. Reflective fieldnotes record the personal thoughts and insights of the researcher about an observation.

    Review section "Observations" in the textbook

Developing a Leadership Identity: A Grounded Theory

Susan R. Komives   Julie E. Owen   Susan D. Longerbeam
Felicia C. Mainella   Laura Osteen

This grounded theory study on developing a leadership identity revealed a 6-stage developmental process. The thirteen diverse students in this study described their leadership identity as moving from a leader-centric view to one that embraced leadership as a collaborative, relational process. Developing a leadership identity was connected to the categories of developmental influences, developing self, group influences, students' changing view of self with others, and students' broadening view of leadership. A conceptual model illustrating the grounded theory of developing a leadership identity is presented.

Burns (1978) observed that despite the large volume of scholarship on the topic, leadership is not well understood. Recent attempts to classify and make meaning of the evolution of leadership have been generally successful at organizing theories of leadership into conceptual families (Bass, 1990; Northouse, 2003; Rost, 1993). Numerous books and articles focus on leadership theory, behaviors, effective practices, or on particular populations (e.g., women, youth, ethnic groups), specific settings (e.g., civic leadership, business leadership, church leadership), and diverse outcomes (e.g., satisfaction, effectiveness, social responsibility). Despite the broad scope of this literature, there is little scholarship about how leadership develops or how a leadership identity develops over time.

The Scholarship of Leadership

Rost (1993) concluded that most of what has been labeled leadership in the past was essentially good management. Leadership theories that rely on traits, behaviors, and situations to explain leadership worked well in an industrial era when the predominant goals of leadership were production and efficiency. However, Rost and other scholars (Allen & Cherrey, 2000; Bennis, 1989; Heifetz, 1994; Wheatley, 1999) noted that society has shifted to a knowledge-based, networked world. Rapid advancements in technology, increasing globalization, complexity, and interconnectedness reveal the new postindustrial paradigm of a networked world and call for "new ways of leading, relating, learning, and influencing change" (Allen & Cherrey, p. 1; Rost). Many of these "new ways of leading" include components of principle-centered leadership such as collaboration, ethical action, moral purposes, and leaders who transform followers into leaders themselves (Burns, 1978; Covey, 1992; Rost).

The principles involved in postindustrial leadership support a values-centered approach (Chrislip & Larson, 1994; Kouzes & Posner, 2003; Matusak, 1997) and have influenced new pedagogical leadership models. Scholars who have developed models largely designed for college student leadership development

Susan R. Komives is Associate Professor, College Student Personnel Program; Julie E. Owen is Coordinator of Curriculum Development and Academic Partnerships, Maryland Leadership Development Program; each at the University of Maryland. Susan D. Longerbream is Assistant Professor of Educational Psychology at Northern Arizona University. Felicia C. Mainella is Assistant Professor of Leadership Studies at Peace College. Laura Osteen is Director of the LEAD Center at Florida State University. This research was supported by grants from the American College Personnel Association's Educational Leadership Foundation and the James MacGregor Burns Academy of Leadership.

November/December 2005 ◆ vol. 46 no 6

593

Komives, Owen, Longerbeam, Mainella, & Osteen

such as the Eisenhower/UCLA ensemble social change model (Higher Education Research Institute, 1996) assert that collaboration among individuals, groups, and communities is essential for social change to occur. Similarly, the relational leadership model (Komives, Lucas, & McMahon, 1998) defines leadership as "a relational process of people together attempting to accomplish change or make a difference to benefit the common good" (p. 21). This relational leadership model includes elements of inclusiveness, empowerment, ethics, purposefulness, and process orientation. Many leadership educators agree that college students are best informed by learning a postindustrial, relational-values approach to leadership (Higher Education Research Institute; Zimmerman-Oster & Burkhardt, 1999). Although scholarship exists that describes these leadership approaches, none offers a theoretical model of how this kind of relational leadership develops.

Most leadership development scholarship focuses on skill-building or short-term interventions such as retreats or courses, rather than on the process of how leadership capacity or leadership identity is created or changes over time. Although there were conceptual models of leadership development (Brungart, 1996; Velsor & Drath, 2004) at the time of this study there was no known research on how leadership identity was formed. Understanding the process of creating a leadership identity is central to designing leadership programs and teaching leadership. The purpose of this study was to understand the processes a person experiences in creating a leadership identity.

METHOD

Because the purpose of the study was to understand how a leadership identity develops, a grounded theory methodology was chosen. The intent of a grounded theory is to generate

or discover a theory or abstract analytical schema of a phenomenon that relates to a particular situation grounded in the experience and perceptions of the participants (Brown, Stevens, Troiano, & Schneider, 2002; Creswell, 1998; Strauss & Corbin, 1998). The grounded theory in this study reflects the developmental experience of college student participants who had been observed working effectively with others toward shared purposes, that is, who had demonstrated relational leadership (Komives et al., 1998).

Procedures

Sampling. The study employed the purposeful sampling procedures of intensity sampling to identify "intensity-rich cases that manifest the phenomenon intensely, but not extremely" (Patton, 2002, p. 243). Nominators in professional positions that afforded them the opportunity to observe students interacting in group settings at a large mid-Atlantic research university were invited to nominate students who were exemplars of relational leadership.

Participants. From the pool of possible participants, we invited 13 students who exhibited the theoretical dimensions of relational leadership to participate in the study. Eight of the participants were White, 1 was Asian American, 3 were African American, and 1 student was African who immigrated to the United States as a child. Eight of the participants were men and 5 were women. There were 2 sophomores, 9 fourth- or fifth-year seniors, and 2 recent graduates. Two participants identified themselves as gay men; others identified themselves as heterosexual or did not identify their sexual orientation. The group was religiously diverse including Muslim, Bahá'í, Jewish, and Christian students, as well as those without active religious affiliations. There was a range of majors from chemistry to speech communications. Students used their

Leadership Identity

own first name or chose their own pseudonym.

In-Depth Interviews. Each student participated in a series of three interviews with the same interviewer. A research team of five White women conducted the research. A structured interview protocol was designed to ensure continuity across interviewers. After participants gave written informed consent, interviews were tape-recorded and subsequently transcribed. Through constant comparative analysis (Merriam & Associates, 2002; Strauss & Corbin, 1998), the research team modified questions to explore emergent issues. Researchers maintained field notes during each interview.

The three interviews ranged from 1 to 2 hours each. This "three-interview series" followed Seidman's (1991) model focusing on life history, followed by a detailed exploration of the experience, and lastly focusing on "reflection on the meaning" (p. 12). The first interview used a life narrative method (Bruner, 1987; Riessman, 1993) and asked the student to start back in elementary school and reflect on "how you have become the person you are now." This question allowed for the broadest possible story to emerge so researchers could connect various experiences to the emergence of leadership identity. The purpose of the second interview was to identify the students' experiences working with others and to explore their experiences with leadership. The third interview explored how the students' view of leadership changed over time and what influenced that changing view.

Trustworthiness. The research team ensured the trustworthiness and credibility of the study (Strauss & Corbin, 1998) with multiple procedures. Participants reviewed and responded to transcripts of their interviews (i.e., member checking). Research team members served as peer debriefers for the process. The

team sought feedback on the evolving theory and interpretations of the data from diverse colleagues to understand its meaning. Concepts were identified in the data and were examined across the stages of the evolving model. The detail in coding and analysis confirmed saturation in the central category and categories of the theory. Grounded theory does not seek to be generalizable and the degree to which it is transferable is sought through the participant "voices" and the thick descriptions reflected in this study.

Data Analysis

We used open, axial, and selective coding (Strauss & Corbin, 1998) to analyze the data. During open coding, each transcript was analyzed in sentences or groups of sentences reflecting single ideas. These units were given a code to reflect that idea or concept (Strauss & Corbin). The open coding identified 5,922 items that were combined through axial coding into 245 abstract concepts. In selective coding the concepts were ultimately organized into one central category or "what the research is all about" (p. 146), in this case, leadership identity along with five categories: (a) essential developmental influences; (b) developing self; (c) group influences; (d) changing view of self with others; and (e) broadening view of leadership. Properties—also known as attributes of a category—were identified for each of these categories. Strauss and Corbin clarified that "whereas properties are the general or specific characteristics or attributes of a category, dimensions represent the location of a property along a continuum or range" (p. 117). Through constant comparative analysis (Merriam & Associates, 2002; Strauss & Corbin), each participant's response was compared and connected to others as categories, properties, and dimensions emerged.

Komives, Owen, Longerbeam, Mainella, & Osteen

FINDINGS AND EMERGING THEORY

The experiences and reflections of these students revealed the dynamic process of developing a leadership identity. Students had different experiences, came to new awareness of themselves in a leadership context at different ages, identified a variety of ways these experiences and context had an impact on them, yet they engaged with the process in similar ways leading to credibility in the emergent theory. The theory emerged as the relationships between the concepts combined into an integrated framework that explained the phenomenon of leadership identity (Strauss & Corbin, 1998). The categories interact to create a leadership identity as the central category that developed over six identity stages. Developing self interacted with group influences to shape the student's changing view of self with others. This changing view of self in relation to others shaped the student's broadening view of what leadership is and created a leadership identity. Illustrative quotations from the participants are included in each of the categories to tell the story of this theory.

Developmental Influences

The essential developmental influences that fostered the development of a leadership identity included adult influences, peer influences, meaningful involvement, and reflective learning. Each of these four properties has dimension, which means they change across the stages of the central category. For example, how adults influenced newer leaders was a different process than with experienced leaders, and meaningful involvement began with an individual joining a variety of organizations but progressed to more in-depth, responsible experiences with one or two core groups.

Adult Influences. Adults played different roles in influencing student movement through the leadership identity development stages. In the family, adults were very important in building confidence and being an early building block of support. Angela noted, "My family is really what built a lot of my character." Adults created safe spaces in classes and organizations where students learned to communicate and relate to peers. On the importance of his scoutmaster, James noted with relief, "When we had moved houses, we didn't move troops" so he still had access to the same scout master who affirmed him. Students explicitly noted the role of school-teachers and the encouragement found in the continuity of those teachers across grades in school.

In the early stages of their leadership identity, adults were particularly influential as role models. James said,

> Through all this you need that person you look up to, that role model, that figure that you aspire to be like or to be. Doesn't have to be a real person, people usually see qualities of what they aspire to be in different people, I guess like a hero. . . And [when I was little] I wanted to be like Superman and smart like Batman and be in touch with people like Star Trek characters.

Adults were the first to recognize the students' leadership potential. Ed recalled times when he was encouraged to take leadership roles in groups: "[adults said] 'Oh, you'd be good at that', or 'I really think you should apply for that.'" In the early stages, adults affirmed and sponsored students. They often prompted students initially to get involved in organizations and helped them set high expectations for themselves. Joey observed: "Positive reinforcement . . . gave me the drive to get more involved in things."

596

Journal of College Student Development

Leadership Identity

Eventually there was less need for this external affirmation and the students became self-directed. Ed saw that shift in his motivation and said, "I'm going to go ahead and do this. I'm going to feel confident in the things I've done in the past, because I don't want to rely on others to force me forward."

Later, adults continued as models and became actively engaged mentors. Jayme described watching adults as intentional modeling: "I'm going to learn from other people's experience, and I'll at least get some information before I jump in there." Students of color, especially, benefited from the presence of an active adult mentor. Students of color were often apprenticed to an adult and worked in intensive and intentional ways as an assistant or protégé to that adult. Jayme became the "protégé" of Miss [Smith]—a highly involved woman at her church. This woman "adopted" her and took her everywhere including on business and church trips. Jayme observed adult conversation, manners, and how conflicts were resolved. She drew on those experiences when she subsequently became the assistant to the dance teacher in her high school and often chose her own behaviors by asking herself, "What would Miss [Smith] do?"

In college, adults continued as models and mentors, but also become meaning-makers and even evolved into friends. Ed described how he often thought things through with his advisor: "We would always talk after any experience. I would go right to [my advisor] and like, 'Okay, this is what happened, and I'm trying to figure it out.'" Adults were a meaningful part of each stage of developing students' leadership identity. The dimensions of adult influences ranged from being affirmers, models, and sponsors in the early stages to being mentors and ultimately to being meaning makers and colleagues or friends.

Peer Influences. Same-aged peers served as friends and older peers served as role models in early leadership identity stages. Joey emulated an older student who was an officer in his college LGBT group and observed: "That's kind of cool . . . I could do that." Modeling peers served as a motivator for involvement as well as a model of leadership. Jimmy admired the SGA president:

> [She] was one of the first people . . . like my role model, like she was . . . this perfect leader. That's what I'm going to strive to be, because, you know she takes this group of uninvolved kids, and she makes them do so much for the campus. She's so great at like organizing. She's fighting for the students. Like, she has this love. . .very selfless like promotion for students in general.

Numerous students cited older peers as the reason they got involved or interested in an organization in college. These peers served as sponsors and took the student to initial meetings of a group or encouraged them to join or to run for an office. Peers served as sources of affirmation and support. For Corey, this peer affirmation was important. He initially described his preference to be an active member of a group and not the positional leader until he was turned to by peers to be the formal leader:

> [I] started to realize that in fact that's how I was viewed by my peers. I felt like, okay, well, if my peers have put faith in me, faith in the fact that they truly believe that I'm a leader, then I kind of need to take it on. I wasn't pressured into it, but I felt like it would be best, that maybe I do have something to offer, so I started to embrace it more.

Engaging with peers gained depth and meaning as leadership identity developed. With more group experience, peers served as followers, teammates, and ultimately as

Komives, Owen, Longerbeam, Mainella, & Osteen

collaborators and peer meaning-makers.

Meaningful Involvement. Involvement experiences were the training ground where leadership identity evolved. These experiences helped clarify personal values and interests, and helped students experience diverse peers, learn about self, and develop new skills. Early involvements were a way to make friends. Reflecting on his membership on the high school swim team, Joey described his motivation: "It wasn't the athletics event. It was the camaraderie." As they transitioned into new schools and the university, they sought social integration through involvement in sports, band, theater, or service as a source of new friends. Later meaningful involvements showed more complex motivations. Jimmy reported that "SGA was the first kind of goal-oriented group for me . . . I felt like I was working towards something." Other involvements developed values and personal skills. Jayme learned new skills through service: "I've gotten used to just listening like just hearing them talk about their lives."

Team-based involvements such as sports, theater, and band taught students to do their personal best while concurrently supporting others. From playing sports, Corey said, "I learned it is not just about me" and "your individual achievement helps the team. It doesn't help you shine or stand out, and don't ever put yourself on that pedestal." Marie learned in band that "I'm not trying to beat someone else, but like we're trying to sound good together." Some learned the importance of support from older teammates who established a positive group climate. Ed described his swim team experience as always being "on our feet cheering for each other," and "we cheered more for the kids that were struggling."

Reflective Learning. Structured opportunities for critical reflection, such as journal-

ing and meaningful conversations with others, allowed students to uncover their passions, integrity, and commitment to continual self-assessment and learning. This reflection was initially with a parent or sibling; participants described dinner table conversations, family meetings, and the listening ear of close-age siblings. Over time, they began to process their experiences with other adults and peers. Some students preferred journaling and began to share those journals with others.

Experiences in which students intentionally learned about leadership, such as trainings, retreats, or classes, provided them with new language and ideas that aided their development. Students used this new leadership language to assess themselves and differentiate experiences. Ed talks about the power of his first undergraduate leadership classes: "We talked about having some kind of lens or framework, or even the language to describe [leadership], it changes not only the way I think about it, but it changes the way I act as a leader in ways that I don't understand . . . in unconscious ways." Becky clearly saw:

> It's a combination of the experiences I've had, the classes and the theories I've learned. I don't think alone any of it would have influenced me as it has. It has really made it spin together to really understand it, because I could come out of class one day and take something that I learned and really implement it in my experience, but because having experienced it I can also talk about it theory-wise. So I think it's definitely that combination.

Even being a participant in this study supported reflection. Jimmy said, "Now, I feel like having gone through this research study like definitely. . .my interactions are more genuine." As depicted in Figure 1, these developmental influences were the environ-

Leadership Identity

mental context in which leadership identity developed.

Developing Self

The category of developing self contains properties with dimensions of personal growth that changed throughout the development of leadership identity. The properties in this category are deepening self-awareness, building self-confidence, establishing interpersonal efficacy, applying new skills, and expanding motivations.

Deepening Self-Awareness. In the early stages of developing their leadership identity, students recalled a highly vague and diffuse sense of self. Attributions from adults, family, and peers helped them identify aspects of themselves that were strengths and aspects that needed attention. Over time they were able to label aspects of their personal identity on their own. For example, Becky said, "I just

happen to be a very outspoken, share-my-opinion-kind of person." Joey claimed, "I'm more of an interpersonal person."

When asked about their personal identities, students of color identified race as a critical factor. James, an African American student, said, " [the] biggest thing is race"; another African American student, Ray, described how he was motivated to present "a positive image of a Black male," although he tried "not to think about [race] too much." Sammy, an Asian American student, discussed his many identities including the influence of race, ethnicity, and being male, and had come to see them as assets of diversity that he brought to a group. Both gay students felt being male was an asset to their leadership; however, Donald worried that sexual orientation could be a barrier to leadership based on what others might have thought of him.

Gender was a factor in how some ap-

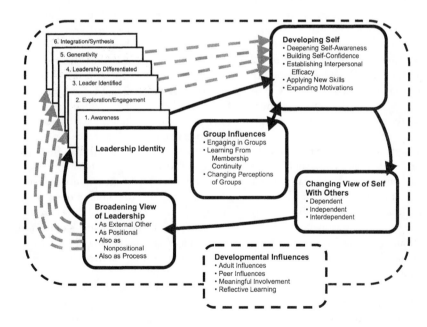

FIGURE 1. Developing a Leadership Identity: Illustrating the Cycle

proached leadership. After being denied membership in a group based upon her gender, Jayme noted, "I decided that I am not going to let anything, anything at all, push me down." Christine became more activist in her youth after completing altar server training in her church only to be denied the opportunity to become an altar "boy." Angela acknowledged that she didn't ever think, "'I can't do [something] because I'm a woman,'" but acknowledged that "[you] have to succeed to the best of your ability to show that you're not inferior."

The awareness of majority aspects of the students' identities was largely taken for granted. For example, most of the White students did not identify race until asked about it. Donald, a White male, reflected what many White men in the study shared that: "Race and gender does sort of make it easier. . . . People sort of expect you to take on a leadership role." Angela did not think about how being White and heterosexual helped her, although in reflection, said that it probably did. Ed, however, felt truly transformed and enlightened when he "started to understand my own privilege . . . as a White able-bodied male." Those in later stages of developing their leadership identity were generally more complex in their awareness of their multiple identities.

Other aspects of self-awareness were the development of personal values and a sense of personal integrity that became more important over time. James shared that: "The first time I heard the word *integrity* was my Dad saying it; and he was like, 'You know when it comes to integrity it is the most important thing because if everything is gone that is all you have.'"

Building Self-Confidence. Most students described feeling special in their families and with other adults. Even when they went

through periods of self-doubt and low esteem, they knew they mattered to someone. They sought the support and approval of adults in the early stages of their leadership identity development. For example, James commented, "I always wanted the coach's approval." Building their confidence supported developing a positive self-concept, a sense of themselves. Sammy knew when that happened and shared that: "Things started rolling and I was in a groove. . .I knew what needed to get done." Confidence came with meaningful experience. James said "I can do this because I have done similar things to it." Confidence also came with being able to identify their strengths and weaknesses. Jayme said, "I'm not perfect, but I have something to bring."

As their confidence built, they were willing to take risks to get more involved and were empowered to take on more active group roles. Jayme reflected, "Eleventh grade was when I started letting myself be open and do what I wanted to do and not think about what other people say." Over time, their growing sense of self-awareness let them take on unpopular issues, stand up for their values, and not need peer affirmation. Ed described antihomophobia programs he did on his residence hall floor as a heterosexual resident assistant, knowing it was the right thing to do so "the alienation doesn't matter as much."

Once they acknowledged that they were leaders or had leadership potential, they began to incorporate that identity into their sense of self. Corey noted: "Sophomore year in college is when I really started to believe and really identify with being a leader—others had been saying it" and Jimmy noticed that "people showed respect. . .[I] started to think of [my]self this way."

Establishing Interpersonal Efficacy. Participants had numerous experiences that contributed to their efficacy in working with

Leadership Identity

other people. Most students described how they learned to make new friends in the normal transitions from elementary school to middle or junior high school, high school, and on to college. Sammy and Joey, who moved often as children, saw the value of those transitions. Sammy said: "I get to know people a lot quicker because I socialize with everybody."

Students noted how important it was that they learned to relate to and communicate with people different from themselves. They developed an appreciation of diverse points of view and valued different perspectives. Ray observed: "I've just been really exposed to a broad range of viewpoints and that's kind of helped me to mature and helped me to be a better person in interacting with people too." Ed came to the realization that he first had to understand himself well before he could

> learn to deal with people who are different from me and have different ideals from what I have, I need to understand more what I represent and what I think. So the more work I do about what I value and what biases I have already that I've been culturally or socially conditioned to have, the better.

Students who felt different or who worked closely with people different from themselves (such as Becky, Ed, and Donald who worked weekly with youth with severe disabilities), later came to value that difference and credit it with the importance of empathy and their commitment to involving others who may be marginalized in groups. According to Becky, "All my work with people with special needs has really opened my eyes to an entirely different world of respect." Donald observed: "I think that [being gay] does make me more sensitive towards other people and what . . . their needs are in a group situation."

Students recognized that working with others on shared tasks required new inter-

personal skills. Ray noted that in leadership: "The trickiest thing was asking one of your peers to do something." When he was in an early leadership position, Sammy described his own struggle with delegation when he stated, "I mean there are certainly times in my life when I feel that . . . I can't trust other people and that I'm going to have to do it myself." With the acceptance of interdependence, developing trust in others became essential. Being a cochair and practicing shared leadership, Becky observed: "I guess it all developed in one big chunk that I started to go through the process of really learning how to build relationships with other people, to help influence them to be a part of the group, and to make the changes [together]." She reflected, "I've gained trust in other people . . . I just took a few years to figure that out."

Each student valued being a self-proclaimed "people-person." They developed an early appreciation of harmonious relationships with others. Few of the participants liked conflict and each had learned to be mediators. Jimmy, for example, described himself as a "smoother" and Joey saw himself as "the connector, the bridge builder." Marie observed:

> I'm just a big believer . . . in the power of personal relationships . . .it's one thing to work with someone in a group or with a campus committee or whatever but if you can get to know that person and they can get to know you outside of that professional or academic experience and have a social bond on top of everything else I think that that personal relationship when you take that into the academic/ professional scenario will lead to maybe bigger and better results.

Applying New Skills. Participants worked to develop new skills as they developed their leadership identity. When they first started joining groups, they were conscious they were

Komives, Owen, Longerbeam, Mainella, & Osteen

learning how to work with other people and knew this required new skills. They found developmental opportunities in many experiences; for example, Jimmy spoke about his high school play experience. "The play was the first time I learned how to completely interact with other people." When first serving as positional leaders, they practiced more directive leadership styles and approaches, all with the goal of getting tasks accomplished. Practical skills dominated that stage of their leadership identity. Donald noted he was "a good time framer, practical, an organizer," and Becky developed her public speaking skills. Practicing included learning difficult tasks such as delegation, member motivation, and member recognition.

When they became aware of interdependence, they came to need new skills such as trusting others, and being open to diverse ideas and perspectives. They recognized the need to develop team-building skills and learned how to work alongside others toward common purposes. Becky asserted: "If the group is working together, there needs to be a common set of values, so everyone is working toward the same goal and everyone has the same ideas." Key to the facilitator role was learning to listen actively to others. They knew listening was a learned skill. Jimmy reflected on his awareness of how he was developing this skill with the support of his advisor:

> Sometimes I think I don't realize what I say or what I do can offend other people . . . like . . . for me coming from like a White male background. So working with [an advisor] has really put a spin like I see myself acting differently. Then it comes out in more like not talking, but more listening.

Expanding Motivations. Students' indiscriminant early interests to get involved included personal motivations such as making

friends or doing interesting things. Goals were refined as they narrowed their focus to joining or remaining in groups that meant something to them. As they developed personally and gained more experience, they sought a deep sense of commitment to something and knew that passion would be a strong motivation to action. James observed, "I like [having a] passion about things, [but] I didn't know what I was passionate about." Jayme observed that "Every single person needs something bigger than just their everyday life, because then it makes things all worthwhile." As participants' commitments to a change or a passion emerged, they took on a catalyst or a change agent role.

Group Influences

The category of developing self interacted with the category of group influences (see the double arrow in Figure 1). The category of group influences includes the properties of engaging in groups, learning from membership continuity, and changing perceptions of groups.

Engaging in Groups. Students often sought groups for a "sense of place." Ed captured many students' early childhood group experiences when he said, "I had feelings of being an outsider." They sought to find organizations that fit their developing self-image. James observed that "Working at scout camp made me feel like I could do anything."

Students sought a sense of belonging in groups. Donald's college church group was even called "The Welcoming Place." These core groups included identity-based groups such as LGBT organizations or the Black Student Union. As he became more purposeful in his membership, Joey observed he sometimes felt

> the weight of the world on your shoulders . . .you feel like you're alone and there's

Leadership Identity

points where you feel like you need to have a safe space where there's people like you that can identify with you, who are experiencing the same struggle and have the same objectives.

Participants were also becoming increasingly clear about the conditions under which they would participate in groups and the role of groups in their development. They were developing convictions and narrowing their interests. Donald dropped out of scouts when he feared being "outed" as gay because the group was hostile toward gay students. Ed described dropping out of a sports club because "the more that I learned about myself and who I wanted to be, and what I wanted to do, it just didn't align with kind of their priorities." He shared the painful story of being at dinner with several members of that group who were telling insensitive jokes so he just got up and walked away and never went back to practice again. In reflection, he told us that he wished he had the capacity to tell them why he was upset but he did not know how to say those things then.

Many kinds of group experiences were critical. Experiences with group projects such as class projects contributed to trust and relationship building when successful and resulted in resentment toward others when not successful. Ed described a bad group experience in a class: "It was a dismal experience. I hated it, and I think some students really hated it since they are the ones that ended up taking on most of the work." Most shared Christine's comment that "[class] group projects are terrible." Conversely, Ray eventually came to learn a lot in group settings: "Everyone has different concerns in the groups that I work with, so that's kind of opened my mind . . . I've been able to understand where people are coming from a lot better."

We were fascinated by the relationship of a strong group culture to the individual's view of themselves and how that culture influenced developing a leadership identity. Becky described being the chair of a senior honor society committee going into her first meeting with a highly structured agenda and a set of ideas about how the task should be accomplished. The group slowed the process down by affirming that they were all leaders with good ideas and wanted to build a vision together of how the committee should approach its task. The group pulled Becky back from being too directive and supported her in practicing shared leadership. Becky reflected that she actually was very relieved. In a similar way, Jayme described her experience in her work with the local African immigrant community. The group continually reminded her that she and others were there to serve the group, not stand out as leaders themselves. Jayme observed:

> It keeps you grounded, because they'll easily call you out . . . So you don't get too cocky. It doesn't make you think . . ."I'm a leader." They're quick to tell you, . . . "What are you doing? A leader is the one who serves the community. Are you serving us?"

Learning From Membership Continuity. To gain more time and energy to invest in organizations they cared about, students started to narrow down their numerous organizational involvements to a few that were more meaningful. They went deep into these organizations. Corey chose to stay highly involved in his fraternity and reflected on this experience: "[It] . . . just changed my entire life." Students who were committed to a group or organization over time readily gained relational skills such as dealing with conflict, handling transition issues, and sustaining organizations. They increasingly became aware

Komives, Owen, Longerbeam, Mainella, & Osteen

of their responsibility for the development of younger group members. They assumed responsibility and took on positional leadership roles and active member roles. Students often maintained their membership in other groups, while retaining a primary group as their main source of identification; a concept that Marie called her "core group." They eventually became wise senior members and continued their support of their core groups even when less active in the group's leadership. Some sports team experiences were particularly powerful developmental environments, which offered opportunities to develop group spirit, encouraged bonding and morale, and were sustained over time. On some teams, they learned to work with people they might not even like but had to learn to function together. That continuity of being known provided a core group—a safe space—to try on roles and practice processes.

Students' interaction with others in groups influenced their own self-awareness as well as shaped how they viewed groups and their role with others in groups. Angela, for example, had been used to doing things by herself in most groups but as tasks became more complex in one of her high school organizations, she came to realize she had to depend on others in the group to accomplish their goals. She had learned that working along with others was more productive than working alone. Subsequently, in her first year of college, she was one of several vice presidents of her residence hall association. When the president abruptly resigned, the group of vice presidents decided to share the role as copresidents until a new president was elected some months later.

Changing Perceptions of Groups. Students initially viewed groups as just collections of friends or people they knew. As they began to realize those groups had purposes and objectives, this collection of people began to be

seen as an organization with structure and roles. Eventually they saw that those organizations were entities to develop. Becky saw this as a new responsibility in her developing leadership identity: "I really try to . . . make it a better organization . . . [and make] simple changes that maybe in the long run would affect the organization." Organizations were also viewed as communities of people working together. Becky observed that the feeling of "community is necessary to do anything." As they developed in their leadership identity, they had a new sense of how their group was linked to other organizations in a system, and they became interested in how the system worked. Students became aware of those who worked in other groups on campus-wide or community-wide issues, and of those who functioned well in coalitions. These systems views led them to see the contributions of diverse roles of stakeholders in those systems and the complexity of different groups within a system. By gaining a systems-view, Ray even gained a new view of administrators: "Working with administrators [I'm] now . . . able to see where they're coming from. . . . I'm a little bit more open-minded about sometimes why they can't get things done."

Changing View of Self With Others

Developing self interacted with group influences to effect how participants changed their view of themselves in relation to other people. In the early stages of engaging in groups, they were *dependent* on others. Even when developing personal efficacy to accomplish their goals, they depended on adults and older peers for sponsorship, affirmation, and support. As students began to be involved in leadership contexts and take on member or leader roles, they engaged in groups from one of two primary pathways: *independent* or *dependent*. On the independent path, students aspired to

Leadership Identity

be the positional leader or had a strong motivation to change something in a group or organization of which they were a part. Others continued to be dependent and preferred to be members or followers in groups. Corey said, "I didn't want to lead, but be part of a team that did." Many functioned on both pathways and clearly saw that they had different roles (independent leader or dependent follower). Whether students entered groups from an independent or dependent position, they shared a leader-centric view of leadership, believing only positional leaders did leadership. Donald said it succinctly, "Leadership is what the leader does." The key transition to a more differentiated view of leadership was facilitated by the awareness that group participants were interdependent with each other. The students continued a consciousness of the interdependence of themselves with others across the final stages of their leadership identity. They believed that leadership came from anywhere in the group and worked to develop their own and their peers' capacity for leadership.

Broadening View of Leadership

Students' changing view of themselves with others influenced their broadening view of leadership and their personal definitions of leadership. The final category concerned participants' construction of leadership and the mental models that framed that construct. In the early stages of leadership identity, the construction of leadership was not yet a personal identity. The initial view of leader was an external adult and it broadened to include an older peer. That view could be stated as: "I am *not* a leader." Leadership then became leader-centric with the belief that a positional leader does leadership. Jayme said,

When I was a girl, I thought leadership was the person who could boss everyone around, and make them do what they wanted to do. Because you saw all the people around you, those in charge were like, "Do this, do that, do this, do that."

That individual leader takes on responsibility, organizes tasks, and gets things done. Taking on a position meant one was the leader. In their independent or dependent approaches to leadership, students acknowledged they were the leader in some contexts and also knew there were other contexts in which they were not the leader, they were "just" a member or follower. As students recognized they could not do everything themselves as positional leaders and that they valued the diversity of talents and perspectives brought by group members to accomplish goals, they began to engage with others in more meaningful, interdependent ways. This led to differentiation in the concept of leadership acknowledging that leadership could come from those in nonpositional roles (i.e., members) and increasingly was seen as a process among people in the group. Leaders were people facilitating the groups' progress from anywhere in the organization.

A leadership identity had become a more stable part of self. This led to the view represented by stating: "I can be *a* leader even when not being *the* leader." Evidence for this transition can be seen in Marie commenting: "There is a difference between having a position and being a leader," and in Ed's philosophy that "leadership is more of a fluid thing, it wasn't just rested in one person." From viewing leadership as a process comes the awareness that people can learn to engage in leadership. Sammy summed it up: "You know, everyone has leadership qualities, and everyone can be a leader in some avenue." Ultimately leadership became an integrated part of self-concept.

Komives, Owen, Longerbeam, Mainella, & Osteen

Leadership Identity

The central category of this grounded theory was leadership identity and it developed in six stages. Each stage ended with a transition, which signaled leaving that stage and beginning the next stage. The process of developing a leadership identity was informed by the interaction of developing self through group influences that changed one's view of self with others and broadened the view of leadership in the context of the supports of the developmental influences. These stages are briefly described with student voices as illustrations.

Awareness. The first stage was the early recognition that leaders existed. As children, participants were particularly aware of parent figures and of national, historic, or charismatic leaders. Angela said, "I always thought of my mom as a huge leader just because in times of hardship she always was the one that pulled through and seemed to pull everything together, and I think that's a leadership quality." This view of leadership was external to the self and participants did not personally identify as a leader or even differentiate group roles. Becky said, "I would say that my lower school and middle school parts of my life, I was not a leader. I wasn't much, I wasn't really a follower, I was kind of just there."

Exploration/Engagement. The second stage was a time of intentional involvement, experiencing groups, and taking on responsibilities, though not generally in a positional leadership role. They often engaged in a myriad of organizations and activities such as swim teams, church bible study groups, dance, Boy Scouts, student council, and community service, usually for the friendships involved. They liked to belong to groups but their involvement was often unfocused. Ray observed, "I always wanted to be doing things," but, "I wasn't ready for a huge role yet." This was a significant skill development stage, when they were seeking to learn anything they could from their participation in groups, including observing adult and peer models of leadership.

Leader Identified. In this third stage, all participants perceived that groups were comprised of leaders and followers and believed the leaders did leadership—that leaders were responsible for group outcomes. In this leader-centric stage, one was a leader only if one held a leadership position; indeed, one was *the* leader. When Marie became a positional leader as captain of the swim team her junior year in high school, she said to herself, "You are a leader now." Donald saw the responsibility of a leader as "you get a job, and you've got more work than everybody else to make sure everything happened." Students became intentional about their group roles in this stage. Some participants intentionally chose a member role when they joined groups; for example, Christine would "be a member first to see what something is about." As followers, these students might be very active and engaged in the goals of their group, but they still looked to the leader as the person who should be in charge.

Leadership Differentiated. In Stage 4, students differentiated leadership beyond the role of the positional leader and recognized that anyone in the group could do leadership and became aware that leadership was also a process between and among people. Students entered this stage with a new awareness that people in organizations were highly interdependent and that leadership was happening all around them. If they were in a positional leadership role, there was a commitment to engage in a way that invited participation and shared responsibility. They began to view this positional leader role as a facilitator, community builder, and shaper of the group's culture. James realized, "We were actually working together as a group, not under me."

Leadership Identity

When they were in a member role (i.e., a nonpositional role), there was an awareness of their own influence and the responsibility of every member to engage in leadership together to support the group's goals. James observed, "I like the fact that I can be a leader without a title because I think those are the best types of leaders to have." They affirmed their commitment to the groups' responsibility for its goals—as a "we" thing and not the individual leader doing it all. [Note: The complexity of the data in Stages 3 and 4 led us to identify two phases in each of these stages. An *emerging phase* clarified the ways the student "tried on" the identity early in the stage and the *immersion phase* was the practicing or living with that identity. These phases are discussed further in Komives, Owen, Longerbeam, Mainella, and Osteen (2005).

Generativity. In Stage 5, students became actively committed to larger purposes and to the groups and individuals who sustained them. Students entered this stage and sought to articulate a personal passion for what they did. These passions were explicitly connected to the beliefs and values they identified as important in their lives. Describing her experience in residence hall government, Angela felt rewarded to realize that future "freshmen. . .[were] getting something better because of something we did." Service was seen as a form of leadership activism, a way of making a difference and working toward change. Exploring their interdependence further, they began to accept responsibility for developing others and for regenerating or sustaining organizations. They made a commitment to sponsor, support, mentor and develop others. They recognized that younger group members were in a developmental place that they themselves had experienced. Jimmy saw his responsibility from "having a peer mentor and now turning around and being a

peer mentor." They sought to enhance the leadership capacity of newer members so they too could be part of the leadership process, largely to create a leadership pipeline for their groups. Anticipating his graduation, Sammy worked for continuity in the organization so the "person coming after me feels comfortable and can do just as well . . . as I did. . . . My approach to leadership now would have to be a kind of mentoring people."

Integration/Synthesis. Stage 6 was a time of continual, active engagement with leadership as a daily process—as a part of self identity. They were increasing in internal confidence and were striving for congruence and integrity. Ed described this as:

> A conscious shift . . . I feel that I can take ownership and the strengths that I have and the value that I bring to a group of people and have confidence in myself that I can do the things that I could set out to do.

This stage was signaled by many students in the study, but not fully evident in all of them. Those in or approaching this stage were confident that they could work effectively with other people in diverse contexts whether they were the positional leader or as an active group member. Even if they did not own the title of leader, they did have a confident identity of a person who does leadership. They understood organizational complexity and practiced systemic thinking. They were comfortable with contextual uncertainty knowing that because they had internalized leadership into their self-concept they could adapt and contribute to a new, unknown context. Ultimately, they echoed Joey's observation that "I see leadership now as an everyday thing."

A Conceptual Model of the Integration of Categories

The conceptual model in Figure 1 illustrates

Komives, Owen, Longerbeam, Mainella, & Osteen

a cycle of how students engaged in the categories that in turn influenced the development of their leadership identity and how that developed over time. One category, *developmental influences*, defined the supports in the environmental context in which the development of leadership identity was occurring.

As students developed themselves through deepening their self-awareness, building self-confidence, establishing interpersonal efficacy, learning to apply new skills, and expanding their motivations, they changed their perceptions of groups and their role in groups. Similarly, engaging in groups and feedback from group members informed the development of themselves as individuals. This interaction between *developing self* and *group influences* shaped an individual's awareness of who they were in relation to others. Depending on their stage of leadership identity, students saw themselves as dependent on others, independent from others, or interdependent with those around them. Their *changing view of self with others* had a direct bearing on their *broadening view of leadership*. Those who viewed themselves as dependent on others saw leadership as something external to them or as a position someone else held. Those who viewed themselves as independent from others assumed positional leader roles and perceived that the leader does leadership. Those who saw their interdependence with those around them viewed leadership as a relational process and leaders as anyone in the group who was contributing to that process.

An individual's broadening view of leadership has properties that develop through the six stages of the core category, *leadership identity*. Students remained in a stage of leadership identity for varying lengths of time. Either dissonance with the stage they were in or a new view of themselves and how they related to others in groups eventually led them

to a new view of leadership. This new view of leadership signaled a transition to a new stage. These transitions between stages of leadership identity marked a shift in thinking, a very gradual process of letting go of old ways of thinking and acting, and trying on new ways of being. In the new, more complex stage, students repeated the cycle that supported their transition to the next stage of leadership identity. This could be envisioned as a helix where one returns to a category such as *developing self* with a higher level of complexity.

Each student's story across the stages of developing their leadership identity was unique, yet was reflected in this grounded theory. Even those who did not evidence all six stages are represented in the theory. Donald, for example, was a sophomore in the study who saw himself as the positional leader in most groups he was in. Concurrently, he eloquently described the issues he was wrestling with as he tried to be a good team member for a major group research project in his honors class and knew that his next developmental step was to learn to trust classmates more and be an active leader as a member of the team. His story described his identity in Stage 3, *leader identified*, and he was beginning a transition toward Stage 4.

We observed that leadership identity is the cumulative confidence in one's ability to intentionally engage with others to accomplish group objectives. Further, a relational leadership identity appears to be a sense of self as one who believes that groups are comprised of interdependent members who do leadership together. This theory is further applied in a leadership identity model (LID) that integrates these categories (Komives, et al., 2005).

Summary of Results

This grounded theory demonstrated that leadership identity develops through six stages

Leadership Identity

moving from awareness to integration/ synthesis. The process within each stage engaged developing self with group influences, which in turn influenced the changing view of self with others from dependence to interdependence and shaped the broadening view of leadership, shifting from an external view of leadership to leadership as a process. Developmental influences facilitated this identity development.

DISCUSSION AND IMPLICATIONS

After developing an awareness of leadership, the students in this study described their shifting leadership identity as moving from a hierarchical, leader-centric view to one that embraced leadership as a collaborative, relational process. Participants' recognition that they function in an interdependent world was an essential part of having a *leadership differentiated* leadership identity. Students in the *generativity* and *integration/synthesis* stages recognized the systemic nature of leadership. The components of this leadership identity theory connect to the observations of many leadership scholars. Margaret Wheatley (1999) described the zeitgeist of the end of the 21st century as an "awareness that we participate in a world of exquisite interconnectedness. We are learning to see systems rather than isolated parts and players" (p. 158). Allen and Cherrey (2000) stated that "new ways of leading require the ability to think systemically. One cannot make sense of relationships and connections by looking at a small part of the system" (p. 84).

This leadership identity theory affirms Wielkiewicz's (2000) operationalization of Allen, Stelzner, and Wielkiewicz's (1998) ecology of leadership model. Wielkiewicz measured two orthogonal dimensions called hierarchical thinking and systemic thinking.

Both dimensions were clearly present in the leadership identity stages. Hierarchical thinking was the view of leadership held in *leader identified* and systemic thinking emerged in *leadership differentiated*. This theory extended Wielkiewicz's work by indicating that these appear to be developmental dimensions and that one experiences hierarchical thinking before one develops systemic thinking.

Some leadership scholarship (McCall, Lombardo, & Morrison, 1988) asserted the role of key events and critical incidents in the development of leadership. In McCall et al.'s research, they found key events to include challenging assignments, bosses (good and bad), and hardships as the broad categories that impacted leadership growth. We found that the developmental process for these students does include key events but it is more grounded in the psychosocial dimensions of developing their interdependence, establishing healthy interpersonal relationships, and forging a confident sense of self (Baxter-Magolda, 2001; Chickering & Reisser, 1993; Kegan, 1994).

The students in this study had multiple social identities and factors in *developing self* were central to developing a leadership identity. In research about the multiple identities of college students, Jones (1997) found that students' most salient identity was the one identified with a minority status. On the other hand, students did not usually speak about identities associated with a privileged status; this silence indicated a limitation in their development of the identity associated with a privileged status. This finding is consistent with the development of leadership identity; race, for example, was most salient for the students of color in the study. The leadership identity of women, men who were gay, and students of color connected to those aspects of themselves and led them to view

Komives, Owen, Longerbeam, Mainella, & Osteen

leadership contexts differently, particularly when they anticipated attributions made about them based on those personal dimensions. In organizational settings, they were committed to including all members so that no one would feel excluded or marginalized.

The students in this study had a leadership identity that developed over time. Erikson (1968) asserted that people discover, more than create, their identities, and they do it within a social context. Each person discovers and uncovers their identity through a continual process of observation and reflection. "Identity development is the process of becoming more complex in one's personal and social identities" (McEwen, 2003, p. 205). Identity is often viewed as a global sense of self but it can also refer to a particular dimension of one's identity (McEwen), such as a professional identity, an athlete identity, or as it did in this study, a leadership identity.

Limitations and Implications

This theory has direct implications in both advising individual students and in designing programs to develop the leadership efficacy of students in an organizational context. In this study we identified a number of meaningful factors that work together to facilitate the development of a leadership identity. Komives et al. (2005) described a model integrating the categories with the developmental stages and expanding on practice implications.

It must also be recognized that for this study we examined the identity development process for students who were selected because they exhibited a relational leadership approach to others. Although relational leadership is a broad postindustrial approach, the process for identity development might be different for those who espouse other specific leadership philosophies such as servant leadership. Further, the study reflects the developmental

process for students who were involved in organizations that may not be the same for those with little formal group involvement. In addition, more participants of color would have allowed for more saturation in diverse experiences. Although diverse perspectives were incorporated, a more diverse research team might have analyzed the data differently. The transferability of the study is influenced by the methodology, particularly related to the small number of participants from one campus.

The possibilities of research on a new theory such as this one are numerous. For example, more research is needed on environmental interventions that facilitate the key transition from Stage 3 (independence) to the Stage 4 interdependent levels of consciousness (Kegan, 1994). The theory should be tested with students who do not hold extensive organizational involvements as did the students in this study to see if this theory is transferable to the development of their leadership identity; and if so, what the conditions are that facilitate it in non-organizational settings. Further research is needed with those for whom leader-centric approaches are not part of their cultural values in particular, to explore if they experience Stages 3 and 4 differently. As a potential life span model, more research is needed to determine how postcollege adults experience the *integration/synthesis* stage of leadership identity and whether there are additional stages not reflected in this theory. Leadership identity development could also be explored with noncollege adults. In addition, more research is needed to see if groups or organizations function in ways parallel to the core category and what influences those organizational practices; for example, are group leadership practices dependent on the positional leader's style? Do group structures shape the

Leadership Identity

approaches used?

The students in this study shared their stories of how they experienced themselves in groups engaging with others that revealed how their leadership identity developed. The theory has implications for working with individuals as they develop their leadership identity and for groups as they learn to work more effectively to enhance the leadership efficacy of group members.

Correspondence concerning this article should be addressed to Susan R. Komives, 3214 Benjamin Building, University of Maryland, College Park, MD 20742; komives@umd.edu

REFERENCES

Allen, K. E., & Cherrey, C. (2000). *Systemic leadership.* Lanham, MD: University Press of America.

Allen, K. E., Stelzner, S. P., & Wielkiewicz, R. M. (1998). The ecology of leadership: Adapting to the challenges of a changing world. *The Journal of Leadership Studies, 5*(2), 62-82.

Bass, B. M. (1990). *Bass & Stogdill's handbook of leadership* (3rd ed.). New York: Free Press.

Baxter Magolda, M. B. (2001). *Making their own way: Narratives for transforming higher education to promote self-development.* Sterling, VA: Stylus.

Bennis, W. (1989). *On becoming a leader.* Reading, MA: Addison-Wesley.

Brown, S. C., Stevens, R. A., Troiano, P. F., & Schneider, M. K. (2002). Exploring complex phenomena: Grounded theory in student affairs research. *Journal of College Student Development 43,* 173-183.

Brungardt, C. (1996). The making of leaders: A review of the research in leadership development and education *Journal of Leadership Studies, 3*(3), 81-95.

Bruner, J. (1987). Life as narrative. *Social Research, 54*(1), 11-32.

Burns, J. M. (1978). *Leadership.* New York: Harper & Row.

Chickering, A. W., & Reisser, L. (1993). *Education and identity* (2nd ed.). San Francisco: Jossey-Bass.

Chrislip, D. D., & Larson, C. E. (1994). *Collaborative leadership.* San Francisco: Jossey-Bass.

Covey, S. R. (1992). *Principle-centered leadership.* New York: Simon & Schuster.

Creswell, J. W. (1998). *Qualitative inquiry and research design: Choosing among five traditions.* Thousand Oaks, CA: Sage.

Erikson, E. (1968). Identity: Youth and crisis. New York: W. W. Norton.

Heifetz, R. (1994). *Leadership without easy answers.* Cambridge, MA: Belknap Press.

Higher Education Research Institute. (1996). *A social change model of leadership development, guidebook III.* Los Angeles: Author.

Jones, S. R. (1997). Voices of identity and difference: A qualitative exploration of the multiple dimensions of identity development in women college students. *Journal of College Student Development, 38,* 376-386.

Kegan, R. (1994). *In over our heads: The mental demands of modern life.* Cambridge, MA: Harvard University Press.

Komives, S. R., Lucas, N., & McMahon, T. R. (1998). *Exploring leadership: For college students who want to make a difference.* San Francisco: Jossey-Bass.

Komives, S. R., Owen, J. E., Longerbeam, S., Mainella, F. C., & Osteen, L. (2005) *Leadership identity development model.* Manuscript submitted for publication.

Kouzes, J., & Posner, B. (2003). *The leadership challenge* (3rd ed.). San Francisco: Jossey-Bass.

Matusak, L. R. (1997). *Finding your voice: Learning to lead anywhere you want to make a difference.* San Francisco: Jossey-Bass.

McCall, M. W., Lombardo, M. M., & Morrison, A. M. (1988). *Lessons of experience.* New York: Free Press.

McEwen, M. K. (2003). New perspectives on identity development. In S. R. Komives & D. B. Woodard, Jr. (Eds.), *Student services: A handbook for the profession* (4th ed., pp. 203-233). San Francisco: Jossey Bass.

Merriam, S. B., & Associates (2002). *Qualitative research in practice.* San Francisco: Jossey-Bass.

Northouse, P. G. (2003). *Leadership: Theory and practice* (3rd ed.). Thousand Oaks, CA: Sage.

Patton, M. Q. (2002). *Qualitative evaluation and research methods* (3rd ed.). Newbury Park, CA: Sage.

Riessman, C. K. (1993). *Narrative analysis.* Newbury Park, CA: Sage.

Rost, J. (1993). *Leadership for the 21st century.* Westport, CT: Praeger.

Seidman, I. E. (1991). *Interviewing as qualitative research: A guide for researchers in education and the social sciences.* New York: Teachers College, Columbia University.

Strauss, A., & Corbin, J. (1998). *Basics of qualitative research* (2nd ed.). Newbury Park, CA: Sage.

Velsor, E. V., & Drath, W. H. (2004). A lifelong developmental perspective on leader development. In C. D. McCauley & E. V. Velsor (Eds.), *The Center for Creative Leadership handbook of leadership development* (pp. 383-414). San Francisco: Jossey-Bass.

Wheatley, M. J. (1999). *Leadership and the new science.* San Francisco: Berrett-Koehler.

Wielkiewicz, R. M. (2000). The Leadership Attitudes and Beliefs Scale: An instrument for evaluating college students' thinking about leadership and organizations. *Journal of College Student Development, 41,* 335-347.

Zimmerman-Oster, K., & Burkhardt, J. C. (1999). *Leadership in the making.* Battle Creek, MI: W. K. Kellogg Foundation.

Chapter 9

Analyzing and Interpreting Qualitative Data

After completing your study of Chapter 9, you should be able to:

1. Name the steps involved in conducting an analysis of qualitative data.

2. Describe how to organize and transcribe qualitative data.

3. Read through and form initial impressions of text data.

4. Conduct coding of a transcript or text file.

5. Develop a detailed qualitative description.

6. Generate a qualitative theme.

7. Create a visual image that represents your data.

8. Write a paragraph describing a theme.

9. Make a qualitative interpretation from your data.

10. Check the accuracy of your findings and interpretation.

Practice in Understanding Key Concepts

Important Terms and Concepts

The following items represent important concepts relating to analyzing and interpreting qualitative data. Using your own words, record definitions for the items in the space provided.

Transcription: _____

_____

_____

Hand analysis of qualitative data: _____

_____

_____

Computer analysis of qualitative data: _____

_____

_____

Qualitative data analysis computer program: _____

_____

_____

Preliminary exploratory analysis: _____

_____

_____

Coding process: _____

_____

_____

Text segment: _____

_____

_____

Codes: _____

_____

_____

In vivo codes: _____

_____

_____

Lean coding: _____

_____

_____

Themes: _____

_____

_____

Chapter 9

Description: _____

_____

_____

Describing and developing themes from the data: _____

_____

_____

Multiple perspectives: _____

_____

_____

Contrary evidence: _____

_____

_____

Saturation: _____

_____

_____

Layering the analysis: _____

_____

_____

Interconnecting themes: _____

_____

_____

Narrative discussion: _____

_____

_____

Interpretation: _____

_____

_____

Validating findings: _____

_____

_____

Triangulation: _____

_____

_____

Member checking: _____

_____

_____

External audit: _____

_____

_____

Applying the Concepts as a Consumer of Research

Carefully re-read the "Methodology," "Findings," and "Discussion" sections of Sample Study #4 (SG pages 85–103). As you read, look for the following features of the study's data analysis and interpretation and make corresponding notes in the margins:

- Preparing the data
- Preliminary reading of the data
- Coding
- Building description from the data
- Building themes from the data

- Summarizing findings
- Conveying personal reflections
- Comparing to the literature
- Offering limitations
- Suggesting future research

Now carefully consider your definitions and descriptions of the key concepts for this chapter as you answer questions 1–2 for Sample Study #4.

1. Describe the coding process used in this study. _____

_____

_____

_____

_____

2. Describe the thematic analysis discussed in this passage. What themes emerged from the study? _____

_____

_____

_____

_____

Chapter 9

Carefully re-read the "Method," "Findings and Emerging Theory," and "Discussion and Implications" sections of Sample Study #6 (SG pages 157–175). As you read, look for the following features of the study's data analysis and interpretation and make corresponding notes in the margins:

- Coding
- Building themes from the data
- Interrelating themes
- Validating findings

- Summarizing findings
- Comparing to the literature
- Offer limitations
- Suggest future research

Now carefully consider your definitions and descriptions of the key concepts for this chapter as you answer questions 3–9 for Sample Study #6.

3. Describe the coding process used in this study. _____

_____

_____

_____

_____

4. List examples of the major themes that emerged from the data: _____

_____

_____

_____

_____

5. List an example of the use of multiple perspectives: _____

_____

_____

_____

6. Give an example of the authors' use of quotes from individuals: _____

_____

_____

_____

7. Did the authors reach saturation? Describe what this means for this study. _____

_____

_____

_____

8. How did the authors represent their findings? _____

_____

_____

9. How did the authors validate their findings? _____

_____

_____

Activity Feedback!

This study implemented data analysis and interpretation in the following ways:

- Coding Process: The authors describe a three-step coding process using open, axial, and selective coding to identify text segments, combine them into categories, and organize them into themes.
- Major Themes: Themes include Developmental Influences, Developing Self, Group Influences, Changing View of Self with Others, Broadening View of Leadership, and Leadership identity.
- Use of Multiple Perspectives: One example is in the discussion of "Adult Influences" where the perspectives include those of Angela (influenced by family), James (influenced by his scoutmaster), and others (influenced by schoolteachers).
- Use of Quotes: Quotes appear extensively throughout discussion of themes.
- Reached Saturation: Discussed in subsection with heading "Trustworthiness"
- Representing the Findings: Findings were described in the theme passages; the themes were interrelated in the conceptual model given in Figure 1.
- Validation of Findings: The authors discussed the strategies of using member checking and peer debriefers as well as their attention to reaching saturation.

Applying the Concepts as a Producer of Research

You will now practice applying the important concepts of this chapter to a new research problem. Assume that you are a researcher who is working on a qualitative research project to explore how graduate students think about vacations. On the next two pages, you will find documents that two graduate students prepared in response to the following directions: *Write a 1–2 page letter to a friend describing your ultimate vacation. That is, if money and logistics were not limited, what would you do?*

Complete a hand analysis of these documents by completing the following steps and answering the questions that follow the two documents.

1. Conduct a preliminary exploratory analysis to obtain a general sense of the data. Record your initial impressions in the space provided for question 10.

2. Reread the text, and this time identify text segments and code the document. Place boxes around key words that might be used as codes or possibly themes. Use bracketing to identify sentences that seem to fit together. Record codes on the left side of the transcript. List the codes you identified in question 11.

3. Organize the codes into groups that represent similar ideas. From these groups, identify 2–4 potential themes for this study on the right side of the transcript. List the themes you identified in the space provided for question 12.

4. Record your ideas and highlight good quotes on the right side of the transcript. Explain why you think the identified quote(s) is good in the space provided for question 13.

Chapter 9

Activity Hint!

- See Chapter 9 section *"Think-Aloud About Coding a Transcript"* for advice on analyzing qualitative data.

Codes Here   **Themes (and Other**
                                                                    Ideas) Here

Participant #1

Dear Journal,

My dream vacation starts with a trip to Disney World with my wife and kids. I take the kids on every thrill ride there is (a couple of times) and then we go to the interesting informational spots that deal with the mind, space, history, and all of the wide-ranging curiosities mankind has dabbled in.

At night, my wife and I go out and eat fine cuisine and sip tropical drinks while we watch a show. We go dancing around the hot spots in Florida and watch the sunrise on the beach.

The next day we go to see the NASA space center which we have reserved for our own personal shuttle to the International Space Center orbiting earth. We go through an abbreviated training regiment for the trip and load up into the shuttle after a few days of preparation. The blast-off will be quite an experience, I expect. I better bring my camera.

The flight and docking at the International Space Center will begin a 3-day stay where we will get a full tour of the facilities. I might have to help out the astronauts with some things so I'll be going outside in a spacesuit. That will be awesome. I have always dreamed about seeing the earth and space from that perspective. What would it be like? How would it feel to be out there gazing at the earth and the moon and the cosmos?

I know three days will go fast. But we have to get back if we're going to make it to our final destination: Australia. Landing on earth after being in space for that amount of time will mean we'll need to adjust to gravity again. We can't take too long though because the flight for Australia leaves at 11:30 two days after we land and you know how security is. I think we better pack light.

When we arrive in Australia, I have arranged a guide to take us to the far reaches to the continent and show us the wonders of this beautiful and mysterious place. I want to see the diverse ecosystems that work in harmony there since I do not know much about the place. It will be, for me, an exploration of a new people and new world. After sightseeing Australia with our guide for about two weeks, I guess we'll have to return home.

I guess this trip is mostly about seeing how big the world, actually the universe is. Many times we forget just how wondrous and special this place we live in is. We forget the length and breadth of it. I hope this trip revives that sense in us.

Codes Here

Participant #2

Dear Jenny,

I've decided that it's time to get out of dodge and head for the hills for the ultimate vacation. Well, not really the hills but more like the long lost land of Africa. You know that I have desired to travel abroad, see the world, and experience life elsewhere. Well, the time has come. I came across a couple thousand dollars a few weeks ago. Of course, I had to sell my car—but I thought—why keep a car when I have a scooter and public transportation?

Well, I'll get to the point! I met some wonderful people on campus a couple of weeks ago. They were here to discuss an exchange program for American students to teach, travel, and provide public assistance to the people of the land. I thought this would be a great opportunity to visit the area and get an idea of what is there to see if I would be interested in becoming an American student abroad.

I'm going to depart Omaha on August 2 for Chicago where I will board a flight destined for the country of Chad. Once in Chad, I will travel via bus to Zambia. The flight is going to be around 48 hours all together. Whoosh! I can't even imagine what that is going to feel like! However, I hear the people in Zambia are very generous and love Americans who are there for public assistance purposes so I have a feeling that it will be well worth it.

While in Zambia, I am going to visit the famous Victoria Falls for 2 or 3 days— one of the natural wonders of the world situated on the banks of the upper Zambezi. Within the next week, I plan to go on a Zambian safari, which starts in Livingstone where I will spend two nights on the banks of the Zambezi River at Sussi and Chuma lodge. Next, I will be transferred to the Lower Zambezi National Park for a two-night stay at Kulefu Tented Camp. On day 3 I will be transferred to Chichele Presidential Lodge in South Luangwa National Park. On day ten I will be transferred back to Mfuwe for my flight back to Lusaka.

I realize that this all sounds like a super safari vacation. However, after my safari, I will return to Lusaka and begin my charity work with the people of the area. I plan to meet with the gentlemen of the University of Zambia and get my assignment for the next few weeks. I believe I will be working with many HIV/AIDS patients and attending to their needs. From what I gather, this work will entail educating the people on possible health risks associated with HIV/AIDS and educating children on preventive measures. I'm so excited to finally be doing this. I've been looking forward to this type of vacation and work for many years.

I plan to return to the states after about two months. I will keep you posted as best as possible while I am away. You can look forward to many stories and pictures when I return.

I better go now. I have an appointment at the Health Center to get all my immunizations for the trip. Please write when you have a chance.

My love to you!
Stephanie

Chapter 9

Exploring how graduate students think about vacations

10. What were your initial impressions upon reading these documents? _____

_____

_____

_____

_____

_____

11. List all of the codes that you assigned to text segments (around 8–15 codes): _____

_____

_____

_____

_____

_____

12. Group similar codes together and give a name to each of these themes (around 2–5 code groupings). List which

codes make up each theme: _____

_____

_____

_____

_____

_____

_____

_____

13. Give an example of a good quote and explain why you think this quote is good. _____

_____

_____

_____

_____

_____

_____

Practice Test Items

Answer the following items to check your understanding of the important concepts related to analyzing and interpreting qualitative data. Once you have answered all of the items, you can check your ideas with the provided solutions.

1. Suppose you have a qualitative data set to be analyzed. Put the following five steps in the order that you would do them, starting with the first step. Use the letters found to the left of the choices to designate each step in the provided blanks.

   a. Explore the data
   b. Develop a description from the data
   c. Connect and interrelate themes
   d. Define themes from the data
   e. Code text data

   First step _____   _____   _____   _____   _____   Last step

2. Which of the following best describes the qualitative analysis process? Circle the letter to the left of the correct response.

   a. Going in circles
   b. Going along the path that feels best
   c. Going from the general to the particular
   d. Going from the particular to the general

3. Which of the following is not an acceptable way of validating findings in a qualitative study? Circle the letter to the left of the correct response.

   a. Testing interview questions for content validity
   b. Triangulation of data sources
   c. Member checking of test data
   d. External audit of research process

4. Which of the following best describes the use of contrary evidence in a narrative discussion? Circle the letter to the left of the correct response.

   a. It demonstrates that a theory is wrong
   b. It presents at least two perspectives about a theme
   c. It helps convey the complexity of the phenomenon
   d. It helps to interconnect different themes

5. For a study, which of the following should be least in number? Circle the letter to the left of the correct response.

   a. Text segments
   b. Codes
   c. Data
   d. Themes

Chapter 9

Read the following two excerpts from the study "*Depression and Substance Use in Two Divergent High School Cultures: A Quantitative and Qualitative Analysis.*" You will use these paragraphs to answer questions 6–8.

[A] Our interview analyses consisted of detailed readings of students' perspectives on substance use and their reasons for choosing to use or abstain from use. [B] Typical of many qualitative approaches, our method involved a content analysis in which interview data were partitioned into content domains for the comparison of themes across individual cases (Strauss, 1987). [C] Three trained readers independently read for common themes in students' descriptions of their substance use patterns. [D] Themes were identified and compared within and across schools. [E] Only those themes that were identified by all three readers independently were considered common themes in the interviews. [F] The following results section describes the common themes detected from the interviews of the urban and suburban depressed sample by the three data analysts. (Way, Stauber, Nakkula, & London, 1994, pp. 344–345)

[G] Our qualitative study of depressed students' beliefs and attitudes about substance use suggests that depressed urban and suburban students may differ in their views about substance use. [H] These different attitudes and beliefs may be centrally important to understanding why depression and substance use are differently related across schools. [I] However, in future studies, it would be important to examine beliefs and attitudes concerning substance use held by a broader population of students, including those reporting no, low, or moderate levels of depression. [J] Such an examination could help determine whether the attitudes and beliefs revealed in our qualitative analyses are unique to depressed students (and somehow related to "being depressed") or whether these beliefs are typical of the larger student body in each school. (Way, Stauber, Nakkula, & London, 1994, pp. 354–355)

When answering questions 6–8, you should refer to specific sentences in the passage. You should refer to each individual sentence by the reference letter (e.g., [A]) given at the start of each sentence.

6. In which sentence(s) did the authors give evidence of using data transcriptions? Explain.

_____

_____

_____

7. In which sentence(s) did the authors give evidence of using a coding process? Explain.

_____

_____

_____

8. In which sentence(s) did the authors give suggestions for future research? Explain.

_____

_____

_____

186

9. Briefly describe the difference between the role of personal reflections in a typical quantitative study and in a typical qualitative study.

_____

_____

_____

_____

_____

10. Briefly describe the difference between "exploring the data" in a typical quantitative study and in a typical qualitative study.

_____

_____

_____

_____

_____

Practice Test Items - Answer Key

1. Suppose you have a qualitative data set to be analyzed. Put the following five steps in the order that you would do them, starting with the first step.

    First step: a.   Explore the data
                   e.   Code text data
                   b.   Develop a description from the data
                   d.   Define themes from the data
    Last step: c.   Connect and interrelate themes

    Review section "How Do You Explore and Code the Data in Analysis?" in the textbook

2. Which of the following best describes the qualitative analysis process?

    d.   Going from the particular to the general

    Review section "How Do You Analyze Qualitative Data?" in the textbook

3. Which of the following is not an acceptable way of validating findings in a qualitative study?

    a.   Testing interview questions for content validity

    Review section "How Do You Validate the Accuracy of Your Findings?" in the textbook

4. Which of the following best describes the use of contrary evidence in a narrative discussion?

    c.   It helps convey the complexity of the phenomenon

    Review section "Themes" in the textbook

5. For a study, which of the following should be least in number?

    d.   Themes

    Review section "Themes" in the textbook

6. In which sentence(s) did the authors give evidence of using data transcriptions? Explain.

    Evidence was given in sentences [A], [C], and [E]. These sentences give evidence that the interviews were transcribed because they refer to "readers" and "detailed readings."

    Review section "How Do You Analyze Qualitative Data?" in the textbook

7. In which sentence(s) did the authors give evidence of using a coding process? Explain.

    Evidence was given in sentence [B]. The authors describe their "method" during which "interview data were partitioned into content domains for the comparison of themes across individual cases."

    Review section "How Do You Explore and Code the Data in Analysis?" and Figure 9.4 in the textbook

8. In which sentence(s) did the authors give suggestions for future research? Explain.

    Suggestions were given in sentences [I] and [J]. The authors describe what could be done next if data were collected with a different sampling strategy.

    Review section "How Do You Interpret Findings?" in the textbook

9. Briefly describe the difference between the role of personal reflections in a typical quantitative study and in a typical qualitative study.

    In a qualitative study, personal reflections are an important part of interpreting the findings of a study where an author's personal views can never be kept separate from interpretations.
    In a quantitative study, personal reflections are typically not considered as part of the interpretation of the results.

    Review section "Convey Personal Reflections" in the textbook

10. Briefly describe the difference between "exploring the data" in a typical quantitative study and in a typical qualitative study.

    In a qualitative study, exploring the data consists of reading through all the information, memoing ideas, thinking about the overall organization of the data, and considering whether more data is needed.
    In a quantitative study, exploring the data consists of cleaning the data and calculating descriptive statistics.

    Review section "How Do You Explore and Code the Data in Analysis?" and Figure 9.4 in the textbook

Chapter 10

Reporting and Evaluating Research

After completing your study of Chapter 10, you should be able to:

1. Define the purpose of a research report.

2. Identify factors important in writing for audiences.

3. Distinguish among the different types of research reports and proposals: dissertations or theses, journal articles, conference papers, and policy and school-oriented reports.

4. Describe the physical structure of quantitative and qualitative research reports.

5. Identify discriminatory language in a research report.

6. Use scholarly writing strategies to help readers understand your research.

7. List criteria for evaluating a research report.

Practice in Understanding Key Concepts

Important Terms and Concepts

The following items represent important concepts relating to reporting and evaluating research. Using your own words, record definitions for the items in the space provided.

Research report: _____

_____

_____

Dissertation and thesis: _____

_____

_____

Chapter 10

Dissertation or thesis proposal: _____

_____

_____

Purpose of a proposal: _____

_____

_____

Journal article: _____

_____

_____

Conference paper: _____

_____

_____

Conference proposal: _____

_____

_____

Physical structure of a study: _____

_____

_____

Qualitative scientific structure: _____

_____

_____

Qualitative storytelling structure: _____

_____

_____

Encoding: _____

_____

_____

Linking devices: _____

_____

_____

Applying the Concepts as a Consumer of Research

Carefully consider your definitions and descriptions of the key concepts for this chapter as you complete the following activities based on the sample studies.

Reporting and evaluating quantitative research

1. Examine the structure used in the three quantitative sample studies (Sample Studies #1, 3, and 5). To what extent did the studies utilize a structure typical of quantitative research as illustrated in Figure 10.3?

Activity Hint!
   ▪ See Chapter 10 section "*Useful Information for Consumers of Research*" for advice on examining and evaluating research reports.

Sample Study #1: _____

_____

_____

Sample Study #3: _____

_____

_____

Sample Study #5: _____

_____

_____

2. State how the authors referred to their participants in the three quantitative sample studies. Did the authors use nondiscriminatory language? Do you have any suggestions for improvements?

Sample Study #1: _____

_____

_____

Sample Study #3: _____

_____

_____

Sample Study #5: _____

_____

_____

3. Select one of the quantitative sample studies. Evaluate this study's process of research using the checklist that follows. You might use the following notation:

   +   Element done well
   ✓   Element present and satisfactory
   −   Element missing or inadequate

Chapter 10

Checklist for Evaluating the Process of a Quantitative Study (Figure 10.6 in the textbook)

Study evaluated: _____

Title for the Study

_____ Does it reflect the major independent and dependent variables?
_____ Does it express either a comparison among groups or a relationship among variables?
_____ Does it convey the participants and site for the study?

Problem Statement

_____ Does it indicate an educational issue to study?
_____ Has the author provided evidence that this issue is important?
_____ Is there some indication that the author located this issue through a search of past literature or from personal experiences?
_____ Does the research problem fit a quantitative approach?
_____ Are the assumptions of the study consistent with an approach?

Review of the Literature

_____ Are the studies about the independent and dependent variables clearly reviewed?
_____ Does the review end with how the author will extend or expand the current body of literature?
_____ Does the study follow the American Psychological Association style?

Purpose, Hypotheses, and Research Questions

_____ Does the author specify a purpose statement?
_____ Is the purpose statement clear, and does it indicate the variables, their relationship, and the people and site to be studied?
_____ Are either hypotheses or research questions written?
_____ Do these hypotheses or questions indicate the major variables and the participants in a study?
_____ Do the purpose statement and hypotheses or research questions contain the major components that will help a reader understand the study?
_____ Has the author identified a theory or explanation for the hypotheses or questions?

Data Collection

_____ Does the author mention the steps taken to obtain access to people and sites?
_____ Is a rigorous probability sampling strategy used?
_____ Has the author identified good, valid, and reliable instruments to use to measure the variables?
_____ Are the instruments administered so that bias and error are not introduced into the study?

Data Analysis and Results

_____ Are the statistics chosen for analysis consistent with the research questions, hypotheses, variables, and scales of measurement?
_____ Is the unit of analysis appropriate to address the research problem?
_____ Are the data adequately represented in tables and figures?
_____ Do the results answer the research questions and address the research problem?
_____ Are the results substantiated by the evidence?
_____ Are generalizations from the results limited to the population of participants in the study?

Writing

_____ Is the structure of the overall study consistent with the topics addressed in a quantitative study?
_____ Are educational and social science terms carefully defined?
_____ Are variables labeled in a consistent way throughout the study?
_____ Is the study written using extensive references?
_____ Is the study written using an impersonal point of view?
_____ Is the study written appropriately for intended audiences(s)?

Reporting and evaluating qualitative research

4. Examine the structure used in the three qualitative sample studies (Sample Studies #2, 4, and 6). To what extent did the studies utilize a qualitative scientific or storytelling structure as illustrated in Figures 10.4 and 10.5?

Activity Hint!
- See Chapter 10 section "***Design an Appropriate Qualitative Structure***" for advice on examining and evaluating qualitative research report structures.

Sample Study #2: _____

_____

_____

_____

Sample Study #4: _____

_____

_____

_____

Sample Study #6: _____

_____

_____

_____

5. State how the authors referred to their participants in the three quantitative sample studies. Did the authors use nondiscriminatory language? Do you have any suggestions for improvements?

Sample Study #2: _____

_____

_____

Sample Study #4: _____

_____

_____

Sample Study #6: _____

_____

_____

6. Select one of the qualitative sample studies. Evaluate this study's process of research using the checklist that follows. You might use the following notation:
- \+   Element done well
- ✓   Element present and satisfactory
- −   Element missing or inadequate

Chapter 10

Checklist for Evaluating the Process of a Qualitative Study (Figure 10.7 in the textbook)

Study evaluated: _____

Title for the Study

_____ Does it reflect the central phenomenon being studied?
_____ Does it reflect the people and site being studied?

Problem Statement

_____ Does it indicate an educational issue to study?
_____ Has the author provided evidence that this issue is important?
_____ Is there some indication that the author located this issue through a search of past literature or from personal experience?
_____ Does the research problem fit a qualitative approach?
_____ Are the assumptions of the study consistent with a qualitative approach?

Review of the Literature

_____ Has the author provided a literature review of the research problem under study?
_____ Has the author signaled that the literature review is preliminary or tentatively based on the findings in the study?
_____ Does the study follow the American Psychological Association style?

Purpose and Research Questions

_____ Does the author specify both a purpose statement and a central research question?
_____ Do the purpose statement and central question indicate the central phenomenon of study and the people and place where the study will occur?
_____ Are subquestions written to narrow the central question to topic areas or foreshadow the steps in data analysis?

Data Collection

_____ Has the author taken steps to obtain access to people and sites?
_____ Has the author chosen a specific purposeful sampling strategy for individuals or sites?
_____ Is the data collection clearly specified and is it extensive?
_____ Is there evidence that the author has used a protocol for recording data?

Data Analysis and Findings

_____ Were appropriate steps taken to analyze the text or visual data into themes, perspectives, or categories?
_____ Was sufficient evidence obtained (including quotes) to support each theme or category?
_____ Were multiple layer themes or categories derived?
_____ Did the findings answer the research questions?
_____ Were the findings realistic and accurate? Were steps taken to support this conclusion through verification?
_____ Were the findings represented in the themes or categories so that multiple perspectives can be easily seen?
_____ Were the findings represented in narrative discussions or in visuals?

Writing

_____ Was the account written persuasively and convincingly?
_____ Was the overall account consistent with one of the many forms for presenting qualitative research?
_____ Was the account written to include literacy approaches, such as the use of metaphor, surprises, detail, dialogue, and complexity?
_____ Was it written using a personal point of view?
_____ Is the study written appropriately for intended audience(s)?

Applying the Concepts as a Producer of Research

You will now practice applying the important concepts of this chapter to a new research problem of your choice. Assume that you are a researcher who is working on a quantitative or qualitative research project. Consider how you will report and evaluate this study by answering the following questions.

7. Who will be the audience(s) for your research report? _____

_____

_____

8. What types of research report(s) and proposal(s) do you expect to prepare for this study? _____

_____

_____

_____

9. What nondiscriminatory terms will you use to refer to the individuals who participate in your study? _____

_____

_____

_____

10. Will you use an impersonal or personal point of view? Why? _____

_____

_____

11. What will be the overall structure (i.e., major headings) for your research report? _____

_____

_____

_____

_____

_____

_____

_____

_____

_____

Practice Test Items

Answer the following items to check your understanding of the important concepts related to reporting and evaluating research. Once you have answered all of the items, you can check your ideas with the provided solutions.

1. Which of the following is **not** a typical evaluation standard for a quantitative study? Circle the letter to the left of the correct response.

   a. Were the limitations of the study stated?
   b. Did the text honestly convey the position of the author?
   c. Was an appropriate sampling strategy used?
   d. Was the validity of the data gathering procedures discussed?
   e. Were the data gathering methods described clearly?

2. Which of the following is **not** a typical evaluation standard for a qualitative study? Circle the letter to the left of the correct response.

   a. Were the participants' voices heard?
   b. Does the work contribute to our understanding of social life?
   c. Was the reliability of the data gathering procedures discussed?
   d. Is the text written persuasively?
   e. Did the researcher reciprocate to the study participants?

Examine the physical structure of the article by Feen-Calligan (1999) given below to answer items 3–4.

> Title
> Introduction
> Chemical Addiction
> Data Collection and Analysis
> The Experience of Enlightenment in Art Therapy
> Art Interventions
> Intervening Conditions
> Consequences
> Propositions
> Conclusion
> References

3. Do you think this is a qualitative or quantitative article? _____

4. Explain your answer to item 3. _____

_____

_____

_____

_____

Examine the physical structure of the article by Schelske and Deno (1994) given below to answer items 5–6.

Title
Abstract
Introduction
Method
Results
Discussion
References

5. Do you think this is a qualitative or quantitative article? _____

6. Explain your answer to item 5. _____

_____

_____

_____

7. Consider the passage: "Data collected on types of reading materials preferred by students were summarized by category and the most and least preferred materials presented as percentages." (Gallik, 1999, p. 484). What was the point of view used in this passage? Record your answer and a brief explanation in the provided space.

_____

_____

_____

8. Consider the passage: "In Naomi's story we are presented with an explicit example of the dilemmas and sense of split existence which become shaped by a teacher's movement between these two profoundly different places of knowing, defined by dramatically different moral qualities" (Huber & Whelan, 1999, p. 388). What was the point of view used in this passage? Record your answer and a brief explanation in the provided space.

_____

_____

_____

9. Briefly describe the difference between a dissertation and a journal article.

_____

_____

_____

10. List three ways in which quantitative and qualitative reports tend to be similar.

_____

_____

_____

Practice Test Items - Answer Key

1. Which of the following is not a typical evaluation standard for a quantitative study?

    b. Did the text honestly convey the position of the author?

    Review section "How Do You Evaluate the Quality of Your Research?" in the textbook

2. Which of the following is not a typical evaluation standard for a qualitative study?

    c. Was the reliability of the data gathering procedures discussed?

    Review section "How Do You Evaluate the Quality of Your Research?" in the textbook

3. This structure appears more typical of a qualitative article.

4. This structure is more flexible and unusual than a typical quantitative study. It seems to emphasize description and it deemphasizes the standard quantitative structure.

    Review section "How Should You Structure Your Report?" in the textbook

5. This structure appears typical of a quantitative article.

6. This structure emphasizes the five major sections typically found in quantitative reports.

    Review section "How Should You Structure Your Report?" in the textbook

7. Consider the passage: "Data collected on types of reading materials preferred by students were summarized by category and the most and least preferred materials presented as percentages." (Gallik, 1999, p. 484). What was the point of view used in this passage? Record your answer and a brief explanation in the provided space.

    This passage uses an impersonal point of view, the past tense, and passive construction.

    Review section "Use an Appropriate Point of View" in the textbook

8. Consider the passage: "In Naomi's story we are presented with an explicit example of the dilemmas and sense of split existence which become shaped by a teacher's movement between these two profoundly different places of knowing, defined by dramatically different moral qualities" (Huber & Whelan, 1999, p. 388). What was the point of view used in this passage?

    This passage uses a personal point of view with the authors present in the foreground (i.e., "we"), the present tense, persuasive writing, and the use of a first name to refer to the participant.

    Review section "Use an Appropriate Point of View" in the textbook

9. Briefly describe the difference between a dissertation and a journal article.

A dissertation is written as part of a doctoral program. The intended audience is faculty and graduate committees. They are typically long reports, often going over 100 pages. On the other hand, a journal article is a shorter, more polished description of research work that is typically reviewed before publication. The intended audience is the readers of scholarly journals.

Review section "What Are the Types of Research Reports?" in the textbook

10. List three ways in which quantitative and qualitative reports tend to be similar.

Possible answers include:
1. They both address the six steps in the research process.
2. They both attempt to balance the emphasis on research process and on the content.
3. They both should use appropriate research terms.

Review sections "How Should You Structure Your Report?" and "How Do You Write in a Sensitive and Scholarly Way?" in the textbook

Chapter 11

Experimental Designs

After completing your study of Chapter 11, you should be able to:

1. Define the purpose of an experiment and identify when you use experimental research.

2. Describe the reasons for random assignment in experiments.

3. Identify the types of procedures used to control for extraneous factors in an experiment.

4. Describe how experimental researchers manipulate the treatment condition.

5. Define an outcome variable in an experiment.

6. Explain how researchers compare groups in an experiment.

7. Define the types of internal and external validity threats in an experiment.

8. Distinguish between between-group and within-group experiments.

9. Describe steps in conducting an experimental or quasi-experimental study.

10. Identify criteria for evaluating an experimental study.

Practice in Understanding Key Concepts

Important Terms and Concepts

The following items represent important concepts relating to experimental designs. Using your own words, record definitions for the items in the space provided.

Research designs (from Part III introduction): _____

_____

_____

_____

Experiment: _____

_____

_____

Random assignment: _____

_____

_____

Equating the groups: _____

_____

_____

Random selection: _____

_____

_____

Extraneous factors: _____

_____

_____

Pretest: _____

_____

_____

Posttest: _____

_____

_____

Covariates: _____

_____

_____

Matching: _____

_____

_____

Homogeneous samples: _____

_____

_____

Chapter 11

Blocking variable: _____

_____

_____

Experimental treatment: _____

_____

_____

Levels: _____

_____

_____

Intervene (or manipulate): _____

_____

_____

Outcome: _____

_____

_____

Group comparison: _____

_____

_____

Threat to validity: _____

_____

_____

Threats to internal validity: _____

_____

_____

History: _____

_____

_____

Maturation: _____

_____

_____

Regression: _____

_____

_____

Selection: _____

_____

_____

Mortality: _____

_____

_____

Interactions with selection: _____

_____

_____

Diffusion of treatments: _____

_____

_____

Compensatory equalization: _____

_____

_____

Compensatory rivalry: _____

_____

_____

Resentful demoralization: _____

_____

_____

Testing: _____

_____

_____

Instrumentation: _____

_____

_____

Chapter 11

Threats to external validity: _____

_____

_____

Interaction of selection and treatment: _____

_____

_____

Interaction of setting and treatment: _____

_____

_____

Interaction of history and treatment: _____

_____

_____

True experiments: _____

_____

_____

Quasi-experiments: _____

_____

_____

Factorial designs: _____

_____

_____

Main effects: _____

_____

_____

Interaction effects: _____

_____

_____

Within-group experimental design: _____

_____

_____

Within-individual design: _____

_____

_____

Time series design: _____

_____

_____

Interrupted time series design: _____

_____

_____

Equivalent time series design: _____

_____

_____

Repeated measures design: _____

_____

_____

Single-subject research: _____

_____

_____

A/B design: _____

_____

_____

Multiple baseline design: _____

_____

_____

Alternating treatment design: _____

_____

_____

Experimental unit of analysis: _____

_____

_____

Chapter 11

Applying the Concepts as a Consumer of Research

Carefully consider your definitions and descriptions of the key concepts for this chapter as you respond to the following items about the experimental study described in Sample Study #3 (SG pages 55–59) or the sample experimental study in the textbook. Each item represents a key characteristic of the designs described in this chapter. For each item, explain how the characteristic was implemented within the study.

Activity Hint!
- See Chapter 11 section "*What Are Key Characteristics of Experiments?*" for information about each key characteristic.

Key characteristics of experimental designs

1. Participants are assigned to groups. _____

_____

_____

_____

2. Control for extraneous factors. _____

_____

_____

_____

_____

3. Manipulation of treatment conditions. _____

_____

_____

_____

_____

4. Outcomes are measured after a treatment. _____

_____

_____

_____

5. Comparisons of different groups are conducted. _____

_____

_____

_____

6. Procedures are designed that address potential threats to validity. _____

_____

_____

_____

_____

Evaluating experimental research

The following items represent criteria for evaluating research using the designs described in this chapter. In each case, explain the meaning of the statement and critique the implementation of an experimental design within Sample Study #3 (SG pages 55–59) or the sample experimental study in the textbook.

7. Does the experiment have a powerful intervention? _____

_____

_____

_____

8. Does the study employ few treatment groups? _____

_____

_____

_____

9. Will participants gain from the intervention? _____

_____

_____

_____

10. Did the researcher derive the number of participants per group in some systematic way? _____

_____

_____

_____

11. Were an adequate number of participants used in the study? _____

_____

_____

_____

12. Were valid, reliable, and sensitive measures or observations used? _____

_____

_____

_____

_____

13. Did the study control for extraneous factors? _____

_____

_____

_____

14. Did the researcher control for threats to internal validity? _____

_____

_____

_____

_____

Applying the Concepts as a Producer of Research

You will now practice applying the important concepts of this chapter to a new research problem of your choice. Assume that you are a researcher who is going to undertake a research study using an experimental design. Select a research topic and use the following steps to design this experiment.

Activity Hint!
- ▪ See Chapter 11 section "*What Are the Steps in Conducting Experimental Research?*" for information about each step.

My research topic: _____

_____

Step 1 – Explain why an experiment addresses your research problem. _____

_____

_____

_____

_____

Step 2 – Form hypotheses to test cause-and-effect relationships among variables. _____

_____

_____

_____

_____

_____

Step 3 – Select an experimental unit and identify the study participants. _____

_____

_____

_____

Step 4 – Describe the levels of the experimental treatment. _____

_____

_____

_____

Step 5 – Choose a type of experimental design. _____

_____

_____

_____

_____

Step 6 – Describe the procedures you will use in conducting the experiment. _____

_____

_____

_____

_____

_____

Step 7 – Describe how you will analyze the data. _____

_____

_____

_____

Chapter 11

Step 8 – List what aspects of your study you will include in your written report. _____

_____

_____

_____

_____

_____

_____

Practice Test Items

Answer the following items to check your understanding of the important concepts related to experimental designs. Once you have answered all of the items, you can check your ideas with the provided solutions.

1. Put the following historical developments related to experimental designs in chronological order, starting with the earliest. Use the letters found to the left of the choices to designate each step in the provided blanks.

    a. Development of improved statistical procedures allowing for multiple dependent and independent variables
    b. Idea of random assignment of participants to treatment conditions
    c. Use of experimental and control group
    d. Designation and description of experiments and quasi-experiments

    Earliest _____   _____   _____   _____   Most recent

2. Which of the following is a difference between true experiments and quasi-experiments? Circle the letter to the left of the correct response.

    a. How participants are assigned to groups
    b. Use of statistical comparisons
    c. Measurement of an outcome
    d. Use of a treatment

3. Which of the following describes the purpose of using random assignment of participants to treatment conditions? Circle the letter to the left of all correct responses.

    a. To control extraneous factors
    b. To facilitate the use of repeated measures
    c. To equate the groups
    d. To allow for generalizations to be made to the population

4. Which of the following describes the purpose of using matching? Circle the letter to the left of the correct response.

    a. To facilitate the use of repeated measures
    b. To control extraneous factors
    c. To reduce threats to external validity
    d. To allow for generalizations to be made to the population

5. Consider Sample Study #3 in this Study Guide for this question. Identify the following aspects of that study.

    a. Treatment variable: _____

    b. Levels: _____

6. Which of the following design types can be used to study one group over time? Circle the letter to the left of the correct response.

    a. Between-group experiment
    b. True experiment
    c. Factorial design
    d. Within-group design

7. List three potential threats to the internal validity of an experimental study.

    a. _____

    b. _____

    c. _____

8. Which of the following describes the major intention of choosing an experimental design? Circle the letter to the left of the correct response.

    a. Measure the association between the treatment variable and the outcome
    b. Provide evidence of a cause-and-effect relationship between the treatment variable and outcome
    c. To quantitatively describe the different levels of a treatment variable
    d. To describe the process of implementing a treatment variable

9. Which of the following design types can be used with intact groups? Circle the letter to the left of the correct response.

    a. A/B design
    b. True experiment design
    c. Factorial design
    d. Quasi-experiment design

10. Which of the following design types can be used to measure interaction effects? Circle the letter to the left of the correct response.

    a. A/B design
    b. True experiment design
    c. Factorial design
    d. Quasi-experiment design

Practice Test Items - Answer Key

1. Put the following historical developments related to experimental designs in chronological order, starting with the earliest. Use the letters found to the left of the choices to designate each step in the provided blanks.

   Earliest: c. Use of experimental and control group
         b. Idea of random assignment of participants to treatment conditions
         d. Designation and description of experiments and quasi-experiments
   Most recent: a. Development of improved statistical procedures allowing for multiple dependent and independent variables

   Review section "What Is an Experiment?" in the textbook

2. Which of the following is a difference between true experiments and quasi-experiments?

   a. How participants are assigned to groups

   Review section "Between-Group Designs" in the textbook

3. Which of the following describes the purpose of using random assignment of participants to treatment conditions?

   c. To equate the groups

   Review section "Random Assignment" in the textbook

4. Which of the following describes the purpose of using matching?

   b. To control extraneous factors

   Review section "Control over Extraneous Variables" in the textbook

5. Consider Sample Study #3 in this Study Guide for this question. Identify the following aspects of that study.

   a. Treatment variable: Type of instruction
   b. Levels: (1) Received the eating disorder prevention program (Prevention group); (2) Did not receive the eating disorder prevention program (Control group)

   Review section "Manipulating Treatment Conditions" in the textbook

6. Which of the following design types can be used to study one group over time?

   d. Within-group design

   Review section "Within-Group or Individual Designs" in the textbook

7. List three potential threats to the internal validity of an experimental study. Possible threats include:

    a. History   b. Selection   c. Mortality

    Review section "Threats to Validity" in the textbook

8. Which of the following describes the major intention of choosing an experimental design?

    b. Provide evidence of a cause-and-effect relationship between the treatment variable and outcome

    Review section "What Is an Experiment?" in the textbook

9. Which of the following design types can be used with intact groups?

    d. Quasi-experiment design

    Review section "What Are the Types of Experimental Designs?" in the textbook

10. Which of the following design types can be used to measure interaction effects?

    c. Factorial design

    Review section "What Are the Types of Experimental Designs?" in the textbook

Chapter 12

Correlational Designs

Learning Objectives

After completing your study of Chapter 12, you should be able to:

1. Define the purpose and use of correlational research.

2. Distinguish between the explanatory and prediction correlational designs.

3. Draw a scatterplot of scores and create a correlation matrix of scores.

4. Analyze correlational coefficients for two sets of scores in terms of direction, form, degree, and the strength of the association.

5. Explain the reasons for using partial correlations and multiple regression in correlational research.

6. Identify steps in conducting a correlational study.

7. List the criteria for evaluating a correlational study.

Practice in Understanding Key Concepts

Important Terms and Concepts

The following items represent important concepts relating to correlational designs. Using your own words, record definitions for the items in the space provided.

Correlational research designs: _____

_____

_____

Correlation: _____

_____

_____

Co-vary: _____

_____

_____

Product-moment correlation coefficient: _____

_____

_____

Explanatory research design: _____

_____

_____

Prediction research design: _____

_____

_____

Predictor variable: _____

_____

_____

Criterion variable: _____

_____

_____

Scatterplot (scatter diagram): _____

_____

_____

Correlation matrix: _____

_____

_____

Positive correlation: _____

_____

_____

Negative correlation: _____

_____

_____

Chapter 12

Positive linear relationship: _____

_____

_____

Negative linear relationship: _____

_____

_____

Uncorrelated relationship: _____

_____

_____

Curvilinear or nonlinear relationship: _____

_____

_____

Spearman rho: _____

_____

_____

Point-biserial correlation: _____

_____

_____

Phi-coefficient: _____

_____

_____

Degree of association: _____

_____

_____

_____

Coefficient of determination: _____

_____

_____

Partial correlations: _____

_____

_____

Regression line: _____

_____

_____

Multiple regression (or multiple correlation): _____

_____

_____

Regression table: _____

_____

_____

Beta weight: _____

_____

_____

Applying the Concepts as a Consumer of Research

Carefully consider your definitions and descriptions of the key concepts for this chapter as you respond to the following items about the correlational study described in Sample Study #5 (SG pages 117–130) or the sample correlational study in the textbook. Each item represents a key characteristic of the designs described in this chapter. For each item, explain how the characteristic was implemented within the study.

Activity Hint!
- See Chapter 12 section "***What Are the Key Characteristics of Correlational Designs?***" for information about each key characteristic.

Key characteristics of correlational designs

1. Using scatterplots and matrices to display scores. _____

_____

_____

2. Assessing the direction, form, and strength of the association between scores. _____

_____

_____

3. Using multiple variable analysis. _____

_____

_____

_____

Evaluating a correlational study

The following items represent criteria for evaluating research using the designs described in this chapter. In each case, explain the meaning of the statement and critique the implementation of a correlational design within Sample Study #5 (SG pages 117–130) or the sample correlational study in the textbook.

4. Is the size of the sample adequate for hypothesis testing? _____

_____

_____

5. Does the researcher adequately display the results in matrices or graphs? _____

_____

_____

_____

6. Is there an interpretation about the direction and magnitude of the association between two variables? _____

_____

_____

_____

7. Is there an assessment of the magnitude of the relationship based on the coefficient of determination, p values,

effect size, or the size of the coefficient? _____

_____

_____

_____

8. Is the researcher concerned about the form of the relationship so that an appropriate statistic is chosen for

analysis? _____

_____

_____

_____

9. Has the researcher identified the predictor and the criterion variables? _____

_____

_____

10. If a visual model of the relationships is advanced, does the researcher indicate the expected direction of the

relationships among variables? Or the predicted direction based on observed data? _____

_____

_____

_____

11. Are the statistical procedures clearly identified? _____

_____

_____

Applying the Concepts as a Producer of Research

You will now practice applying the important concepts of this chapter to a new research problem of your choice. Assume that you are a researcher who is going to undertake a research study using a correlational design. Select a research topic and use the following steps to design this correlational study.

Activity Hint!
- See Chapter 12 section "*How Do You Conduct a Correlational Study?*" for information about each step.

My research topic: _____

_____

Step 1 – Explain why a correlational study best addresses the research problem. _____

_____

_____

_____

Step 2 – Identify individuals to study. _____

_____

_____

Step 3 – Identify two or more measures to be used with each individual in the study. _____

_____

_____

Step 4 – Collect data and monitor potential threats to being able to draw valid inferences from the data. _____

_____

_____

_____

Step 5 – Describe how you will analyze the data and represent the results. _____

_____

_____

_____

Step 6 – Describe how you will interpret your results. _____

_____

_____

_____

Practice Test Items

Answer the following items to check your understanding of the important concepts related to correlational designs. Once you have answered all of the items, you can check your ideas with the provided solutions.

1. Put the following historical developments related to correlational designs in chronological order, starting with the earliest. Use the letters found left of the choices to designate each step in the provided blanks.

   a. Development of the use of regression techniques to predict scores
   b. Advent of path analysis to fit data to a theoretical model
   c. Pearson published his correlation statistic
   d. Discussion of the correlational research design by Campbell and Stanley

   Earliest _____   _____   _____   _____   Most recent

2. Which of the following is an important difference between correlational research and true experiments? Circle the letter to the left of the correct response.

   a. Use of random sampling
   b. Use of statistical comparisons
   c. Use of an intervention

3. Which of the following describes the major intention of choosing a correlational design? Circle the letter to the left of the correct response.

   a. Measure the association between two variables
   b. Provide evidence of a cause-and-effect relationship between two variables
   c. To descriptively describe each of two variables
   d. To compare two groups

Four different predictor variables (a, b, c, and d) were measured and correlated with a criterion variable for the same group of participants. The resulting coefficients are summarized in the following table. Use these results to answer questions 4–7.

Variable	r	r^2
a	+0.30*	0.09
b	−0.98**	0.96
c	−0.55**	0.30
d	+0.01	0.00

$* p < .05; ** p < .01$

4. Which predictor variable has the strongest linear relationship with the criterion variable? Record your response.

    Variable _____

5. Which predictor variable has the most positive linear relationship with the criterion variable? Record your response.

    Variable _____

6. Which predictor variable is uncorrelated with the criterion variable? Record your response.

    Variable _____

7. Which predictor variable explains 30% of the variability of the criterion variable? Record your response.

    Variable _____

8. Which of the following design types would you use if you wanted to forecast future behavior? Circle the letter to the left of the correct response.

    a. Between-group experiment
    b. Explanatory correlational design
    c. Prediction correlational design
    d. Within-group design

9. Which of the following should a researcher use if the data are normally distributed? Circle the letter to the left of the correct response.

    a. Phi-coefficient
    b. Spearman rho
    c. Point-biserial correlation
    d. Pearson product-moment correlation coefficient

10. Which of the following is a common difference between a correlational study and a quasi-experiment? Circle the letter to the left of the correct response.

    a. Use of two (or more) groups for comparison
    b. Use of statistical comparisons
    c. Measurement of variables
    d. Determining p-values for statistics

Practice Test Items - Answer Key

1. Put the following historical developments related to correlational designs in chronological order, starting with the earliest. Use the letters found to the left of the choices to designate each step in the provided blanks.

   Earliest: c.   Pearson published his correlation statistic
                a.   Development of the use of regression techniques to predict scores
                d.   Discussion of the correlational research design by Campbell and Stanley
   Most recent: b.   Advent of path analysis to fit data to a theoretical model

   Review section "How Did Correlational Research Develop?" in the textbook

2. Which of the following is an important difference between correlational research and true experiments?

   c.   Use of an intervention

   Review section "What Is Correlational Research?" in the textbook

3. Which of the following describes the major intention of choosing a correlational design?

   a.   Measure the association between two variables

   Review section "When Do You Use Correlational Research?" in the textbook

4. Which predictor variable has the strongest linear relationship with the criterion variable?

   Variable b

   Review section "Associations between Scores" in the textbook

5. Which predictor variable has the most positive linear relationship with the criterion variable?

   Variable a

   Review section "Associations between Scores" in the textbook

6. Which predictor variable is uncorrelated with the criterion variable?

   Variable d

   Review section "Associations between Scores" in the textbook

7. Which of the predictor variables explains 30% of the variability of the criterion variable?

    Variable c

    Review section "Associations between Scores" in the textbook

8. Which of the following design types would you use if you wanted to forecast future behavior?

    c. Prediction correlational design

    Review section "What Are the Types of Correlational Designs?" in the textbook

9. Which of the following should a researcher use if the data are normally distributed?

    d. Pearson product-moment correlation coefficient

    Review section "Associations between Scores" in the textbook

10. Which of the following is a common difference between a correlational study and a quasi-experiment?

    a. Use of two (or more) groups for comparison

    Review section "How Do You Conduct a Correlational Study?" in the textbook

Chapter 13

Survey Designs

After completing your study of Chapter 13, you should be able to:

1. Identify the intent and the use of surveys.

2. Describe the use of cross-sectional and longitudinal survey designs.

3. Distinguish among the population, the target population, and the sample.

4. Identify the types of interviews and questionnaires used in survey research.

5. Identify the elements that go into writing good questions on a survey instrument.

6. Describe the steps researchers take to develop a high return rate on a mailed questionnaire.

7. Describe how to construct a good mailed questionnaire.

8. Describe how to design and conduct an interview survey.

9. List the steps in conducting survey research.

10. Identify criteria useful for evaluating survey research.

Practice in Understanding Key Concepts

Important Terms and Concepts

The following items represent important concepts relating to survey designs. Using your own words, record definitions for the items in the space provided.

Survey research designs: _____

_____

_____

_____

Cross-sectional survey design: _____

_____

_____

Longitudinal survey design: _____

_____

_____

Trend study: _____

_____

_____

Cohort study: _____

_____

_____

Panel study: _____

_____

_____

Questionnaire: _____

_____

_____

Interview survey: _____

_____

_____

Mailed questionnaire: _____

_____

_____

Electronic questionnaire: _____

_____

_____

One-on-one interviews in survey research: _____

_____

_____

Chapter 13

Focus group interviews in survey research: _____

_____

_____

Telephone interview surveys: _____

_____

_____

Closed-ended questions in surveys: _____

_____

_____

Open-ended questions in a survey: _____

_____

_____

Semi-closed-ended questions in a survey: _____

_____

_____

Pilot test: _____

_____

_____

Response return rate: _____

_____

_____

Response bias: _____

_____

_____

_____

Wave analysis: _____

_____

_____

_____

Applying the Concepts as a Consumer of Research

Carefully consider your definitions and descriptions of the key concepts for this chapter as you respond to the following items about the survey study described in Sample Study #1 (SG pages 11–25) or the sample survey study in the textbook. Each item represents a key characteristic of the designs described in this chapter. For each item, explain how the characteristic was implemented within the study.

Activity Hint!
- See Chapter 13 section "*What Are the Key Characteristics of Survey Research?*" for information about each key characteristic.

Key characteristics of survey designs

1. Sampling from a population. _____

_____

_____

_____

_____

2. Collecting data through questionnaires or interviews. _____

_____

_____

_____

_____

3. Designing instruments for data collection. _____

_____

_____

_____

_____

4. Obtaining a high response rate. _____

_____

_____

_____

_____

Chapter 13

Evaluating survey research

The following items represent criteria for evaluating research using the designs described in this chapter. In each case, explain the meaning of the statement and critique the implementation of a survey design within Sample Study #1 (SG pages 11–25) or the sample survey study in the textbook.

5. Was the target population or sampling frame clearly described and specified? _____

_____

_____

_____

6. Were the sampling procedures specified? If the authors did not use simple random sampling, did they explain the

reason for other sampling procedures? _____

_____

_____

_____

7. Was the sample clearly identified and the basis on which it was selected explained? _____

_____

_____

_____

_____

8. Did the type of survey match the questions or hypotheses? _____

_____

_____

_____

9. Was the form of data collection clear and was the basis for selecting or developing an instrument identified? ____

_____

_____

_____

10. Was information on the reliability and validity of scores from past use of the instrument reported? _____

_____

_____

_____

11. Were the instrument administration procedures fully described? _____

_____

_____

_____

12. Did the study indicate how high response rates were ensured? _____

_____

_____

_____

13. Were sample items provided? And if so, did they demonstrate good item construction? _____

_____

_____

_____

_____

14. Did the data analysis match the research questions and hypotheses? _____

_____

_____

_____

_____

15. Was the study written scientifically and ethically? _____

_____

_____

_____

Applying the Concepts as a Producer of Research

You will now practice applying the important concepts of this chapter to a new research problem of your choice. Assume that you are a researcher who is going to undertake a research study using a survey design. Select a research topic and use the following steps to design this survey study.

Activity Hint!
-   See Chapter 13 section "***What Are the Steps in Conducting Survey Research?***" for information about each step.

Chapter 13

My research topic: _____

_____

Step 1 – Explain why a survey design best addresses your research problem. _____

_____

_____

_____

_____

_____

Step 2 – Identify the research questions or hypotheses. _____

_____

_____

_____

_____

_____

Step 3 – Identify the population, the sampling frame, and the sample. _____

_____

_____

_____

_____

_____

Step 4 – Determine the survey design and data collection procedures. _____

_____

_____

_____

_____

_____

Step 5 – Describe whether you will develop or locate an instrument. _____

_____

_____

_____

Step 6 – Describe your procedures for administering the instrument. _____

_____

_____

_____

_____

Step 7 – Describe how you will analyze the data to address the research questions or hypotheses. _____

_____

_____

_____

_____

Step 8 – List what aspects of your study you will include in your written report. _____

_____

_____

_____

_____

Practice Test Items

Answer the following items to check your understanding of the important concepts related to survey designs. Once you have answered all of the items, you can check your ideas with the provided solutions.

1. Put the following historical developments related to survey designs in chronological order, starting with the earliest. Use the letters found to the left of the choices to designate each step in the provided blanks.

    a. Development of electronic surveys
    b. Advancements in large-scale data collection by polling organizations
    c. Development of sampling techniques and scales of measurement
    d. 34-page survey of national education systems conducted in 1817

    Earliest _____ _____ _____ _____ Most recent

2. Which of the following is an important difference between survey research and experiments? Circle the letter to the left of the correct response.

    a. Need for good construct validity
    b. Random sampling techniques
    c. Treatment given to participants
    d. Use of measurement instruments

Chapter 13

3. Which of the following describes the major intention of choosing a survey design? Circle the letter to the left of the correct response.

    a. Establish a cause-and-effect relationship
    b. Measure the impact of a treatment on an outcome
    c. Make predictions based on the relationship between two variables
    d. Describe characteristics of a population

4. Which of the following design types would you use if you wanted to study a population at one point in time? Circle the letter to the left of the correct response.

    a. Cohort study
    b. Cross-sectional study
    c. Panel study
    d. Trend study

5. Which of the following design types would you use if you wanted to study the same individuals over time? Circle the letter to the left of the correct response.

    a. Cohort study
    b. Cross-sectional study
    c. Panel study
    d. Trend study

6. Which of the following is an important difference between a questionnaire and an interview in a survey study? Circle the letter to the left of the correct response.

    a. The use of close-ended or open-ended items
    b. The sensitive nature of the items
    c. The number of questions
    d. Who actually records the information on the data collection form

7. Which of the following statements explains why a high response rate is important in survey research? Circle the letter to the left of the correct response.

    a. It gives evidence that your instrument has high content validity
    b. It will give you a larger sampling frame
    c. It will result in an increase of response bias
    d. It allows you to make stronger claims about the population

8. Which of the following sampling strategies is preferred in survey research? Circle the letter to the left of the correct response.

    a. Random sampling
    b. Typical sampling
    c. Maximal variation sampling
    d. Theoretical sampling

9. Briefly describe what it means to have response bias in a survey study.

_____

_____

_____

_____

_____

10. Briefly describe the difference between a cohort survey study and a trend study?

_____

_____

_____

_____

_____

Practice Test Items - Answer Key

1. Put the following historical developments related to survey designs in chronological order, starting with the earliest. Use the letters found to the left of the choices to designate each step in the provided blanks.

   Earliest: d.   34-page survey of national education systems conducted in 1817
                   c.   Development of sampling techniques and scales of measurement
                   b.   Advancements in large-scale data collection by polling organizations
   Most recent: a.   Development of electronic surveys

   Review section "How Did Survey Research Develop?" in the textbook

2. Which of the following is an important difference between survey research and experiments?

   c.   Treatment given to participants

   Review section "What Is Survey Research?" in the textbook

3. Which of the following describes the major intention of choosing a survey design?

    d.   Describe characteristics of a population

Review section "What Is Survey Research?" in the textbook

4. Which of the following design types would you use if you wanted to study a population at one point in time?

    b.   Cross-sectional study

Review section "What Are the Types of Survey Designs?" in the textbook

5. Which of the following design types would you use if you wanted to study the same individuals over time?

    c.   Panel study

Review section "What Are the Types of Survey Designs?" in the textbook

6. Which of the following is an important difference between a questionnaire and an interview in a survey study?

    d.   Who actually records the information on the data collection form

Review section "Questionnaires and Interviews" in the textbook

7. Which of the following statements explains why a high response rate is important in survey research?

    d.   It allows you to make stronger claims about the population

Review section "Response Rate" in the textbook

8. Which of the following sampling strategies is preferred in survey research?

    a.   Random sampling

Review section "Sampling from a Population" in the textbook

9. Briefly describe what it means to have response bias in a survey study.

Response bias occurs when the obtained responses do not accurately reflect the views of the overall sample and population. This can happen when the individuals who do not return the questionnaire have attitudes more positive (or more negative) than the overall sample and population. These missing data will result in the conclusions being biased, that is the results will be more negative (or more positive) than they would have been had all individuals responded.

Review section "Response Rate" in the textbook

10. Briefly describe the difference between a cohort survey study and a trend study?

A cohort study is a longitudinal survey study of the changes in a subpopulation group. Although different individuals may be sampled at different times, all participants will share a common characteristic, making them all part of the identified subpopulation. A trend study is a longitudinal survey study of the changes in the same population over time.

Review section "What Are the Types of Survey Designs?" in the textbook

Review #1: The Quantitative Research Designs

Carefully consider your definitions and descriptions of the key concepts for the three quantitative research designs discussed in Chapters 11, 12, and 13. Using these ideas, complete the following questions to review and compare these three designs.

1. When do you choose to use each design?

Activity Hint!
- Review the sections on "***When Do You Use… Research?***" at the start of Chapters 11, 12, and 13.

Experimental Design:	Correlational Design:	Survey Design:

2. What are the different types of each design?

Activity Hint!
- Review the sections on "***What Are the Types of… Designs?***" in Chapters 11, 12, and 13.

Experimental Design:	Correlational Design:	Survey Design:

3. What sample size is appropriate for each design?

Activity Hint!
- Review the section on "***Sample Size***" in Chapter 6.

Experimental Design:	Correlational Design:	Survey Design:

Review #1: The Quantitative Research Designs

4. The data are typically analyzed to address what type of research question?

Activity Hint!
- Review the sections on "***Writing Quantitative Research Questions***" in Chapter 5 and "***When Do You Use... Research?***" at the start of Chapters 11, 12, and 13.

Experimental Design:	Correlational Design:	Survey Design:

5. What are the key characteristics of each design?

Activity Hint!
- Review the sections on "***What Are the Key Characteristics of...?***" in Chapters 11, 12, and 13.

Experimental Design:	Correlational Design:	Survey Design:

6. Write a research question for a study that you might want to conduct using each design.

Activity Hint!
- Review the sections on "***Writing Quantitative Research Questions***" in Chapter 5 and "***When Do You Use... Research?***" at the start of Chapters 11, 12, and 13.

Experimental Design:	Correlational Design:	Survey Design:

Chapter 14

Grounded Theory Designs

Learning Objectives

After completing your study of Chapter 14, you should be able to:

1. Define grounded theory and indicate when to use it in research.

2. Distinguish among three types of grounded theory designs.

3. Identify a process studied in grounded theory research.

4. Illustrate how theoretical sampling works in grounded theory research.

5. Describe the process of making a constant comparative data analysis.

6. Identify a core category for a grounded theory model.

7. Draw a theory generated from the data analysis.

8. Explain the importance of memoing in grounded theory research.

9. Describe how to conduct a grounded theory study.

10. Evaluate the quality of a grounded theory study.

Practice in Understanding Key Concepts

Important Terms and Concepts

The following items represent important concepts relating to grounded theory designs. Using your own words, record definitions for the items in the space provided.

Grounded theory design: _____

_____

_____

_____

Chapter 14

Systematic design in grounded theory: _____

_____

_____

Open coding: _____

_____

_____

Properties: _____

_____

_____

Dimensionalized properties: _____

_____

_____

Axial coding: _____

_____

_____

Coding paradigm: _____

_____

_____

Selective coding: _____

_____

_____

Process in grounded theory research: _____

_____

_____

Categories in grounded theory designs: _____

_____

_____

In vivo codes: _____

_____

_____

Theoretical sampling: _____

_____

_____

Emerging design: _____

_____

_____

Saturation: _____

_____

_____

Constant comparison: _____

_____

_____

Core category: _____

_____

_____

Theory in grounded theory research: _____

_____

_____

Theoretical propositions: _____

_____

_____

Memos: _____

_____

_____

Discriminant sampling: _____

_____

_____

Chapter 14

Applying the Concepts as a Consumer of Research

Carefully consider your definitions and descriptions of the key concepts for this chapter as you respond to the following items about the grounded theory study described in Sample Study #6 (SG pages 157–175) or the sample grounded theory study in the textbook. Each item represents a key characteristic of the designs described in this chapter. For each item, explain how the characteristic was implemented within the study.

Activity Hint!
- See Chapter 14 section *"What Are the Key Characteristics of Grounded Theory Research?"* for information about each key characteristic.

Key characteristics of grounded theory designs

1. A process approach. _____

_____

_____

_____

2. Theoretical sampling. _____

_____

_____

_____

_____

3. Constant comparative data analysis. _____

_____

_____

_____

4. A core category. _____

_____

_____

_____

5. Theory generation. _____

_____

_____

_____

6. Memos. _____

_____

_____

_____

_____

Evaluating grounded theory research

The following items represent criteria for evaluating research using the designs described in this chapter. In each case, explain the meaning of the statement and critique the implementation of a grounded theory design within Sample Study #6 (SG pages 157–175) or the sample grounded theory study in the textbook.

7. Is there an obvious connection or fit between the categories and the raw data? _____

_____

_____

8. Is the theory useful as a conceptual explanation for the process being studied? In other words, does it work? ___

_____

_____

9. Does the theory provide a relevant explanation of actual problems and a basic process? _____

_____

_____

10. Is the theory modified as conditions change or the researcher collects additional data? _____

_____

_____

11. Is a theoretical model developed or generated? Is the intent of this model to conceptualize a process, an action,

or an interaction? _____

_____

_____

12. Is there a core category specified at the heart of the theoretical model? _____

_____

_____

13. Does the model emerge through phases of coding? _____

_____

_____

_____

14. Does the researcher interrelate the categories? _____

_____

_____

_____

15. Does the researcher gather extensive data to develop a detailed conceptual theory well saturated in the data? ___

_____

_____

_____

16. Does the study show that the researcher validated the evolving theory by comparing it to data, examining how

the theory supports or refutes existing theories in the literature, or checking the theory with participants? _____

_____

_____

_____

Applying the Concepts as a Producer of Research

You will now practice applying the important concepts of this chapter to a new research problem of your choice. Assume that you are a researcher who is going to undertake a research study using a grounded theory design. Select a research topic and use the following steps to design this grounded theory study.

Activity Hint!
- See Chapter 14 section "***What Are the Steps in Conducting Grounded Theory Research?***" for information about each step.

My research topic: _____

_____

Step 1 – Explain why a grounded theory design best addresses the research problem. _____

_____

_____

_____

Step 2 – Identify a process to study. _____

_____

_____

_____

Step 3 – Describe the kinds of approvals and access that will be required of your study. _____

_____

_____

_____

_____

Step 4 – Describe your theoretical sampling strategy. _____

_____

_____

_____

_____

Step 5 – Describe the process you will use to code your data. _____

_____

_____

_____

_____

Step 6 – Describe the process you will use for selective coding and developing the theory. _____

_____

_____

_____

_____

Step 7 – Describe how you will validate your theory. What steps will you take? _____

_____

_____

_____

_____

Chapter 14

Step 8 – List what aspects of your study you will include in your written report. _____

_____

_____

_____

_____

_____

Practice Test Items

Answer the following items to check your understanding of the important concepts related to grounded theory designs. Once you have answered all of the items, you can check your ideas with the provided solutions.

1. Put the following historical developments related to grounded theory designs in chronological order, starting with the earliest. Use the letters found to the left of the choices to designate each step in the provided blanks.

    a. Introduction of grounded theory using predetermined categories
    b. Introduction of the constructivist method of grounded theory
    c. Glaser and Strauss publish *Discovery of Grounded Theory*
    d. Criticism of approaches that do not allow the theory to emerge from the data

    Earliest   _____   _____   _____   _____   Most recent

2. Which of the following designs uses open, axial, and selective coding? Circle the letter to the left of the correct response.

    a. Systematic design
    b. Emerging design
    c. Constructivist design

3. In which of the following analysis steps do researchers focus on one category as the central phenomenon? Circle the letter to the left of the correct response.

    a. Describing dimensionalized properties
    b. Axial coding
    c. Selective coding
    d. Open coding

4. Which of the following grounded theory designs emphasizes the following criteria for evaluating a theory: fit, work, relevance, and modifiability? Circle the letter to the left of the correct response.

    a. Systematic design
    b. Emerging design
    c. Constructivist design

5. Which of the following grounded theory designs attempts to explain the feelings of individuals as they experience a process? Circle the letter to the left of the correct response.

   a. Systematic design
   b. Emerging design
   c. Constructivist design

6. Which of the following best describes the major intention of choosing a grounded theory design? Circle the letter to the left of the correct response.

   a. To test a published theory using qualitative data
   b. To create a theory of a cultural viewpoint
   c. To explain individual's views about a particular theory
   d. To develop a theory when one does not already exist

7. Which of the following types of codes are always labeled using the exact words of participants? Circle the letter to the left of the correct response.

   a. *In vivo* codes
   b. Categories
   c. Axial codes
   d. Selective codes

8. Which of the following sampling strategies is most appropriate for an emerging grounded theory design? Circle the letter to the left of the correct response.

   a. Maximal variation sampling
   b. Disconfirming sampling
   c. Critical sampling
   d. Theoretical sampling

9. Which of the following strategies is most appropriate for validating the findings of a grounded theory design? Circle the letter to the left of the correct response.

   a. Maximal variation sampling
   b. Discriminant sampling
   c. Critical sampling
   d. Theoretical sampling

10. Which of the following grounded theory designs is most similar to a quantitative research approach? Circle the letter to the left of the correct response and explain why in the space provided.

    a. Systematic design
    b. Emerging design
    c. Constructivist design

    Why? _____

    _____

Practice Test Items - Answer Key

1. Put the following historical developments related to experimental designs in chronological order, starting with the earliest. Use the letters found to the left of the choices to designate each step in the provided blanks.

   Earliest: c.   Glaser and Strauss publish *Discovery of Grounded Theory*
                  a.   Introduction of grounded theory using predetermined categories
                  d.   Criticism of approaches that do not allow the theory to emerge from the data
   Most recent: b.   Introduction of the constructivist method of grounded theory

   Review section "How Did Grounded Theory Develop?" in the textbook

2. Which of the following designs uses open, axial, and selective coding?

   a.   Systematic design

   Review section "Types of Grounded Theory Designs" in the textbook

3. In which of the following analysis steps do researchers focus on one category as the central phenomenon?

   b.   Axial coding

   Review section "The Systematic Design" in the textbook

4. Which of the following grounded theory designs emphasizes the following criteria for evaluating a good theory: fit, work, relevance, and modifiability?

   b.   Emerging design

   Review section "The Emerging Design" in the textbook

5. Which of the following grounded theory designs attempts to explain the feelings of individuals as they experience a process?

   c.   Constructivist design

   Review section "The Constructivist Design" in the textbook

6. Which of the following best describes the major intention of choosing a grounded theory design?

   d.   To develop a theory when one does not already exist

   Review section "What Is Grounded Theory Research?" in the textbook

7. Which of the following types of codes are always labeled using the exact words of participants?

   a. *In vivo* codes

   Review section "A Process Approach" in the textbook

8. Which of the following sampling strategies is most appropriate for an emerging grounded theory design?

   d. Theoretical sampling

   Review section "Theoretical Sampling" in the textbook

9. Which of the following strategies is most appropriate for validating the findings of a grounded theory design?

   b. Discriminant sampling

   Review section "What Are the Steps in Conducting Grounded Theory Research?" in the textbook

10. Which of the following grounded theory designs is most similar to a quantitative research approach?

    a. Systematic design

    Why? This design is closest to a quantitative approach because it sometimes uses predetermined categories and frameworks.

    Review section "The Systematic Design" in the textbook

Chapter 15

Ethnographic Designs

Learning Objectives

After completing your study of Chapter 15, you should be able to:

1. Define ethnographic research and identify when to use it.

2. Distinguish among three types of ethnographic designs.

3. Identify a cultural theme in an ethnographic study.

4. List the characteristics of a culture-sharing group.

5. Explain the types of shared patterns of behaviors, beliefs, and language studied in an ethnography.

6. Describe several forms of ethnographic data collected during fieldwork.

7. Describe the three components of description, themes, and interpretation in ethnography.

8. Illustrate the aspects of context reported in ethnography.

9. Identify approaches ethnographers might use to document their reflexivity.

10. Identify steps in conducting an ethnography study.

11. List criteria useful for evaluating an ethnographic research report.

Practice in Understanding Key Concepts

Important Terms and Concepts

The following items represent important concepts relating to ethnographic designs. Using your own words, record definitions for the items in the space provided.

Ethnographic design: _____

_____

_____

Culture: _____

_____

_____

Realist ethnography: _____

_____

_____

Case study: _____

_____

_____

Intrinsic case: _____

_____

_____

Instrumental case: _____

_____

_____

Collective case study: _____

_____

_____

Critical ethnography: _____

_____

_____

Cultural theme: _____

_____

_____

Culture-sharing group: _____

_____

_____

Shared pattern: _____

_____

_____

Chapter 15

Behavior (in an ethnography): _____

_____

_____

Belief (in an ethnography): _____

_____

_____

Language (in an ethnography): _____

_____

_____

Fieldwork: _____

_____

_____

Emic data: _____

_____

_____

Etic data: _____

_____

_____

Negotiation data: _____

_____

_____

Description in ethnography: _____

_____

_____

Thematic data analysis in ethnography: _____

_____

_____

Interpretation in ethnography: _____

_____

_____

Context: _____

_____

_____

Reflexivity in ethnography: _____

_____

_____

Applying the Concepts as a Consumer of Research

Carefully consider your definitions and descriptions of the key concepts for this chapter as you respond to the following items about the case study described in Sample Study #2 (SG pages 26–33) or the sample ethnographic study in the textbook. Each item represents a key characteristic of the designs described in this chapter. For each item, explain how the characteristic was implemented within the study.

Activity Hint!
- See Chapter 15 section "***What Are the Key Characteristics of an Ethnographic Design?***" for information about each key characteristic.

Key characteristics of ethnographic designs

1. Cultural themes. _____

_____

_____

_____

2. A culture-sharing group. _____

_____

_____

_____

3. Shared patterns of behavior, belief, and language. _____

_____

_____

_____

_____

4. Fieldwork. _____

_____

_____

_____

_____

5. Description, themes, and interpretation. _____

_____

_____

_____

_____

_____

6. Context or setting. _____

_____

_____

_____

_____

_____

7. Researcher reflexivity. _____

_____

_____

_____

Evaluating ethnographic research

The following items represent criteria for evaluating research using the designs described in this chapter. In each case, explain the meaning of the statement and critique the implementation of an ethnographic design within Sample Study #2 (SG pages 26–33) or the sample ethnographic study in the textbook.

8. Is the culture-sharing group or the case clearly identified and specified? _____

_____

_____

_____

9. Are patterns identified for the group or case? _____

_____

_____

_____

10. Is the group or the case described in detail? _____

_____

_____

_____

11. Do you learn about the context surrounding the group or the case? _____

_____

_____

_____

12. Does the author reflect on his or her role in the study? _____

_____

_____

_____

13. Is there a broader interpretation made of the meaning of the patterns or the case? _____

_____

_____

_____

_____

14. Does the interpretation naturally flow from the description and the themes? _____

_____

_____

_____

15. Do you have a sense about how the culture works from the participants' or researcher's viewpoint? _____

_____

_____

_____

16. Has the author checked the accuracy of the study by using procedures such as triangulating among data sources

or taking the study back to participants for review? _____

_____

_____

_____

Applying the Concepts as a Producer of Research

You will now practice applying the important concepts of this chapter to a new research problem of your choice. Assume that you are a researcher who is going to undertake a research study using an ethnographic design. Select a research topic and use the following steps to design this ethnography.

Activity Hint!
- See Chapter 15 section "***What Are the Steps in Conducting an Ethnography?***" for information about each step.

My research topic: _____

_____

Step 1 – Describe the intent of your study and explain why an ethnographic study addresses your research problem.

_____

_____

_____

_____

Step 2 – Discuss the approval and access considerations that will be part of your study. _____

_____

_____

_____

_____

Step 3 – Describe your data collection procedures and explain why they are appropriate. _____

_____

_____

_____

_____

Step 4 – Describe how you will analyze and interpret the data within the design type. _____

_____

_____

_____

_____

_____

Step 5 – What aspects of your study will you include in your written report to make it consistent with your design?

_____

_____

_____

_____

_____

Practice Test Items

Answer the following items to check your understanding of the important concepts related to ethnographic designs. Once you have answered all of the items, you can check your ideas with the provided solutions.

1. Put the following historical developments related to ethnographic designs in chronological order, starting with the earliest. Use the letters found to the left of the choices to designate each step in the provided blanks.

    a. Margaret Mead studied childrearing, adolescence, and the influence of culture on personality in Samoa
    b. Acceptance by sociologists of the importance of studying a single case
    c. Call for flexible evaluation standards embedded within the participants, historical, and cultural influences
    d. Development of educational anthropology

    Earliest _____   _____   _____   _____   Most recent

2. Which of the following is an important aspect of ethnographies? Circle the letter to the left of the correct response.

    a. Study of a process
    b. Collection of data through fieldwork
    c. Theoretical sampling
    d. Using predetermined categories to code the data

3. Which of the following describes the major intention of choosing a case study design? Circle the letter to the left of the correct response.

    a. Describe and interpret the story of one individual
    b. Address inequities in our society
    c. In-depth exploration of an event or activities
    d. Describe characteristics of a population

4. Which of the following design types would you use if you wanted an objective account of a culture-sharing group? Circle the letter to the left of the correct response.

    a. Case study
    b. Cohort study
    c. Realist ethnography study
    d. Critical ethnography study

5. Which of the following design types would you use if you wanted a non-neutral account of a culture-sharing group with an advocacy perspective? Circle the letter to the left of the correct response.

    a. Case study
    b. Cohort study
    c. Realist ethnography study
    d. Critical ethnography study

6. Which of the following is an example of etic data? Circle the letter to the left of the correct response.

    a. The number of individuals within the group under study
    b. A quote from one of the study participants
    c. A description of the data collection procedures
    d. A theme that emerged during data analysis

7. In which design might the interpretation include a discussion of the generalizability of the findings? Circle the letter to the left of the correct response.

    a. Case study
    b. Realist ethnography study
    c. Critical ethnography study

8. Which of the following sampling strategies would be most useful in case study research? Circle the letter to the left of the correct response.

    a. Typical sampling
    b. Random sampling
    c. Multistage cluster sampling

9. Which of the following data collection strategies is an important feature of critical ethnographies? Circle the letter to the left of the correct response.

    a. Spend extensive time at the site
    b. Emphasize observations
    c. Actively involve participants
    d. Verify the reliability of the data sources

10. Briefly describe the difference in the point of view of realist ethnographic and critical ethnographic studies.

_____

_____

_____

_____

Practice Test Items - Answer Key

1. Put the following historical developments related to survey designs in chronological order, starting with the earliest. Use the letters found to the left of the choices to designate each step in the provided blanks.

    Earliest: a.   Margaret Mead studied childrearing, adolescence, and the influence of culture on personality in Samoa
                   b.   Acceptance by sociologists of the importance of studying a single case
                   d.   Development of educational anthropology
    Most recent: c.   Call for flexible evaluation standards embedded within the participants, historical, and cultural influences

    Review section "How Did Ethnographic Research Develop?" in the textbook

2. Which of the following is an important aspect of ethnographies?

    b.   Collection of data through fieldwork

    Review section "What Are the Key Characteristics of an Ethnographic Design?" in the textbook

Chapter 15

3.   Which of the following describes the major intention of choosing a case study design?

    c.   In-depth exploration of an event or activities

Review section "What Are the Types of Ethnographic Designs?" in the textbook

4.   Which of the following design types would you use if you wanted an objective account of a culture-sharing group?

    c.   Realist ethnography study

Review section "What Are the Types of Ethnographic Designs?" in the textbook

5.   Which of the following design types would you use if you wanted a non-neutral account of a culture-sharing group with an advocacy perspective?

    d.   Critical ethnography study

Review section "What Are the Types of Ethnographic Designs?" in the textbook

6.   Which of the following is an example of etic data?

    d.   A theme that emerged during data analysis

Review section "Fieldwork" in the textbook

7.   In which design might the interpretation include a discussion of the generalizability of the findings?

    a.   Case study

Review section "What Are the Steps in Conducting an Ethnography?" in the textbook

8.   Which of the following sampling strategies would be most useful in case study research?

    a.   Typical sampling

Review section "What Are the Steps in Conducting an Ethnography?" in the textbook

9.   Which of the following data collection strategies is a vital feature of critical ethnographies?

    c.   Actively involve participants

Review section "What Are the Types of Ethnographic Designs?" in the textbook

10.   Briefly describe the difference in the point of view of realist ethnographic and critical ethnographic studies.

    In a realist ethnography, the researcher will write from an objective point of view, keeping personal views and biases in the background. In a critical ethnography, the researcher will include personal points of view and openly discuss the biases and views that he or she brought to the study. A critical ethnographer will also include a "call to action" to address the issue that has been studied.

Review sections "What Are the Types of Ethnographic Designs?" and "What Are the Steps in Conducting an Ethnography?" in the textbook

Chapter 16

Narrative Research Designs

After completing your study of Chapter 16, you should be able to:

1. Describe the major types of narrative studies.

2. Define what it means to explore the experiences of an individual.

3. Describe the type of information that goes into building a chronology of an individual's experiences.

4. Identify the aspects of a "story" and the types of data used to report the "story."

5. Describe the process of restorying in narrative research.

6. Identify the use of themes in a narrative study.

7. Define the setting or context that goes into a narrative study.

8. Identify strategies for collaboration with participants in narrative research.

9. Identify several types of issues that may arise in gathering narrative stories.

10. Describe the steps used in conducting a narrative study.

11. List criteria for evaluating a narrative study.

Practice in Understanding Key Concepts

Important Terms and Concepts

The following items represent important concepts relating to narrative research designs. Using your own words, record definitions for the items in the space provided.

Narrative research designs: _____

_____

_____

Chapter 16

Biography: _____

_____

_____

Autobiography: _____

_____

_____

Life history: _____

_____

_____

Personal experience story: _____

_____

_____

Teachers' stories: _____

_____

_____

Theoretical lens: _____

_____

_____

Experiences: _____

_____

_____

Chronology: _____

_____

_____

Story in narrative research: _____

_____

_____

Field texts: _____

_____

_____

Restorying: _____

_____

_____

Setting: _____

_____

_____

Collaboration: _____

_____

_____

Applying the Concepts as a Consumer of Research

Carefully consider your definitions and descriptions of the key concepts for this chapter as you respond to the following items about the narrative study described in Sample Study #4 (SG pages 85–103) or the sample narrative research study in the textbook. Each item represents a key characteristic of the designs described in this chapter. For each item, explain how the characteristic was implemented within the study.

Activity Hint!
▪ See Chapter 16 section "***What Are the Key Characteristics of Narrative Designs?***" for information about each key characteristic.

Key characteristics of narrative research designs

1. Focusing on individual experiences. _____

_____

_____

_____

2. Reporting a chronology of the experiences. _____

_____

_____

_____

3. Collecting individual stories. _____

_____

_____

_____

4. Restorying. _____

_____

_____

_____

_____

5. Coding the stories for themes. _____

_____

_____

_____

6. Describing the context or setting of the stories. _____

_____

_____

_____

7. Collaborating with participants. _____

_____

_____

_____

Evaluating narrative research

The following items represent criteria for evaluating research using the designs described in this chapter. In each case, explain the meaning of the statement and critique the implementation of a narrative design within Sample Study #4 (SG pages 85–103) or the sample narrative research study in the textbook.

8. Does the researcher focus on individual experiences? _____

_____

_____

_____

9. Is there a focus on a single individual or a few individuals? _____

_____

_____

_____

10. Did the researcher collect the story of an individual's experience? _____

_____

_____

_____

_____

11. Did the researcher restory the participant's story? _____

_____

_____

_____

_____

12. In the restorying, was the participant's voice as well as the researcher's voice heard? _____

_____

_____

_____

_____

13. Did the researcher identify themes that emerged from the story? _____

_____

_____

_____

14. Did the story include information about place or setting of the individual? _____

_____

_____

_____

_____

15. Did the story have a temporal, chronological sequence including the past, present, and future? _____

_____

_____

_____

_____

16. Is there evidence that the researcher collaborated with the participant? _____

_____

_____

_____

17. Does the story adequately address the purpose and questions of the researcher? _____

_____

_____

_____

Applying the Concepts as a Producer of Research

You will now practice applying the important concepts of this chapter to a new research problem of your choice. Assume that you are a researcher who is going to undertake a research study using a narrative research design. Select a research topic and use the following steps to design this narrative study.

Activity Hint!
- See Chapter 16 section "***What Are the Steps in Conducting Narrative Research?***" for information about each step.

My research topic: _____

_____

_____

Step 1 – Identify a phenomenon to explore that addresses a research problem. _____

_____

_____

_____

_____

Step 2 – Describe how you will purposefully select an individual from whom you can learn about the phenomenon.

_____

_____

_____

_____

_____

_____

Step 3 – Describe how you will collect the story from that individual. _____

_____

_____

_____

_____

_____

Step 4 – Describe how you will restory or retell the individual's story. What steps will you take? _____

_____

_____

_____

_____

_____

Step 5 – Describe how you will collaborate with the participant-storyteller. _____

_____

_____

_____

_____

Step 6 – Describe what aspects you will include in your written story about the participant's experiences. _____

_____

_____

_____

_____

_____

Step 7 – Describe how you will validate the accuracy of the report. _____

_____

_____

_____

_____

Chapter 16

Answer the following items to check your understanding of the important concepts related to research designs and narrative designs in particular. Once you have answered all of the items, you can check your ideas with the provided solutions.

1. Put the following research designs in order starting with the one with the most flexible research process to the one with the most formalized and structured research process. Use the letters found to the left of the choices to designate each step in the provided blanks.

    a. Case study
    b. Narrative study
    c. Systematic grounded theory study
    d. Quasi-experimental study

    Most flexible   _____   _____   _____   _____   Most structured

2. Which of the following best applies to narrative research studies in educational research? Circle the letter to the left of the correct response.

    a. Focus on exploring an event
    b. Focus on a group's experiences and beliefs
    c. Focus on an individual's experiences
    d. Focus on a life history

3. Narrative research often uses a theoretical lens. Which of the following research designs also uses this guiding perspective? Circle the letter to the left of the correct response.

    a. Systematic grounded theory
    b. Critical ethnography
    c. Constructivist grounded theory
    d. Case study

4. List two examples of how narrative researchers may attempt to validate the accuracy of their findings.

    a._____

    b._____

5. Which of the following steps is not part of a restorying process? Circle the letter to the left of the correct response.

    a. Analyze the story for key elements
    b. Choose a core category
    c. Gather field texts
    d. Resequence the order of the events

6. Which of the following are part of Clandinin and Connelly's (2000) Three-Dimensional Space Narrative Structure? Circle the letter to the left of all of the correct responses.

    a. Interaction
    b. Situation
    c. Properties
    d. Continuity

7. In which of the following designs is collaboration and negotiation between researchers and participants considered especially crucial? Circle the letter to the left of all the correct responses.

    a. Critical ethnography
    b. Realist ethnography
    c. Case study
    d. Narrative

When answering questions 8–10, think about Ting's (2000) correlational study that was presented in Chapter 12 of the textbook. As you may recall, this study was concerned with the challenges facing Asian American students in universities such as racism, insufficient mastery of English, loneliness, and isolation. The intent of this correlational study was to predict Asian American students' GPA and retention in the first year of college.

8. Think of a study that you could conduct to address the problem of challenges facing Asian American college students that would utilize a narrative design. Briefly describe this study and explain why this design would be appropriate.

_____

_____

_____

_____

9. Which of the following best describes your proposed study? Circle the letter to the left of all of the correct responses.

    a. Autobiography
    b. Personal experience story
    c. Life history
    d. Teacher's story

10. Would your proposed story have a theoretical lens? If not, explain why not. If yes, then describe this theoretical lens.

_____

_____

_____

_____

Practice Test Items - Answer Key

1. Put the following research designs in order starting with the one with the most flexible research process to the one with the most formalized and structured research process. Use the letters found to the left of the choices to designate each step in the provided blanks.

    Most flexible: b.   Narrative study
                         a.   Case study
                         c.   Systematic grounded theory study
    Most structured: d.   Quasi-experimental study

    Review section "What Is Narrative Research?" in the textbook

2. Which of the following best applies to narrative research studies in educational research?

    c.   Focus on an individual's experiences

    Review section "What Are the Types of Narrative Designs?" in the textbook

3. Narrative research often uses a theoretical lens. Which of the following research designs also uses this guiding perspective?

    b.   Critical ethnography

    Review section "What Are the Types of Narrative Designs?" in the textbook

4. List two examples of how narrative researchers may attempt to validate the accuracy of their findings.

    Two possible responses are:
    a. Member checking
    b. Searching for disconfirming evidence

    Review section "What Are the Steps in Conducting Narrative Research?" in the textbook

5. Which of the following steps is not part of a restorying process?

    b.   Choose a core category

    Review section "Restorying" in the textbook

6. Which of the following are part of Clandinin and Connelly's (2000) Three-Dimensional Space Narrative Structure?

    a.   Interaction
    b.   Situation
    d.   Continuity

    Review section "Restorying" in the textbook

7. In which of the following designs is collaboration and negotiation between researchers and participants considered especially crucial?

    a. Critical ethnography
    d. Narrative

Review section "Collaborating with Participants" in the textbook

When answering questions 8–10, think about Ting's (2000) correlational study that was presented in Chapter 12 of the textbook. As you may recall, this study was concerned with the challenges facing Asian American students in universities such as racism, insufficient mastery of English, loneliness, and isolation. The intent of this correlational study was to predict Asian American students' GPA and retention in the first year of college.

8. Think of a study that you could conduct to address the problem of challenges facing Asian American college students that would utilize a narrative design. Briefly describe this study and explain why this design would be appropriate.

    Here is one possible study:
    A narrative study on this topic could include collecting and analyzing the stories on one Asian American college student during the first year of attending college. His or her individual stories would describe his or her personal experiences of being an Asian American college student and the adjustments made and challenges faced during freshmen orientation and throughout the freshman year of college.

Review section "Individual Experiences" in the textbook

9. Which of the following best describes your proposed study? [Answered for the study described above in #8.]

    b. Personal experience story

Review section "What Are the Types of Narrative Designs?" in the textbook

10. Would your proposed story have a theoretical lens? If not, explain why not. If yes, then describe this theoretical lens. [Answered for the study described above in #8.]

    This study could have a theoretical lens because it could be guided by the perspective of wanting to advocate and give voice to Asian American college students whose voices may not be heard adequately in education.

Review section "Is a Theoretical Lens Being Used?" in the textbook

---

Review #2: The Qualitative Research Designs

Carefully consider your definitions and descriptions of the key concepts for the three qualitative research designs discussed in Chapters 14, 15, and 16. Using these ideas, complete the following questions to review and compare these three designs.

1. When do you choose to use each design?

Activity Hint!
- Review the sections on "**When Do You Use... Research?**" at the start of Chapters 14, 15, and 16.

Grounded Theory Design:	Ethnographic Design:	Narrative Research Design:

2. What are the different types of each design?

Activity Hint!
- Review the sections on "**What Are the Types of... Designs?**" in Chapters 14, 15, and 16.

Grounded Theory Design:	Ethnographic Design:	Narrative Research Design:

3. What sample size is appropriate for each design?

Activity Hint!
- Review the section on "**Sample Size or Number of Research Sites**" in Chapter 8 as well as discussions within Chapters 14, 15, and 16.

Grounded Theory Design:	Ethnographic Design:	Narrative Research Design:

4. The data are typically analyzed to address what type of research question?

Activity Hint!
- Review the sections on "***Writing Qualitative Research Questions***" in Chapter 5 and "***When Do You Use...Research?***" at the start of Chapters 14, 15, and 16.

Grounded Theory Design:	Ethnographic Design:	Narrative Research Design:

5. What are the key characteristics of each design?

Activity Hint!
- Review the sections on "***What Are the Key Characteristics of...?***" in Chapters 14, 15, and 16.

Grounded Theory Design:	Ethnographic Design:	Narrative Research Design:

6. Write a research question for a study that you might want to conduct using each design.

Activity Hint!
- Review the sections on "***Writing Qualitative Research Questions***" in Chapter 5 and "***When Do You Use...Research?***" at the start of Chapters 14, 15, and 16.

Grounded Theory Design:	Ethnographic Design:	Narrative Research Design:

Chapter 17

Mixed Methods Designs

Learning Objectives

After completing your study of Chapter 17, you should be able to:

1. Define mixed methods research and identify when you use it.

2. Distinguish among four types of mixed methods designs.

3. Identify three reasons for conducting mixed methods research.

4. List types of quantitative and qualitative data collected in a mixed methods study.

5. Define priority of quantitative or qualitative research as a design decision in mixed methods research.

6. Define sequence of qualitative or quantitative research as a design decision in mixed methods research.

7. Describe the data analysis strategies for each of the types of mixed methods designs.

8. Illustrate mixed methods procedures with a diagram.

9. Describe steps in conducting a mixed methods study.

10. List criteria useful in evaluating a mixed methods design.

Practice in Understanding Key Concepts

Important Terms and Concepts

The following items represent important concepts relating to mixed methods research designs. Using your own words, record definitions for the items in the space provided.

Mixed methods research design: _____

_____

_____

Triangulation (or concurrent or parallel) mixed methods design: _____

_____

_____

Embedded mixed methods design: _____

_____

_____

Explanatory mixed methods design: _____

_____

_____

Exploratory mixed methods design: _____

_____

_____

Weight (or priority): _____

_____

_____

Sequence: _____

_____

_____

Visualization (or diagram): _____

_____

_____

Applying the Concepts as a Consumer of Research

Carefully consider your definitions and descriptions of the key concepts for this chapter as you respond to the following items about the sample mixed methods study in the textbook. Each item represents a key characteristic of the designs described in this chapter. For each item, explain how the characteristic was implemented within the study.

Activity Hint!
- See Chapter 17 section "***What Are the Key Characteristics of Mixed Methods Designs?***" for information about each key characteristic.

Chapter 17

Key characteristics of mixed methods designs

1. Rationale for using the mixed methods design. _____

_____

_____

_____

_____

2. Collecting both quantitative and qualitative data. _____

_____

_____

_____

_____

3. The priority given to the quantitative and qualitative data. _____

_____

_____

_____

4. The sequence given to the quantitative and qualitative data collection. _____

_____

_____

_____

5. Data analysis matches the particular mixed methods design type. _____

_____

_____

_____

_____

6. Inclusion of a visual diagram that portrays the study's procedures. _____

_____

_____

_____

_____

Evaluating mixed methods research

The following items represent criteria for evaluating research using the designs described in this chapter. In each case, explain the meaning of the statement and critique the implementation of a mixed methods design within the sample mixed methods research study in the textbook.

7. Does the study employ at least one method associated with quantitative research and one method associated with

qualitative research? _____

_____

_____

_____

8. Is it called a mixed methods (or a similar term) study? _____

_____

_____

_____

9. Is there a reason why the author intends to mix methods in a single study? _____

_____

_____

_____

_____

_____

10. Does the author indicate the type of mixed methods study? Alternatively, can you identify the type from

reading the rationale or from a visual figure depicting the flow of data collection activities? _____

_____

_____

_____

_____

11. Does the author mention the priority given to the quantitative and qualitative data and the sequence of their use

in the study? _____

_____

_____

_____

12. Is the study feasible, given the amount of data to be collected and the monies, time, and expertise required? ___

_____

_____

_____

_____

13. Has the author written research questions for the quantitative and the qualitative methods and the mixed

methods procedures? _____

_____

_____

_____

_____

_____

14. Has the author clearly identified the quantitative and qualitative data collection procedures? _____

_____

_____

_____

_____

_____

15. Is the procedure for data analysis consistent with the type of mixed methods study? _____

_____

_____

_____

_____

16. Is the written structure of the study consistent with the type of mixed methods design? _____

_____

_____

_____

_____

_____

Applying the Concepts as a Producer of Research

You will now practice applying the important concepts of this chapter to a new research problem of your choice. Assume that you are a researcher who is going to undertake a research study using a mixed methods research design. Select a research topic and use the following steps to design this mixed methods study.

Activity Hint!
- See Chapter 17 section "*What Are the Steps in Conducting a Mixed Methods Study?*" for information about each step.

My research topic: _____

_____

_____

Step 1 – Determine if a mixed methods study is feasible. What skills and resources will you need? _____

_____

_____

_____

_____

_____

Step 2 – Identify a rationale for mixing methods. What is your reason for using this design? _____

_____

_____

_____

_____

_____

_____

Step 3 – Describe your data collection strategy. What priority and sequence will you use? _____

_____

_____

_____

_____

_____

_____

Step 4 – Develop quantitative, qualitative, and mixed methods research questions. _____

_____

_____

_____

_____

_____

_____

Step 5 – Describe your procedures for collecting quantitative and qualitative data. _____

_____

_____

_____

_____

_____

Step 6 – Describe your procedures for analyzing the data separately or concurrently. What steps will you take?

_____

_____

_____

_____

Step 7 – Describe what aspects you will include in your written report. Will you write it as a one-phase or two-

phase study? _____

_____

_____

_____

_____

Practice Test Items

Answer the following items to check your understanding of the important concepts related to research designs and mixed methods designs in particular. Once you have answered all of the items, you can check your ideas with the provided solutions.

1. Put the following historical developments related to mixed methods designs in chronological order, starting with the earliest. Use the letters found to the left of the choices to designate each step in the provided blanks.

   a. Advocacy for a distinct mixed methods design
   b. Debate as to whether it is legitimate to mix methods based on different worldviews
   c. Idea of combining quantitative and qualitative data to neutralize weaknesses in each kind of data
   d. Use of multiple methods in quantitative research was advocated to increase a study's validity

   Earliest _____ _____ _____ _____ Most recent

2. Which of the following designs can be represented with this notation: QUAL → quan ? Circle the letter to the left of the correct response.

   a. Explanatory design
   b. Exploratory design
   c. Embedded design
   d. Triangulation design

3. Which of the following best describes the major intention of using a triangulation mixed methods design? Circle the letter to the left of the correct response.

   a. To turn qualitative textual data into quantitative numerical data for easier analysis
   b. To use qualitative data to design an instrument and quantitative data to build on the findings
   c. To use quantitative data to describe a general picture and the qualitative data to explain this picture
   d. To attempt to offset the weaknesses of each method of data collection

4. Which of the following best describes the major issue in the paradigm debate? Circle the letter to the left of the correct response.

   a. The quantitative worldview is better than the qualitative worldview
   b. The qualitative worldview is better than the quantitative worldview
   c. Quantitative and qualitative methods should not be combined because they reflect different worldviews
   d. Analyzing both quantitative and qualitative data can be difficult

5. If a mixed methods study emphasizes prediction in the purpose statement, which type of priority will it most likely use? Circle the letter to the left of the correct response.

   a. Equal weight
   b. Quantitative data of greater weight
   c. Qualitative data of greater weight
   d. Only use quantitative data

Chapter 17

6. If a mixed methods study emphasizes exploration in the purpose statement, which type of sequence will it most likely use? Circle the letter to the left of the correct response.

    a. Quantitative and qualitative data are concurrent
    b. Quantitative data first
    c. Qualitative data first
    d. Only use qualitative data

7. In which of the following designs is the collection of quantitative and qualitative data simultaneous? Circle the letter to the left of all the correct responses.

    a. Explanatory design
    b. Exploratory design
    c. Triangulation design

8. Think about Ting's (2000) correlational study that was presented in Chapter 12. This study was concerned with the challenges facing Asian American students in universities such as racism, insufficient mastery of English, loneliness, and isolation. The intent of this study was to identify variables that predict Asian American students' GPA and retention in the first year of college. Suppose the author had conducted open-ended interviews with Asian American students during the same year they measured the variables and compared the quantitative and qualitative results. This would have been an example of which of the following design types? Circle the letter to the left of the correct response.

    a. Explanatory design
    b. Exploratory design
    c. Triangulation design
    d. Embedded design

9. Think about Gallik's (1999) survey study that was presented in Chapter 13. This study was concerned with the recreational reading habits of college students. The intent of this study was to describe college student recreational reading habits and to look for evidence that recreational reading is related to academic achievement. Suppose the author had conducted focus group interviews with students to extend the results found from the analysis of the surveys. This would have been an example of which of the following design types? Circle the letter to the left of the correct response.

    a. Explanatory design
    b. Exploratory design
    c. Triangulation design
    d. Embedded design

10. Think about Feen-Calligan's (1999) grounded theory study that was presented in Chapter 14. This study worked to generate a theory to explain the process of art therapy in addiction treatment. Suppose the author had conducted a survey with therapists and recovering individuals after the theory was generated. This survey may have attempted to generalize and/or test the theory with a broader audience. This would have been an example of which of the following design types?

    a. Explanatory design
    b. Exploratory design
    c. Triangulation design
    d. Embedded design

Practice Test Items - Answer Key

1. Put the following historical developments related to mixed methods designs in chronological order, starting with the earliest. Use the letters found to the left of the choices to designate each step in the provided blanks.

   Earliest: d. Use of multiple methods in quantitative research was advocated to increase a study's validity
                c. Idea of combining quantitative and qualitative data to neutralize weaknesses in each kind of data
                b. Debate as to whether it is legitimate to mix methods based on different worldviews
   Most recent: a. Advocacy for a distinct mixed methods design

   Review section "How Did Mixed Methods Research Develop?" in the textbook

2. Which of the following designs can be represented with this notation: QUAL → quan ?

   b. Exploratory design

   Review section "What Are the Types of Mixed Methods Designs?" and Figure 17.2 in the textbook

3. Which of the following best describes the major intention of using a triangulation mixed methods design?

   d. To attempt to offset the weaknesses of each method of data collection

   Review section "What Are the Types of Mixed Methods Designs?" in the textbook

4. Which of the following best describes the major issue in the paradigm debate?

   c. Quantitative and qualitative methods should not be combined because they reflect different worldviews

   Review section "How Did Mixed Methods Research Develop?" in the textbook

5. If a mixed methods study emphasizes prediction in the purpose statement, which type of priority will it most likely use?

   b. Quantitative data of greater weight

   Review section "Priority" in the textbook

Chapter 17

6. If a mixed methods study emphasizes exploration in the purpose statement, which type of sequence will it most likely use?

    c. Qualitative data first

    Review section "What Are the Types of Mixed Methods Designs?" in the textbook

7. In which of the following designs is the collection of quantitative and qualitative data simultaneous?

    c. Triangulation design

    Review section "What Are the Types of Mixed Methods Designs?" in the textbook

8. Think about Ting's (2000) correlational study that was presented in Chapter 12. This study was concerned with the challenges facing Asian American students in universities such as racism, insufficient mastery of English, loneliness, and isolation. The intent of this study was to identify variables that predict Asian American students' GPA and retention in the first year of college. Suppose the author had conducted open-ended interviews with Asian American students during the same year they measured the variables and compared the quantitative and qualitative results. This would have been an example of which of the following design types?

    c. Triangulation design

    Review section "What Are the Types of Mixed Methods Designs?" in the textbook

9. Think about Gallik's (1999) survey study that was presented in Chapter 13. This study was concerned with the recreational reading habits of college students. The intent of this study was to describe college student recreational reading habits and to look for evidence that recreational reading is related to academic achievement. Suppose the author had conducted focus group interviews with students to extend the results found from the analysis of the surveys. This would have been an example of which of the following design types?

    a. Explanatory design

    Review section "What Are the Types of Mixed Methods Designs?" in the textbook

10. Think about Feen-Calligan's (1999) grounded theory study that was presented in Chapter 14. This study worked to generate a theory to explain the process of art therapy in addiction treatment. Suppose the author had conducted a survey with therapists and recovering individuals after the theory was generated. This survey may have attempted to generalize and/or test the theory with a broader audience. This would have been an example of which of the following design types?

    b. Exploratory design

    Review section "What Are the Types of Mixed Methods Designs?" in the textbook

Chapter 18

Action Research Designs

Learning Objectives

After completing your study of Chapter 18, you should be able to:

1. Define the purpose and the uses of action research.

2. Describe practical and participatory action research designs.

3. Identify types of practical issues studied in action research.

4. Define how action research is self-reflective.

5. Describe collaboration in action research.

6. Summarize the activities in the dynamic process used in action research.

7. Identify the types of plans developed in action research.

8. Describe typical audiences for sharing action research.

9. Identify the steps in conducting an action research study.

10. List the criteria for evaluating an action research report.

Practice in Understanding Key Concepts

Important Terms and Concepts

The following items represent important concepts relating to action research designs. Using your own words, record definitions for the items in the space provided.

Action research designs: _____

_____

_____

Chapter 18

Practical action research: _____

_____

_____

Participatory action research: _____

_____

_____

Practical issues: _____

_____

_____

Participatory or self-reflective research: _____

_____

_____

Collaborate with others: _____

_____

_____

Dynamic process: _____

_____

_____

Plan of action: _____

_____

_____

Share reports: _____

_____

_____

Applying the Concepts as a Consumer of Research

Carefully consider your definitions and descriptions of the key concepts for this chapter as you respond to the following items about the sample action research study in the textbook. Each item represents a key characteristic of the designs described in this chapter. For each item, explain how the characteristic was implemented within the study.

Activity Hint!
- See Chapter 18 section "*What Are the Key Characteristics of Action Research?*" for information about each key characteristic.

Key characteristics of action research designs

1. A practical focus. _____

_____

_____

_____

2. The educator-researcher's own practices. _____

_____

_____

_____

3. Collaboration. _____

_____

_____

_____

4. A dynamic process. _____

_____

_____

_____

5. Identification of a plan of action. _____

_____

_____

_____

6. Sharing the report locally. _____

_____

_____

_____

Evaluating action research

The following items represent criteria for evaluating research using the designs described in this chapter. In each case, explain the meaning of the statement and critique the implementation of an action research design within the sample action research study in the textbook.

7. Does the project clearly address a problem or issue in practice that needs to be solved? _____

_____

_____

_____

8. Did the action researcher collect sufficient data to address the problem? _____

_____

_____

_____

9. Did the action researcher collaborate with others? Was there respect for all collaborators? _____

_____

_____

_____

10. Did the plan of action advanced by the researcher build logically from the data? _____

_____

_____

_____

11. Is there evidence that the plan of action contributed to the researcher's reflection as a professional? _____

_____

_____

_____

12. Has the research enhanced the lives of participants by empowering them, changing them, or providing them

with new understandings? _____

_____

_____

_____

13. Did the action research actually lead to a change or did a solution to a problem make a difference? _____

_____

_____

_____

14. Did the author report the action research to audiences who might use the information? _____

_____

_____

Applying the Concepts to a New Research Problem

You will now practice applying the important concepts of this chapter to a new research problem of your choice. Assume that you are a professional (or even a graduate student) who is going to undertake a research study using an action research design. Select a research topic and use the following steps to design this action research study. If it is difficult to choose a topic, then think about how you could have conducted an action research project as part of this educational research course.

Activity Hint!
- See Chapter 18 section "***What Are the Steps in Conducting an Action Research Study?***" for information about each step.

My research topic: _____

_____

Step 1 – Explain why action research is the best design to use to address this problem. _____

_____

_____

_____

Step 2 – Identify a problem to study. _____

_____

_____

_____

Step 3 – Describe what resources you could locate to help address the problem. _____

_____

_____

_____

Step 4 – Describe the information you will need. _____

_____

_____

_____

Step 5 – Describe how you will collect data. What steps will you take? _____

_____

_____

_____

Step 6 – Describe how you will analyze the data. What steps will you take? _____

_____

_____

_____

Step 7 – Describe how you will develop a plan for action based on the data. _____

_____

_____

_____

_____

Step 8 – How will you implement the plan of action? Upon which aspects will you reflect? With whom will you

share the plan? _____

_____

_____

_____

_____

Practice Test Items

Answer the following items to check your understanding of the important concepts related to research designs and action research designs in particular. Once you have answered all of the items, you can check your ideas with the provided solutions.

1. Put the following historical developments related to action research designs in chronological order, starting with the earliest. Use the letters found to the left of the choices to designate each step in the provided blanks.

    a. Emphasis on experiments and systematic research
    b. Use of action research to address societal issues during the Depression and War years
    c. Emphasis on educators reflecting on their own practices
    d. Movement toward having in-service days for teacher staff development activities

    Earliest   _____   _____   _____   _____   Most recent

2. Which of the following does not apply to practical action research studies in educational research? Circle the letter to the left of the correct response.

   a. Study of a local problem
   b. Inquiry by an individual teacher
   c. Attempt to generate a theory about a process
   d. Focus on teacher development

3. Participatory action research has been referred to as "critical action research." Which of the following suggests how this form of research is similar to critical ethnographic research? Circle the letter to the left of the correct response.

   a. Goal of wanting to empower individuals and groups
   b. Use of an object, impersonal point of view
   c. Emphasis on quantitative data (even if some qualitative is included)
   d. Study of teachers

4. Describe what it means that action research is often a dynamic process.

   _____

   _____

   _____

   _____

5. Which of the following are reasons why action research is sometimes criticized as lacking scientific rigor? Circle the letter to the left of all the correct responses.

   a. The study of an educational issue
   b. Results are typically not reported to scholarly journals
   c. Methods are adapted and changed instead of systematic
   d. Collecting and organizing the data

6. Consider the following two types of research designs: experimental and action research. Identify whether each of the following design features is more appropriate for an experimental study, an action research study, or if it is equally appropriate for both. Write "experiment," "action," or "both" after each as appropriate.

   a. Control for extraneous factors.   _____

   b. Use of random assignment.   _____

   c. Focus on practical issues.   _____

   d. Reduce threats to internal validity.   _____

7. Consider the following two types of research designs: narrative and action research. Identify whether each of the following design features is more appropriate for a narrative study, an action research study, or if it is appropriate for both. Write "narrative," "action," or "both" after each as appropriate.

    a. Emphasis on collaboration between researcher and participant(s). _____

    b. Collecting stories of life experiences. _____

    c. Use of a theoretical lens or guiding perspective. _____

    d. Addressing a practical issue. _____

8. Consider the following two types of research designs: ethnography and action research. Identify whether each of the following design features is more appropriate for an ethnography, an action research study, or if it is appropriate for both. Write "ethnography," "action," or "both" after each as appropriate.

    a. Emphasis on self-reflection. _____

    b. Limiting the impact of the researcher on the research site. _____

    c. Use of a theoretical lens or guiding perspective. _____

    d. Developing a plan for action. _____

9. Suppose you are a teacher undertaking an action research project to improve the motivation of your students to study mathematics. As part of your study, you evaluate the scores your students received on their annual standardized test. This is an example of what kind of action research data? Circle the letter to the left of the correct response.

    a. Experiencing
    b. Enquiring
    c. Examining

10. Suppose you are a teacher undertaking an action research project to improve the motivation of your students to study mathematics. As part of your study, you find and read a journal article about a quasi-experiment that compared two mathematics lessons. This is an example of what kind of action research data? Circle the letter to the left of the correct response.

    a. Experiencing
    b. Enquiring
    c. Examining

Practice Test Items - Answer Key

1. Put the following historical developments related to action research designs in chronological order, starting with the earliest. Use the letters found to the left of the choices to designate each step in the provided blanks.

    Earliest: b.   Use of action research to address societal issues during the Depression and War years
                    a.   Emphasis on experiments and systematic research
                    d.   Movement toward having in-service days for teacher staff development activities
    Most recent: c.   Emphasis on educators reflecting on their own practices

    Review section "How Did Action Research Develop?" in the textbook

2. Which of the following does not apply to practical action research studies in educational research?

    c.   Attempt to generate a theory about a process

    Review section "What Are the Types of Action Research Designs?" in the textbook

3. Participatory action research has been referred to as "critical action research." Which of the following suggests how this form of research is similar to critical ethnographic research?

    a.   Goal of wanting to empower individuals and groups

    Review section "What Are the Types of Action Research Designs?" in the textbook

4. Describe what it means that action research is often a dynamic process.

    Action research is a dynamic process because the educator-researcher uses iterations of activities. For example, this has been called a "spiral," where the researcher goes between reflection, data collection, and action. This dynamic process is very different from the process used in a design like an experiment where the research has a clear linear path of posing a hypothesis, applying an intervention, measuring an outcome, and testing the hypothesis.

    Review section "What Are the Key Characteristics of Action Research?" in the textbook

5. Which of the following are reasons why action research is sometimes criticized as lacking scientific rigor?

    b.   Results are typically not reported to scholarly journals
    c.   Methods are adapted and changed instead of systematic

    Review section "How Did Action Research Develop?" in the textbook

6. Consider the following two types of research designs: experimental and action research. Identify whether each of the following design features is more appropriate for an experimental study, an action research study, or if it is appropriate for both. Write "experiment," "action," or "both" after each as appropriate.

    a.   Control for extraneous factors.   <u>experiment</u>
    b.   Use of random assignment.   <u>experiment</u>
    c.   Focus on practical issues.   <u>action</u>
    d.   Reduce threats to internal validity.   <u>experiment</u>

Review sections "What Are the Key Characteristics of Action Research Designs?" and "Experimental Designs" in the textbook

7. Consider the following two types of research designs: narrative and action research. Identify whether each of the following design features is more appropriate for a narrative study, an action research study, or if it is appropriate for both. Write "narrative," "action," or "both" after each as appropriate.

    a.   Emphasis on collaboration between researcher and participant(s).   <u>both</u>
    b.   Collecting stories of life experiences.   <u>narrative</u>
    c.   Use of a theoretical lens or guiding perspective.   <u>both</u>
    d.   Addressing a practical issue.   <u>action</u>

Review sections "What Are the Key Characteristics of Action Research Designs?" and "Narrative Designs" in the textbook

8. Consider the following two types of research designs: ethnography and action research. Identify whether each of the following design features is more appropriate for an ethnography, an action research study, or if it is appropriate for both. Write "ethnography," "action," or "both" after each as appropriate.

    a.   Emphasis on self-reflection.   <u>both</u>
    b.   Limiting the impact of the researcher on the research site.   <u>ethnography</u>
    c.   Use of a theoretical lens or guiding perspective.   <u>both</u>
    d.   Developing a plan for action.   <u>action</u>

Review sections "What Are the Key Characteristics of Action Research Designs?" and "Ethnographic Designs" in the textbook

9. Suppose you are a teacher undertaking an action research project to improve the motivation of your students to study mathematics. As part of your study, you evaluate the scores your students received on their annual standardized test. This is an example of what kind of action research data?

    b.   Enquiring

Review section "What Are the Steps in Conducting an Action Research Study?" in the textbook

10. Suppose you are a teacher undertaking an action research project to improve the motivation of your students to study mathematics. As part of your study, you find and read a journal article about a quasi-experiment that compared two mathematics lessons. This is an example of what kind of action research data?

    c.   Examining

Review section "What Are the Steps in Conducting an Action Research Study?" in the textbook

Review #3: The Combined Research Designs

Carefully consider your definitions and descriptions of the key concepts for the two combined research designs discussed in Chapters 17 and 18. Using these ideas, complete the following questions to review and compare these two designs.

1. When do you choose to use each design?

Activity Hint!
- Review the sections on "***When Do You Use... Research?***" at the start of Chapters 17 and 18.

Mixed Methods Design:	Action Research Design:

2. What are the different types of each design?

Activity Hint!
- Review the sections on "***What Are the Types of... Designs?***" in Chapters 17 and 18.

Mixed Methods Design:	Action Research Design:

3. What sample size is appropriate for each design?

Activity Hint!
- Review the discussions of typical quantitative and qualitative sample sizes in Chapters 6 and 8.

Mixed Methods Design:	Action Research Design:

Review #3: The Combined Research Designs

4. The data are typically analyzed to address what type(s) of research question?

Activity Hint!
- Review the sections on "*Writing... Research Questions*" in Chapter 5 and "*When Do You Use... Research?*" at the start of Chapters 17 and 18.

Mixed Methods Design:	Action Research Design:

5. What are the key characteristics of each design?

Activity Hint!
- Review the sections on "*What Are the Key Characteristics of...?*" in Chapters 17 and 18.

Mixed Methods Design:	Action Research Design:

6. Write two research questions (one quantitative, one qualitative) for a study that you might want to conduct using each design.

Activity Hint!
- Review the sections on "*Writing... Research Questions*" in Chapter 5 and "*When Do You Use... Research?*" at the start of Chapters 17 and 18.

Mixed Methods Design:	Action Research Design:

References

Abril, C. R., & Gault, B. M. (2006). The state of music in the elementary school: The principal's perspective. *Journal of Research in Music Education, 54*(1), 6–20.

Asmussen, K. J., & Creswell, J. W. (1995). Campus response to a student gunman. *Journal of Higher Education, 66*(5), 575–591.

Carrington, S., Templeton, E., & Papinczak, T. (2003). Adolescents with Asperger syndrome and perceptions of friendship. *Focus on Autism and Other Developmental Disabilities, 18*(4), 211–218.

Favaro, A., Zanetti, T., Huon, G., & Santonastaso, P. (2005). Engaging teachers in an eating disorder preventive intervention. *International Journal of Eating Disorders, 38*(1), 73–77.

Feen-Calligan, H. (1999). Enlightenment in chemical dependency treatment programs: A grounded theory. In C. A. Malchiodi (Ed.), *Medical art therapy with adults* (pp. 137–161). London: Jessica Kingsley Publishers.

Gallik, J. D. (1999). Do they read for pleasure? Recreational reading habits of college students. *Journal of Adolescent and Adult Literacy, 42*(6), 480–488.

Huber, J., & Whelan, K. (1999). A marginal story as a place of possibility: Negotiating self on the professional knowledge landscape. *Teaching and Teacher Education, 15*(4), 381–396.

Kim, R. I., & Goldstein, S. B. (2005). Intercultural attitudes predict favorable study abroad expectations of U.S. college students. *Journal of Studies in International Education, 9*(3), 265–278.

Komives, S. R., Owen, J. E., Longerbeam, S. D., Mainella, F. C., & Osteen, L. (2005). Developing a leadership identity: A grounded theory. *Journal of College Student Development, 46*(6), 593–611.

Rushton, S. P. (2004). Using narrative inquiry to understand a student-teacher's practical knowledge while teaching in an inner-city school. *The Urban Review, 36*(1), 61–79.

Ting, S. R. (2000). Predicting Asian Americans' academic performance in the first year of college: An approach combining SAT scores and noncognitive variables. *Journal of College Student Development, 41*, 442–449.

Way, N., Stauber, H. Y., Nakkula, M. J., & London, P. (1994). Depression and substance use in two divergent high school cultures: A quantitative and qualitative analysis. *Journal of Youth and Adolescence, 23*(3), 331–357.